The Journey from Abandonment to Healing

The Journey from Abandonment to Healing

Susan Anderson, C.S.W.

BERKLEY BOOKS, NEW YORK

In explaining the five phases of abandonment, this book relies upon examples drawn from life. Some of the accounts are composites, some are drawn from my clients' experiences, and some are based on interviews conducted for this book. In all cases the names are fictitious and identifying details have been changes to protect the privacy of the individuals involved.

This book is an original publication of The Berkley Publishing Group.

THE JOURNEY FROM ABANDONMENT TO HEALING

A Berkley Book / published by arrangement with the author

PRINTING HISTORY
Berkley trade paperback edition / March 2000

The Penguin Putnam Inc. World Wide Web site address is
http://www.penguinputnam.com

ISBN: 0-425-17228-7

BERKLEY®
Berkley Books are published by
The Berkley Publishing Group, a division of Penguin Putnam Inc.,
375 Hudson Street, New York, New York 10014.
BERKLEY and the "B" design are trademarks
belonging to Penguin Putnam Inc.

PRINTED IN THE UNITED STATES OF AMERICA

12   11   10

For my mother, Barbara Ruth Griffith
And to my children, Adam and Erika Anderson

Akeru

ONE day, leafing through a Japanese dictionary, I came upon a word that caused me to marvel because it had so many different meanings—and ALL of them pertained to abandonment. The word is *akeru*. It means "to pierce, to open, to end, to make a hole in, to start, to expire, to unwrap, to turn over." When someone leaves, *akeru* refers to the empty space that is created, the opening in which a new beginning can take place. I was amazed at the power of a single word that could suggest that *to begin* and *to end* are the same—part of one never-ending cycle of renewal and healing. I was excited to discover this concept and began to use it immediately in my work in abandonment recovery, delighted to see how readily people responded to its wisdom.

I am not trying to cash in on Eastern philosophy or establish a new martial art. I am grateful to be able to borrow the wonderfully fluid, many-faceted meaning of a single word plucked out of its context from an enlightened tradition.

Contents

Preface

What Is Abandonment?

"WHAT is abandonment?" people ask. "Is it about people in search of their mothers? Or people left on someone else's doorstep as children?"

I answer: Every day there are people who feel as if life itself has left them on a doorstep or thrown them away. Abandonment is about loss of love itself, that crucial loss of connectedness. It often involves breakup, betrayal, aloneness—something people can experience all at once, or one after another over a period of months, or even years later as an aftershock.

Abandonment means different things to different people. It is an extremely personal and individual experience. Sometimes it is lingering grief caused by old losses. Sometimes it is fear. Sometimes it can be an invisible barrier holding us back from forming relationships, from reaching our true potential. It sometimes takes the form of self-sabotage. We get caught up in patterns of abandonment.

This book provides real help for those who have searched but found nothing to ease the pain of abandonment or hasten the speed of recovery. It guides you through what I've observed in years of practice as five universal stages of abandonment. As you continue along this journey, you will perhaps be surprised to discover that the pain you feel when a loved one has left is not an end but the beginning of a time of personal growth.

Abandonment is a psychobiological process. I'll share with you recent findings from the field of brain science that shed new light on the biological and chemical processes that underlie our emotional response to loss.

People going through the anguish of love loss often feel that their lives have been permanently altered, that they will never be the same, will never love again. I'm writing to assure you that as devastated as you may be right now, your feelings of despair and hopelessness are in fact *temporary, and* they are a normal part of grieving over a relationship. In fact, only by grappling with the feeling that your life is over can you begin to rebuild.

Those of you who have been left to pick up the pieces may wonder about your lost partners, who have already replaced you with new lives and new relationships. You've been left to do the soul-searching. You are a part of the chosen group able to undertake this journey. As you continue with the book, you will discover that the pain you are feeling is real, it is part of life, and it is necessary.

Anyone who feels this pain is in a legitimate emotional crisis. Many feel as if they have been stabbed in the heart so many times that they don't know which hole to plug up first. But these overwhelming feelings do not in any way imply that you are weak, dependent, or undeserving. In spite of the intensity of your feelings, you are still the competent, responsible person you thought you were. Your breakup, with all of its emotional excess, has not diminished you. In fact, being able to feel so deeply is a testament to your strength and tenacity. Only by giving yourself over to your feelings can you find your way out of them.

This is a time of personal reckoning, but this soul-searching can also lead to extreme self-doubt and scathing self-recrimination. When someone we love rejects us we often turn the anger we feel toward that person against ourselves and blame ourselves for the loss. In this way, abandonment acts like quicksand, miring us in feelings of worthlessness and despair. No matter how hurtful or demoralizing the circumstances may have been, you are not a victim or undeserving of love. The fact that someone has chosen not to be with you says as much or more about your ex as it does about you and how well you functioned in the relationship. You may be humbled for the moment, but you have not been vanquished.

Facing these issues and putting what you have experienced into perspective prevents you from turning your anger inward. As you learn to resist the gravitational pull on your self-esteem, you gain strength and emotional endurance. Rather than feeling defeated by your experience, you emerge from it wiser, more self-reliant, and more capable of love.

Without guidance, many people don't completely recover from the loss of a love. Their fears and doubts remain unresolved. True recovery means confronting uncomfortable feelings, understanding what they are, and most importantly, learning how to deal with them.

There are some feelings no one wants to talk about because they involve fear, despair, and self-doubt so intense that you're naturally humiliated and ashamed by them. This shame is not just about the embarrassment you may feel over having been rejected; it is about feelings that bewilder you with their potency, induce panic, and have you believing you are weak, dependent, unlovable, even repulsive.

Until these intense feelings are addressed, people tend to suffer them in silence or try to deny them. Eventually, these forgotten, deeply buried feelings are transformed into an elusive grief. Many seek therapy for this grief, but can't seem to overcome that undifferentiated emptiness so often misdiagnosed and treated as depression. (For some people, this persistent grief can involve chemical imbalances that, in some cases, respond to medication.)

Abandonment is a complex issue, and its wound can be deeply entrenched. It is important to realize that your feelings, no matter how intense, do not signify a lack of will or frailty of character. They are normal and part of a process that leads to renewal and change.

The healing process I'll describe doesn't limit itself to your current loss. It gets to the heart of your cumulative wound— the one that contains all of your disappointments and heart-breaks that have been bubbling beneath the surface of your life, perhaps since childhood.

Unresolved abandonment may be the underlying issue responsible for most of the ailments you have been struggling with all along: the insecurity that plagues your relationships, depression and anxiety, obsessive and compulsive behaviors, low energy levels, and the loss of self-esteem that have been holding you back. Yet often people who have been abandoned can't name what they are going through. They may have grown up with an alcoholic parent or felt excluded from their peer group at crucial moments, just as their sense of self was beginning to develop. However detached they may be from the root of their distress, they spend their life energy bargaining with fear and fighting insecurity.

Having lost touch with the source of their wounds, many resort to quick fixes and gratify themselves with everything from food and alcohol to shopping or to other people. Or they become addicted to self-help lectures, books, and tapes. But all of the self-medicating and soothing words in the world will not erase the distress. In order to do that, you must embark upon a journey that addresses the underlying cause—the abandonment wound itself.

Through my own experience and through my years of work with others, I have seen how helpful it is to come out of isolation and commune with others as we learn about the grief process that has gripped our lives. Wherever you are in the five stages this book describes, you are not alone. It is a revelation to discover that the pain debilitates the strongest, smartest, most self-sufficient among us; that it cuts across all ages, cultures, and status levels; and that it ultimately is a universal human experience.

This book is designed to serve as your companion and guide, addressing your most difficult feelings, validating your experience with research from related scientific fields, and giving you the tools you'll need on your journey toward a new outlook and new love.

What Is Abandonment?

A feeling

A feeling of isolation within a relationship

An intense feeling of devastation when a relationship ends

An aloneness not by choice

An experience from childhood

A baby left on the doorstep

A divorce

A woman left by her husband of twenty years for another woman

A man being left by his fiancée for someone "more successful"

A mother leaving her children

A father leaving his children

A friend feeling deserted by a friend

A child whose pet dies

A little girl grieving over the death of her mother

A little boy wanting his mommy to come pick him up from nursery school

A child who feels replaced by the birth of another sibling

A child feeling restless due to his parent's emotional unavailability

A boy realizing that he is gay and anticipating the reaction of his parents and friends

A teenager feeling her heart is actually broken

A teenage boy afraid to approach the girl he loves

A woman who has raised now-grown children, feeling empty, as if she has been deserted

A child stricken with a serious illness watching his friends play while he is confined to a wheelchair or bed

A woman who has lost her job and with it her professional identity, financial security, and status

A man who has been put out to pasture by his company, as if he is obsolete

A dying woman who fears being abandoned by loved ones as much or more than she fears pain and death

Abandonment is all of this and more. Its wound is at the heart of human experience.

Chapter One

The Five Stages of Abandonment

WHEN a relationship ends, it is painful for both people, but the pain is especially debilitating for the one left behind.

"In my case, it happened out of the blue," said Marie. "One night, Lonny didn't come home from work. When I didn't hear from him after only an hour, I started jumping to the worst conclusions—car accident, heart attack. Never mind how much worse these visions got when he still wasn't home six hours later. The last thing I imagined was that he was with someone else. Why would he want to be? We were lifelong companions and lovers, best friends, and happily married for over twenty years.

"Finally, I heard his footsteps crunching along the gravel driveway. I ran to meet him at the door. 'What happened?' I asked. My heart was in my throat.

"There was a pause.

" 'I'm not happy,' he said flatly.

" 'Happy?'

"He vaguely said something about how things were different between us.

" 'Different?' I asked.

" 'Don't interrupt me,' he said. 'That's one of the problems. You always interrupt.'

"My face was suddenly hot and pulsating. This was not Lonny.

"Then he uttered the words that turned my stomach upside down and left my mouth dry.

" 'I'm leaving,' he said.

"I stopped breathing. It was hard to collect a single coherent thought. The only logical explanation I could come up with was that he must have had a head injury sometime during the day. Why would he say what he was saying? I thought briefly but seriously about calling an ambulance.

"When I finally managed to speak, my voice came out deep and hollow, like it belonged to someone else.

" 'You don't really mean this,' was all I managed to say in my strange, unsteady new voice.

" 'I'm leaving this weekend.'

"I leaned on the kitchen table for support and tried to catch my breath from the dagger thrust into my gut. 'Is there someone else?' I asked, my voice coming in a whisper.

"He flatly and angrily denied this. But a month after he actually moved out, I was to learn that in fact there was someone else—another teacher from his school. It lessened the bewilderment but not the wrenching pain.

"I spent the first few weeks alone, trying to grapple with the immensity of it all. This was a man I'd loved with all my heart and soul. He'd always been so tender, his goodness always shining right through. For me, loving him had almost been a religious experience. I'd had such reverence for how he lived his life. He was a kind and caring father, both wise and sensitive.

"At night, I'd attempt to put the agony to rest and go to bed. But sleep was out of the question. I would be tortured by the

empty space next to me in the bed. How I loved to hold Lonny,
my beautiful, sensual Lonny. I hugged my pillow instead, weep-
ing, sometimes screaming into it, because the torment was so
unbearable. I had every right to hate him for what he was do-
ing, but all I could do was miss him and damn myself for letting
this happen."

Abandonment's devastation can stem from many different
circumstances, many different types of relationships. There are
a variety of factors affecting the way we react to the loss: the
nature and duration of our relationship, the intensity of the
feelings, the circumstances of the breakup, and our previous
history of losses. Being left by someone we love can open up
old wounds, stirring up insecurities and doubts that had been
part of our emotional baggage since childhood.

Almost all of us have experienced Marie's feelings. Someone
has chosen not to be with us, not to "keep us." We feel suddenly
cut off, alone, sent into emotional exile. Being alone isn't bad
when it is something we choose for ourselves. When someone
decides to leave us, it is a different story. Bewildered, confused,
outraged, we feel as if we've been handed a life sentence to
which we've been unjustly condemned by virtue of some invisible defect. We yearn and ache for someone who has abandoned
us, as Marie does.

Abandonment is our first fear. It is a primal fear—a fear
universal to the human experience. As infants we lay screaming
in our cribs, terrified that when our mothers left the room they
were never coming back. Abandonment is a fear that we will
be left alone forever with no one to protect us, to see to our
most urgent needs. For the infant, maintaining attachment to
its primary caretaker is necessary for its survival. Any threat or
disruption to that relationship arouses this primal fear, a fear
that is embedded in the hardware of our brains, a fear we carry
into adulthood. When children experience feelings of discon-
nection, they do not have the defenses to fall back on that we

as adults do. Their wounds may not heal but instead float beneath the surface of their lives right into adulthood.

Emotional experience is more painful when it echoes an episode from the past; that's especially true when it comes to rejection and loss. The relationship that ended today may be the fulfillment of your worst nightmares from childhood. Grieving over that lost love opens a primal wound.

Someone deciding to leave you awakens this primal fear, and out of it rises intense anger. You feel angry for having to feel so much fear and desperation. You feel frustrated with yourself for being powerless, for not being able to *hold on to* another's love. You feel utterly and helplessly defeated over the circumstances of losing that love.

In some cases your grief may not come from a recent breakup; sometimes it is rooted in the residual insecurity and fear stemming from long-lost loves that interfere with relationships you're struggling with today.

You may still be with your partner, but you understand that he or she no longer loves you. Though physically present, you grieve the loss. It's a steady throb tinged with feelings of personal failure: "Why can't I make it work? Am I not lovable? Why can't I get him to love me?"

In other cases, like Marie's, a partner leaves you for someone else, in which case your grief is complicated by feelings of betrayal and jealousy.

Sometimes there is no one else; your mate left because he just stopped wanting to be with you, needed his space. Your grief becomes fraught with feelings of self-reproach, anxiety, and lack of closure.

Or your relationship may have simply fallen apart—perhaps you weren't ready, or you just didn't seem to be able to make it work. Perhaps the relationship was so painful that initially you were relieved by the prosect of separation. Feelings of inadequacy came as an aftershock. In these cases, grieving may be complicated by a profound sense of personal disappointment. You may feel remorseful, uncertain about your future.

Or the abandonment was sudden and unexpected, in which case shock and disbelief took over. You must first address the desperate pain and debilitating panic before you can begin to grieve.

The grieving process is similar to bereavement over a death: loss is loss. But abandonment grief has a particular life of its own, stemming from the circumstances that led up to it and from the feelings of rejection and inadequacy that often accompany it.

It is because abandonment's knife cuts all the way through to the self that it is so painful. You lose not just your loved one but your core belief in yourself. You doubt that you are lovable and acceptable as a mate. These feelings can become deeply inscribed, creating an invisible wound that causes you to turn on yourself.

Sometimes people feel the loss of a loved one so deeply and question their own worth so profoundly that it is as if there's an invisible drain deep within that works insidiously to siphon off self-worth, like a slow, internal bleed. The paradox for these folks is that when they try to rebuild self-esteem by doing esteemable things, their deep wound is always draining it away.

This drainage of ego strength is crucial to understanding and working through the abandonment cycle. In fact, it is hard for me to understand why its special type of grief has gone virtually unrecognized, unstudied, and untreated until now. Mental health professionals generally interpret the feelings of abandonment as a symptom of depression or anxiety. But abandonment grief is a syndrome of its own. It is the way in which your fear and anger are turned against yourself that gives abandonment grief its particular character.

The tendency toward self-attack and self-recrimination represents the midway point in the grieving process. But injury to self (or *internalizing the rejection,* as I call it) is interwoven into all of the stages of abandonment. It is a persistent, ongoing process.

WHAT IS AN ABANDONMENT SURVIVOR?

Abandonment survivors are those who have experienced the anguish of lost love and have the courage to go on believing in life and in their own capacity for love. Some are celebrities who have told us their childhood stories; others never make a public disclosure. Some are therapists—probably the majority of therapists have their own abandonment histories. But most are everyday people. There is an abandonment survivor in just about everyone; the insecurity, longing, and fear associated with the loss of a love is universal.

Abandonment survivors are sensitive, caring, and primed for love. But membership to this venerable group is not restricted to those able to achieve success in their relationships. Many continue the struggle to resolve the old abandonment wounds that stand in the way of finding love.

For all abandonment survivors—those who've found love and those still seeking it—the impact of losses past and present can be found in the fragments of unlived life, unreached potential, and unfulfilled dreams still waiting to be redeemed through the process of abandonment recovery.

WHAT IS ABANDONMENT RECOVERY?

Abandonment recovery involves a program of five exercises outlined in this book. I call the program *Akeru*. You take action to heal your abandonment wounds, past and present. In this process, you gain new information, identify unfinished business from the past, and practice hands-on exercises for improving your life.

Abandonment recovery provides a new language and approach compatible with twelve-step recovery programs. Its program is specifically designed to deal with unresolved abandonment—the underlying source of your addictions, compulsions, and distress. It involves taking responsibility for improving your life.

If you've been holding out for the right words or the ultimate insight that will finally free you, beware. The magic bullet is not in any book or program. It is within you. It is that untapped energy that you will learn to redirect. Abandonment recovery is easy, even pleasurable. You must do more than read this book. You must put its wisdom into practice.

WHAT IS AN ABANDONER?

Abandoners come in every possible size, shape, shade, age, gender, and disposition. It is often difficult to tell who is or isn't capable of being emotionally responsible—who is worthy of trust, and who is an abandoner.

What complicates the picture even more is that one person's abandoner might be another's lifelong partner. The circumstances surrounding relationships are so complex and variable that it is neither wise nor fair to make moral judgments, point fingers, or draw generalizations.

Let it be said that many abandoners do not set out to intentionally hurt someone. Many are just human beings struggling to find the answers to life's difficult challenges along with everyone else. But there are serial abandoners, those who get some reward from inflicting emotional pain on those who love them. For them, creating devastation is their way of demonstrating power.

Even those who are *not* motivated by this need might experience a heightened sense of self-importance when the one they leave behind seems so desperate to have them back. In the light of the other person's pain, these folks usually don't admit to feelings of triumph. Instead, they air more humble feelings, like the *guilt* they feel over having caused you pain. They are usually easily distracted from this guilt as they get caught up in their new lives with greater gusto than before.

Some abandoners are able to bypass these pangs of guilt by remaining oblivious to the effect they have on others. They're in a general state of denial about the devastation they've caused. It helps them maintain an image of themselves as decent, caring human beings. This denial often comes across as callousness and cruelty to the one who was left behind to pick up the pieces.

Other abandoners, however, unable to deny the pain they've caused, endure their own genuine grief and remorse, parallel to yours, over the failure of the relationship.

Abandonment recovery is dedicated to all of those who struggle to sustain relationships.

You are about to discover the benefits of working through the various stages of abandonment. As difficult as it sounds, the process will help you avoid the pitfalls of suppressing and avoiding the pain. Burying your feelings leaves them unresolved. Unless you face them, they continue to interfere from within, and you may find yourself caught up in self-defeating relationships that end in abandonment over and over again.

The recovery process that I've come to call *Akeru* is designed to reverse this injury. It provides a program of five exercises described in this book. Abandonment recovery helps you gain something from the intense emotions you are feeling, so that you can turn one of life's most painful experiences into an opportunity to grow and change.

What follows is a bird's-eye view of the stages that will help you get started on your journey. Being able to see the stages as *one process* will, I hope, give you some insight on where you are, where you've been, and what to expect.

SHATTERING

In this devastating first stage, you are in shock, pain, and panic, suddenly bereft of life's worth and meaning. You try to keep the shards of yourself together, but in spite of all your efforts, your faith and trust have been shattered. The severing of this important emotional bond makes you feel (temporarily) that you can't live without your lost love. Suicidal feelings are normal to this period. They are caused by despair that is overwhelming but *only temporary*. Old feelings of helplessness and dependency intrude into your current emotional crisis. Akeru provides a pain management technique that will help you get through the most difficult periods as quickly as possible and gain strength from them, allowing you to enter a time of rebirth.

WITHDRAWAL

Love withdrawal is just like heroin withdrawal, involving intense craving and agitation for the love you are missing. You ache, throb, and yearn for your loved one to return. Human beings are genetically heir to a powerful *need for attachment*; severed relationships do not end your need to bond. In fact, losing your relationship tends to intensify this need. The emotional tear triggers a psychobiological process that can include wakefulness, weight loss, anxiety, and emotional and physical fatigue. Akeru will show you how to work with the bonding instinct that is responsible for the wrenching pain. You can redirect its energy toward making a significant new connection to yourself.

INTERNALIZING

It is during this critical third stage of abandonment that your emotional wound becomes susceptible to infection, which can result in permanent scarring in the form of damage to your self-esteem. This is when you suppress your anger toward your lost partner and beat up on yourself instead. You tend to idealize your abandoner at your own expense. Any implicit or explicit criticism from your ex is taken to heart. You become preoccupied with regrets over the relationship, agonizing over what you *should* have done or what you *could* have done to prevent the loss. No matter how hard you try to fight back, your sense of self takes a beating. Akeru provides the tools to help you access internal energy and build a new whole new concept of self. The exercise is designed to open new windows in your awareness, allow you to make new decisions, and set new goals.

RAGE

Rage is not the first time you encounter anger in this process, but during the first three stages, your anger was victim rage, that useless flailing in space or stabbing your pillow to death. It is not until this *fourth stage* that your beleaguered sense of self, under siege from self-attack, is ready to stand up and fight back, to take on the challenge of the outside world. Only then is your rage of the self-empowering, healthy kind. Its aggression can help you rehabilitate your life.

Rage provides the energy you need to defend your newly born sense of self and to insure your continued survival. Some people have difficulty expressing anger and need help to avoid turning their anger inward into an *agitated depression*. Sometimes you are afraid to express anger toward your lost partner for fear of losing any more love than you already have. Instead, you take your anger out on those closest to you. You can have unrealistic expectations toward others at this time; you expect them to replace the love and nurturance you are so sorely missing. When they fall short, you explode. Fantasies of retaliation and revenge toward your abandoners are also common to this stage, but there are better alternatives. The old saying is true: The best revenge is success. Akeru uses the energy of anger to help you turn your abandonment experience into a triumph of personal growth.

LIFTING

Because rage has helped direct the energy outward, it helps to lift you back into life. You begin to experience a levitation of spirit and intervals of peace and freedom. You feel stronger and wiser for the painful lessons you have learned. Life in all of its fullness begins to distract you. You let go of anger. Akeru provides the tools to help you enhance your capacity for newness and love.

The first letter of each of the five stages spell *SWIRL*. The word *swirl* echoes the cyclonic, continuous, flowing nature of your grief. Like any natural life process, the five stages are circular rather than linear. They represent a single process that is overlapping and recurrent, a process that can take place within an hour, a day, a month, or a period of years. You swirl through them over and over, until the tornado begins to weaken, and you emerge a changed person.

Yes, there is life after abandonment—full, rich intense life— but you will have to work to get there. The guiding hand is there to help you get through the pain, learn from it, and experience a stronger connection to yourself. You will never be as conscious, as acutely alive, as you will once you have applied the principles in this program to your daily life.

Chapter Two

Stage One: Shattering

WHAT IS SHATTERING?

Shattering is a tear in the dense tissues of human attachment.
It is a feeling of devastation, unbearable pain.
It is a powerful neurobiological process.
It is the birth trauma revisited. It is rebirth.
It is the breaking up of the storm clouds, the clearing of new sky.

It is an epiphany of insight, an awakening of the emotional core.

Shattering is a bottom—a transforming bottom—the same bottom from which people over the ages have found redemption.

All of our lives we have been overprepared for a shattering— for an event that is capable of ripping us away from what we hold most dear—attempting to ward off circumstances beyond our control. Most of our life energy is spent making ourselves safe so there won't be a shattering. Then, when it happens, it knocks the wind out of us. But once we catch our breath, we are in a position to rebuild our lives and not just to self-medicate with the illusion of security.

Shattering releases the primitive defenses that have become counterproductive, holding us back. The armor that was once protective becomes restrictive and uncomfortable. For the person no longer crippled, the casts must come off or they become a hindrance.

Shattering is what we feel when a relationship first ends, but it can also be the aftershock of earlier experience, an eruption of old, forgotten feelings. These eruptions are often reported by people who have gone through twelve step programs to fight addictions. They discover, most frequently in the second year of the program, that their addictive behavior served as a primitive defense. It takes that long for the old defenses to break away and for true rehabilitation to take place.

Shattering is not a new phenomenon, but by isolating it, we can better deal with it.

We must honor the power of the shattering and harness that power in a disciplined way to create a truly healing environment.

THE FIRST STAGE OF ABANDONMENT: SHATTERING

ROBERTA'S SHATTERING

Roberta is a sensitive person, intelligent and versatile. She has a gifted sense of irony, which she displays with brilliant timing and subtlety. She has a serious side, too, and loves to intensely debate political issues. She has a mane of golden hair and large, pale green eyes. All of it helped her captivate Travis, a conductor of a city orchestra.

Roberta's main drawback, as her friends would tell you, was her choice in men. Travis was no exception. He claimed possession of the artist's temperament. That was how he rationalized his domineering ways and need for control. He could be demanding at times, highly critical, and self-centered. Roberta had to exercise all of her diplomatic skill to keep their relationship on an even keel.

She agreed she'd probably be making a mistake to marry him, which paradoxically was exactly what she found herself probing him about one night at dinner. "What do you think?" she'd asked, looking down at her plate.

Travis hadn't responded right away. "I'm not ready for that," he finally said. "Roberta, you know I'm just trying to have fun, have a good time." He muttered an apology about how shallow that sounded, while Roberta's heart sank. Why did I have to bring that up?

For the next month, Roberta tried to cajole Travis back into the hot and heavy relationship they'd had. But he had become gradually more and more absorbed in his career. He began limiting their time together to once a week and could be seduced into sex only with effort. Roberta sensed she was losing Travis. Her friends told her it was the best thing, but she couldn't bear to let go. She couldn't bear going back out in the world without him, hated the idea of being alone. I'm too old to be going through this, she told herself. She was thirty-five.

Then it happened. She saw him with another woman.

Roberta walked up to them and hit Travis in the chest with her bag. They exchanged words, his last being, "But Roberta, I was going to tell you. I just didn't know how."

Roberta showed up for therapy, crying and blowing her nose into tissue after tissue. "I never believed anything could be this painful," she said, holding her head in her hands. "It feels like my whole life is over."

Shattering is not unique to abandonment. It is the initial stage of all types of grief where significant loss is involved. But the shattering of abandonment is special. Your loss was not due to a death but because someone acted on free will *not to be with you*. In fact, if rejection, desertion, or betrayal played a part in your loss, it is not just your sense of security that has been shattered but your belief in yourself, your sense of self-worth.

"I feel like a complete failure," said Carlyle, his eyes swollen and bloodshot. He had lost nearly ten pounds in a little over two weeks and claimed not to have slept in days. "When I finally do fall asleep," he said, "I just wake up to the reality that it's over. And then my heart starts pounding, and all I can think of is to end it—just do away with myself. The only thing that stops me is my kids.

"My wife wants me to leave by the end of the month. But how can I leave my family? They are what I've always worked for. They are my life. What have I done to deserve this? Why didn't I see it coming? I just can't face it all. I am too numb to know what to do about any of it—to know what I'm feeling. It's overwhelming."

Roberta and Carlyle are experiencing many of the *S* words common to this stage: the *s*hattering of hopes and dreams, the *s*inking feelings, the *s*leeplessness, the *s*oul-searching, the *s*uicidal feelings, the *s*hock. The important thing to bear in mind is that the intense feelings of shattering are temporary. In fact, shattering is the most short-lived of the five stages.

Shattering is a necessary part of the healing process because it brings you to terms with the fact that your relationship is ending. The pain is wrenching because it represents a tear in dense tissues of an intense emotional bond. It is as if you have to be torn apart before you can rebuild a new self.

For most people shattering is a time of reexperiencing. Any old or lingering losses flood into your current wound. If you have been through a similar breakup, memories of that earlier loss come to the surface, forcing you to deal with not just your current loss but the whole issue of loss in your life. Your whole being is thrown into a kind of emotional time warp. Past, present, and future are thrown into the emotional turbulence.

Shattering brings you in touch with feelings that may seem

pathological when taken out of the context of grief. Freud, in one of his early monographs, *Mourning and Melancholia,* emphasized the difference between grieving and depressive illness. The intense emotions of shattering can sometimes even shake the clinician who hasn't come to appreciate the intensity of the abandonment experience.

Alby reported that his therapeutic relationship fell apart soon after his experience of shattering.

The love of his life had just left him. Later, he went to his therapist's office and released his anguish in deep sobs. He reported feeling like a black tar ball long nestled within him finally broke up and melted away. His therapist, agitated by the display of the intense emotions, tried to refer him for medication.

Alby had a stable job where he was highly regarded, was involved in creative arts and stable friendships, and showed no other signs of psychiatric distress.

Ironically, Alby's ability to withstand the intensity of his feelings was a testament to his emotional health. As one abandonment survivor put it, coming to Alby's defense, *"Only the strong can endure the shattering; the weak need their defenses."*

At first, people tend to *swirl* through all of the stages at once. You may go from the shock and devastation of *shattering,* to the *withdrawal* feelings of desperately needing a love fix and not being able to get it, to the shame and self-condemnation of the *internalizing* stage, to the burning anger of the *rage* stage, to moments of hope and clarity of the *lifting* stage, and then back again, over and over, one stage following another in rapid succession.

I have experienced every one of these feelings myself during different phases of my life: childhood, adolescence, and adulthood. Most recently, my lifelong mate left me in the midst of what I had perceived to be a loving, successful, twenty-year relationship. His leaving was sudden, without warning.

The irony that I had devoted my clinical practice of more than twenty years to treating abandonment survivors was not lost on me. Suddenly, all of those years of experience, research, and study were put to the ultimate test; I'd been abandoned.

Somehow, I had chosen to put all of my trust in a person who, after twenty years—after I had grown accustomed to a deep sense of security—suddenly one day said, "It's time for me to go." I found it hard to accept that I had been in the arms of someone who would abandon me after all of those years together. I knew that in my case, it was no random event, no mere coincidence. I knew that it had something to do with old losses, losses from as far back as my childhood. I would have to reach inside myself and find that last remaining seed, the hardy one that managed to lie dormant for nearly twenty years, and then spread its painful roots in my life again. I had to reach inside, find it, examine it, and uproot it once and for all.

It was hard work, but it helped me to reach a new level of understanding and find a better path to recovery, not just for myself but for those who sought my help. True to my work with my clients, I faced my own abandonment honestly and openly.

AKERU

Through my own experience and in working with others, a conceptual truth has emerged. It is that for all of its pain and intensity, abandonment serves as a catalyst for profound personal growth. To explain this notion, I borrow the Japanese word *akeru*.

Akeru is a word with many meanings, among them, "to pierce, to end, to open." It helps to describe the hidden opportunity in abandonment. Shattering involves a painful transition from oneness with another to a state of sudden and involuntary *separateness*. You are left to experience the powerful forces that are at play as you strive to regain your balance. That a single word, *akeru*, embraces the concepts *to end* and *to begin,* helps us to recognize that there is a positive application for the energy created by shattering.

Shattering, in fact, is an explosion of separateness. Abandonment cuts us to the core, but the core personality survives. During shattering, you know you are alive because it exposes raw nerves. All that remains is raw sensation and the urge to survive. Rather than try to submerge, deny, or ignore its discomfort, the task of the Akeru process is to go with it, take advantage of this raw sensation, and make it work for you.

The secret is to *get into the moment and stay there as often as possible.* This allows you to work with the energy rather than against it, to experience this time of stark and naked separateness for all that it's worth. In the moment, you experience the intensity of life as a separate human being.

Getting into the moment involves opening up your senses and focusing your attention upon the sights and sounds and smells and other sensations within your immediate environment. It means using your eyes and skin and ears to experience the moment in a very conscious way. Some have called this *mindfulness.* Others have called it *Zen.* Abandonment recovery calls the moment a natural refuge from emotional pain.

SHATTERING IS A PERSONAL JOURNEY

My own breakup has taught me never to underestimate the intensity of another's experience but to listen closely and learn from it. Shattering is unique to each person. Its intensity cannot be measured by the length of a relationship. It is something that each of us finds our own way through.

"But why must it be so painful?" some ask. "Where does the intensity of its pain come from?"

I am going to take you on a journey through the shattering stage, exploring answers to that question. I will explain how losing a loved one activates the body's automatic system of self-defense and what this means in terms of stress. I will cover feelings common to this stage, such as suicidal thoughts, symbiotic feelings, shame, and the need for self-nurturance. I will help you identify unfinished business you may have left over from old losses that may be amplifying what you feel right now, and describe childhood losses that may have stayed with you into adulthood. I will share relevant information from the field of brain science that will explain why memories of old losses reemerge during your current crisis, and how stress hormones can effect your childhood memories. I will define some of the characteristics of a syndrome that plagues many abandonment survivors—*post-traumatic stress disorder of abandonment*—and discuss the shock, disorientation, and numbness that are common to this disorder. The journey will conclude with step-by-step instructions to help you to incorporate into your life the Akeru exercise for staying in the moment.

Shattering is a time of stark separateness and, although painful, offers the opportunity for tremendous personal awareness. At no other time are you better positioned to come to terms with your reality as a separate human being. This is why shattering, for many, becomes an epiphany, a portal to a whole new level of awareness.

THE ANATOMY OF SHATTERING

SUSTAINING THE HEART WOUND

During this critical first stage, people often feel they have truly sustained a heart wound. Shattering is when the wound is initially inflicted—the point at which you feel the knife that severs you from your heart's attachment. Your whole body reacts in protest.

You may feel an aching or jabbing in your heart, a feeling of constriction, or a rush of anxiety across your chest. At first you may experience the frequent need to sigh or catch your breath. Your heart pounds when you come up against the re-

ality of your loss. You may wake during the
night in a cold sweat of panic and get up each
day with a knot in your stomach.

YOUR SELF-DEFENSE SYSTEM HAS BEEN AROUSED

All of your physical reactions are the result
of your sympathetic nervous system's response
to your very real injury. Your body prepares
you to fight, flee, or freeze in order to protect
you from what it perceives as imminent danger. A rush of stress hormones flows through
your body to keep your self-defense system
aroused, to sustain your alertness, to keep you
on edge and in a state of action readiness.
Adrenaline is released, heightening your
brain's level of reactivity, supercharging your
sensory apparatus to defend against the threat.

It is no wonder that people refer to abandonment as a knife wound to the heart. Physiologically, your body reacts as if your heart
had truly been stabbed.

| Sustaining a Heart Wound |
| Self-Defense |
| Survival Instinct |
| Split Thinking |
| Symbiotic Feelings |
| Suicidal Thoughts |
| Shame |
| Shock |
| Somatic Sensations |

Anatomy of shattering

SURVIVAL INSTINCT

Shattering indeed brings you in touch with the visceral forces
of life. It exposes your core, arousing your most basic and urgent needs. Like childbirth, abandonment forces a separation;
you're suddenly much more alone than you were before.

It is possible that this experience is powerful enough to activate emotional memories stemming all the way back to your
birth—bits and fragments of which have been encoded within
the deep structure of your brain. The brain of a newborn does
not yet have the fully developed structures it needs to record
images of the actual events of birth. But the brain's emotional

memory system is relatively intact at birth and lays down traces of early experience in the form of feelings and sensations. These feelings may be reactivated when an experience in your adult life bears an emotional resemblance to your birth.

For most of us, birth involved a sudden drop in temperature, glaring lights, noise, and perhaps a spank to get us to take our first breaths. When a loved one leaves you, a different kind of umbilical cord is cut. As when you were an infant, you've been suddenly disconnected from everything that gave you comfort, warmth, and sustenance.

The infant calms when it is wrapped snugly in warm blankets; it reminds the infant of the warmth of the mother's womb. But what about you? You have been cut off as well. Are you in no less need of the comfort and human warmth you are suddenly missing?

The tendency even for adults is to cry out for what is lost as if your very life depend upon it. As an adult, of course, this desperation is a feeling, not a fact. Your life does not depend upon your lost partner. It only feels that way.

Shattering has indeed delivered you to a state of stark separateness. But who is there to receive you this time? Who remains to answer the urgent needs that have been activated?

Only you.

There is no nurse, no caretaker this time. Just you. You are just like the snail out of its protective shell, the cold and hungry infant.

The recovery task for this stage is to take hold of yourself one moment at a time, to recognize that you are a separate person, a fully capable adult, responsible for your own self-care. It is no one else's responsibility to meet your emotional needs; only you can do that. Emotional self-reliance involves accepting the intense feelings of the experience, taking stock of your present reality, and assuring yourself that you will survive.

SPLIT THINKING

Characteristic of the shattering stage is a feeling of hopelessness, an aspect of always-and-never thinking. Things will *never* be the same; you will *always* be alone; you will *never* be able to repair the damages; you will *always* be broken. The always-and-never thinking is part of a catastrophic mental process that represents a temporary return to the concrete either/or thinking patterns of your childhood. Shattering has temporarily thrown you into a time warp. Like a newly developing child, you have no real sense that you will live through this crisis and move on with your life's work or onto other loves. Instead, you are caught in a temporary double exposure. Your childhood perspective is superimposed over your adult self's more mature outlook. You consequently see your current condition as a child would: ever-present, permanent.

You may apply the same either/or thinking to the person who has left you, perceiving him or her as all good one minute and all bad the next. One moment they seem entirely irreplaceable, and the next you are saying, or at least trying to convince yourself, that you *didn't need them anyway*. On one hand you see your lost partners as completely justified for having left you; in fact, you have never respected them more or felt more awestruck by their fortitude of character now that they have dismissed you. On the other hand, you believe your partners have proven themselves to be morally corrupt cowards—that abandoning you was a dastardly deed.

This split thinking also applies to the way you view yourself. One minute you are a worthless failure for having lost the most important person in your life. The next you feel a sense of righteous indignation that someone would have the audacity to dismiss someone of your value. Maintaining a balanced perspective about yourself, your lost partners, and about the healing process of life is difficult at this stage.

Getting into the moment provides an immediate respite from the always-and-never perspective. When you are in the moment, this catastrophic thinking has no place. There is only *now*—a sacred place that you can create out of the bounty of life around you.

SYMBIOTIC FEELINGS

We have seen that during shattering we are flooded with feelings we knew best in our infancy when we began as helpless, dependent children. The reawakening of these feelings has brought you in touch with the oldest, most long forgotten part of yourself. In fact, the severing of your attachment has reactivated your emotional memories and has brought your most primitive feelings to the fore.

Symbiotic feelings are the ones you experienced prenatally and during early infancy when you were in a state of oneness with your mother. You were inseparable, in fact, incapable of surviving without a caretaker. These feelings of dependency, triggered during the shattering stage, place abandonment survivors in a painful emotional paradox: *The more you experience the impact of your loss, the more you are compelled to seek your lost partner.*

"I never wanted my wife so badly until she left," said Carlyle. "I felt I couldn't live without her!"

Your friends and family may wonder how you could want someone so badly who has treated you poorly. What they don't understand is that your partner's leaving automatically aroused symbiotic feelings that had been stored deep in your emotional memory. You are left to cope with feelings that stem from psychobiological processes that operate independently of your conscious thought and beyond your immediate control.

It's common, for example, to become temporarily overreliant upon friends, family, and professionals for nurturance. Some people seek sympathy in ways uncharacteristic of them. They're driven by an internal craving for nurturance they can no longer find in their lost partner.

However independently you may have functioned within your relationship, during the shattering stage you may find being alone intolerable. Especially difficult to face are blocks of unstructured time, especially weekends, major holidays, or anniversaries. At these times, it is especially important to seek the company of others—people who can offer companionship. This compelling need for others eventually subsides as you begin to heal.

Chronic Symbiotic Issues

The symbiotic paradox helps to explain the tendency for many to become emotionally trapped within a relationship in which their partners repeatedly abandon them on either physical or emotional levels.

> *"I can't seem to leave Barry," said Patricia. "I know he is no good for me. I know that he's a prop covered with warts and barnacles I'm holding on to, just to ward off the pain of being separated and all alone. I know all of this on one level, but for some reason, I just can't let him go. The worse he is to me, the more desperately I hold on."*

For those struggling with a situation like Patricia's, symbiotic feelings are reactivated again and again, each time you experience a break in an important bond, even if it is with the same person over and over again. Your neediest feelings—the ones that leave you emotionally helpless—keep flooding your consciousness with primal urgencies. You feel—albeit temporarily—that you can't survive on your own. Each tear in your relationship arouses a new round of intense insecurity. The infant in you cries out to be held and loved—paradoxically, by the very same person who keeps betraying, deserting, and *abandoning* you.

Judith Harris, author of *The Nurture Assumption*, states that abused children tend to reach out to the very person who abused them for comfort. The same is true in other species. According to Harris, a researcher who studied imprinting in ducks, when he accidentally stepped on the feet of a duckling that was imprinted on him, the duckling followed him more closely then ever.

Shattering rekindles symbiotic urges, but it also provides you with an opportunity, now as an adult, to finally break them. When all else is ripped away, it is your true self crying out— raw and entirely vulnerable. Your task is to bring your helpless feelings with you into the moment, to give life to your newly awakened internal core.

SUICIDAL FANTASIES AND THOUGHTS OF DEATH

Michael's shattering:

When Michael's lover first threatened to leave him six months earlier, he tried everything to hold on. He felt like he was fighting for his life. He'd made every possible accommodation to save his failing relationship, even gone into couples therapy and laid bare his emotional soul, but to no avail. One agonizing day, his lover packed up and left. Michael wanted to die.

In spite of all the dread and anxiety leading up to the end, Michael had not begun to let go. In fact, faced with the specter of loss, he'd clung tighter than before. Now alone, he could not find the will to go on living.

A friend urged him to sign up for abandonment recovery workshops. He arrived for the interview unshaven and rumpled. Speaking in a monotone, he explained that he had taken a leave from his job so he could "crawl into a hole and stay drunk as much as possible."

But Michael did manage to get himself to the first meeting, at which he talked at length about his suicidal thoughts. At one point, the members interrupted.

"Do you really want to die?" they asked, "or do you just want the pain to go away?"

"I want the pain to go away," he answered listlessly. "I'm

*only happy when I'm asleep," he continued. "And I only fall
asleep after I've drunk myself into a stupor."*

"There are ways to manage that pain," they told him.

*He waved that off. "It's too far gone for all of that," he said.
"The fact is, except for the pain, I've already died. You can't
save somebody who's already died."*

It is common for people to describe their abandonment as a
kind of death. They report feeling dead, or wanting to be dead,
or going through a spiritual death. As you follow Michael into
the next chapter, you will see that it is important not to act
upon these feelings. As intense as they are, they are temporary
and will dissipate as you progress through the stages that follow. During the shattering stage, the hopelessness you are experiencing is a feeling, not a fact.

Many also experience their abandonment as a physical, even
a *mortal* wound. They make frequent references to words that
describe critical injury and destruction to vital organs, references to *broken hearts, stabs in the gut, knife wounds to the
heart.*

*"After Lonny left, my house had become a tomb, a torture
chamber of loneliness. So I headed for anywhere but home.*

*"On the highways, I didn't meet a stone wall I wouldn't have
minded crashing into, head-on. If I spotted a knife while visiting
a friend's house, especially something in a cleaver or butcher
variety, I'd imagine plunging it deeply into my stomach.*

*At night, I'd rummage through the liquor cabinet in search
of something to guzzle down; it was the only way to fall asleep.
The last thing I worried about at the time was becoming an
alcoholic. I was more interested in inducing a stupor, coma,
lobotomy, death—whatever could end the pain.*

*"I struggled to get myself together to go to work in the morn-
ing, and on the way in, I'd try not to follow my urge to drive
off cliffs.*

"It was a real effort to hold myself together for the classes I

taught. It was hard coming up with new excuses every day for my bulbous red nose. I began to look more haggard by the day. People were always asking me what was wrong. Naturally, most of them were other teachers I didn't know well enough to tell about my problem.

"The good news about my deteriorating physical condition was that I lost weight, something I had always tried to do but couldn't because the truth is, I love food. Now I was more interested in the cutlery than the food. Friends saw me pushing my food around on my plate and asked if I was feeling well and why I looked so thin. My response was to thank them sincerely for the compliment and tell them I was on a special diet (called deathwish).

"When I finally found out that Lonny had left me for another woman, I would have preferred that he just stick a knife in my heart. It would have been less painful, quicker, and saved me from nearly starving myself to death."

We have already seen that during this critical period, many believe their devastation will be permanent. While this feeling persists, it is difficult to recognize that it is part of a process that leads to renewal. Like Michael and Marie, they truly feel their lives are over. The concept of death serves as an escape fantasy; it is the only way they can imagine an end to the pain. Conversations with them are riddled with references to death.

"I would be better off dead."

"I can't survive this."

"I can't sleep. I don't want to eat."

"My life is over."

"It feels like I'm going to die."

"Death would be easier."

Many abandonment survivors engage in fantasies about the impact their death might have upon their lost partners. "It would have been worth dying," said Marie, "just to get Lonny to realize that he really did love me."

For some, suicidal feelings, while not to be acted upon, can serve a purpose. They can help to shore up your ego during this stage. The idea that we could end the pain if we wanted to restores a sense of control that we have temporarily lost. But take pause. As powerful as your desire to end the pain, these feelings are only part of the initial healing process. They will pass soon enough, and you will certainly find love again when you choose to. Your task is to get all of the support you need from the people closest to you, and if needed, from mental health professionals. In the end, you will emerge from the experience better than before.

SOMATIC SENSATIONS

You may not be able to pinpoint the biophysiological changes that are taking place under the surface of your conscious mind, but you may, after reading the next few pages, recognize some indicators of those changes.

Your emotional brain perceives the loss of your partner as a threat to survival. The event triggers significant biological changes. As you progress through the rigors of your emotional crisis, many of the effects are sustained. Your heart rate and blood pressure are increased, sending a greater flow of blood and nutrients to the areas of your body needed for self-defense. Your digestion is turned off; blood flow is diverted from your stomach to major muscle groups so that you will be physically prepared to run away or fight off your attacker as the need arises. During the most stressful moments, structures deep within your brain signal a tightening in your vocal cords, creating the high-pitched voice of intense anxiety. According to Daniel Goleman, these same mechanisms make a dog snarl or a cat arch its back.

Other neural circuits are signaled at certain critical times to put a fearful or angry expression on your face, to freeze movements in some of your muscles, or to cause your breathing to become shallow so that you will be better able to detect important sounds above the sound of your breathing. Other processes cause your respiration rate to increase oxygen supply to your brain so that your mind can sustain its state of hypervigilance and keep your attention riveted upon the emergency. Your bladder and colon prepare to void their contents to rid the body of dead weight so you will be able to move quickly. Your pupils dilate to let in more light, your vision is more acute. The cochlear cells in your ears require less stimulation; you can hear a twig snap off a branch hundreds of feet away. Your brain is unusually alert, even at night, as biochemical systems work to sustain what your body experiences as a life-saving vigil.

Your neocortex continues to scan your memory banks, retrieving similar experiences from the past that it systematically sorts, compares, and analyzes to apply to your body's intensive problem-solving campaign. You experience this as obsessive thinking. Your immune system responds by lowering its production of antibodies, delaying swelling and pain to areas of your body that might become injured (in battle), so that your attention can remain focused on the threat at hand. You may not feel the impact of this lowering of your immune response until a few weeks later—perhaps during a respite from your intense emotional crisis. That's when you are likely to come down with that cold or flu.

Subjectively, you experience many of these symptoms in the form of constant preoccupation with your loss, hypervigilance, a tendency to startle easily, gastrointestinal discomforts, and reminders of past hurts and old insecurities. You have trouble sleeping, relaxing, and eating. Alternately, you may be unable to stop eating, because your body is trying to shore up energy reserves for a sustained crisis.

The threat your body prepares you for is not an attack of vicious wolves or an earthquake but the loss of your primary attachment. There isn't, of course, a real, physical threat to your safety, but there is an intense internal battle going on.

Many of these uncomfortable and unsettling sensations respond to the effects of a well-known drug—one that is legal and readily available—alcohol. Because alcohol is a depressant, it can dampen tensions and the edginess you feel. Even the most moderate of drinkers tend to overmedicate with alcohol to help themselves fall asleep or relax. Since alcohol is highly addictive, it is important to remember that even in small doses it can impair functioning and lead to serious injury.

Try, as an alternative analgesic, to seek the refuge of the moment as described at the end of this chapter. Staying in the moment can help you feel centered and at peace, and it leads you to that state of calm that you need to get you through the most difficult moments, one at a time.

SHAME

An issue that comes up for many people throughout the first stages of the abandonment cycle is shame. I'll discuss the shame of being left in depth in Chapter 4 when I explain *internalizing*. But when you first begin to grieve over a lost partner, you feel shame over emotional excesses you can't seem to control.

"I can't face the world," said Michael. *"All people have to do is look at me and see the condition I am in, and they'll know I'm unable to handle my life."*

We are socialized, men and women alike, to feel ashamed of intensely negative feelings. Many people hate losing control over their emotions, feeling helpless, or in any way dependent. It's easy to overlook the valuable emotional wisdom contained in these feelings. But if you get in touch with them and understand what they are about, these feelings can enhance your future relationships. They allow you to become more emotionally accessible to others.

Rather than accept and nurture these valuable feelings, many condemn themselves for being so desperate and needy. They allow the powerful feelings to throw their whole sense of personal strength and independence into question.

"I felt like a child," reports Richard, a bank president whose wife had recently left him. "I cried for her like a baby crying for its mother when she said she was going. My whole life suddenly revolved around her. I was obsessed with wanting to be with her, wanting to talk with her. I felt so needy and frightened.

"I'm a grown man, but I wasn't able to tolerate being alone in my new apartment—it was too sterile, too empty. I was actually frightened of the pain I was in, afraid I wouldn't be able to live through it. It was shameful how dependent I felt. I couldn't help acting like a desperate child in the throes of a tantrum.

"I began to wonder if my whole adult identity was just a facade. I must, I reasoned, have been a weak, needy person all along. I even thought that it must have been why my wife left me in the first place."

Richard didn't realize it at the time, but the symbiotic needs he was feeling were temporary, normal to the process, and even served a *purpose* during the first stage of his grief. Until he was able to accept his needy and fearful feelings, he degraded himself, lost confidence. "I felt as if I had been utterly vanquished," he said, "like *she* was the stronger one." He was profoundly disappointed in himself for feeling so much pain.

There are several reasons to avoid feeling ashamed and simply *accept* your intense but temporary need for your lost attachment. First, as we have seen with Richard, shame only complicates the grieving process. It's one more way in which you turn against yourself. Second, when you attempt to disown, deny, or suppress feelings, you deny yourself the opportunity to better understand yourself emotionally. Third, burying your feelings delays resolving them within your current or future relationships. In short, picking up emotional baggage only prolongs your grief. If unaccepted and unresolved, feelings generate fear, anxiety, and insecurity when you next try to bring love into your life.

Better to accept the cold, hard facts of the situation: that abandonment is a powerful enough trauma to arouse your body's self-defense system, to reactivate old emotional memories, and to create a temporary condition in which your need for attachment is uncomfortably intense. Coming to terms with the reality that losing your loved one is a real emotional crisis is a way to avoid the shame trap. This acceptance is an important step in the direction of becoming emotionally self-nurturing.

SHOCK

Not everyone is able to stay in touch with the most intense feelings of shattering. Some people report not being able to feel anything at all. "I don't know where I'm at. I'm too disoriented," reported Carlyle. Roberta says, "I know I'm in hell, but I'm numb. Everything around me has gone dead."

Belinda describes her experience:

"I flew to Paris to be with my fiancé, and when I got there, he told me he changed his mind. The engagement was off. I was fractured. Life in Paris, the city I'd had always dreamed of, was going on around me, but I was too numb to see it, to hear it, to participate. Instead, I was in complete shock, standing alone with my whole life crashing down around me. Nothing seemed to matter. I wasn't even sure of who I was."

In their initial shock, people often appear detached from themselves and from the events going on around them. The extreme internal focus of this initial stage encapsulates them in a dissociative bubble through which the world can look distorted and far away.

Shock is one of the many symptoms of traumatic stress, a significant component of the shattering stage. Some of its other symptoms will be outlined in the next section.

POST-TRAUMATIC STRESS DISORDER OF ABANDONMENT

Many people's reactions to abandonment share sufficient features with post-traumatic stress disorder (PTSD) to be considered a subtype of this diagnostic category.

As with other types of posttrauma, *post-traumatic stress disorder of abandonment* can range from mild to severe. It is a psychobiological condition in which earlier separation traumas can interfere with current life. You experience emotional flashbacks that flood you with anxiety in response to triggers that you may not consciously perceive, and this often leaves you with the overwhelming sense that you're no longer in control.

JOHN'S SHATTERING

John arrived for his first session, a compelling figure, tall, good-looking, powerfully built. He had recently met a woman he felt attracted to. They had only one date. The evening felt right to him; he'd felt whole, complete in her company, and he wanted to make a real connection with her. He was sure she felt the same, but she didn't call him back.

"It was only one date!" he said. "I can't believe I am this distraught over one date!"

He expected to be running into her at a professional conference that week and was afraid he'd be too emotional to handle seeing her again. "She'll think I'm a basket case. I won't be able to hide it. What could possibly make me overreact like this?" he said. "I'm obsessing every minute of the day. Not to mention the fact that I can't eat.

"It's not like I'm desperate for a woman or anything. I

haven't even wanted *to date anyone for a long time. And now I'm acting like this one woman not calling is a matter of life or death."* He shrugged his shoulders and looked to me for direction.

"Could it be unresolved grief over another relationship?" I offered.

Point-blank, he confronted the pain that had been holed up inside. He took a deep breath and tried to speak. He made a couple of false starts—he couldn't seem to find his voice or control his facial muscles.

Handing him a box of tissues seemed to help. His words and tears began to pour freely. The painful event happened about ten years ago. His fiancée had broken their engagement a week before the wedding. As he described this shattering experience, he seemed surprised that he could still feel the pain. "I thought I was completely over her," he said. "I haven't given it a moment's thought in years.

"After the breakup, I tried to date other people, but I just didn't feel right with anyone else. I was too insecure, too on guard. After a year or so of getting nowhere, I decided to go it alone for a while."

This he accomplished by staying off the playing field, becoming a "devout bachelor," as he put it. The only side effect of his voluntary isolation was loneliness, but this was a steady throb, a dull ache he got used to. He considered it preferable to the ups and downs of dating. He told himself that there was nobody out there he was interested in, that he was fine by himself.

"So now I finally meet a woman I like, and I find out I'm a basket case," he said. "How could old stuff like this still have so much kick after all these years?"

While not severe, John's case portrays one of the features of post-traumatic stress disorder of abandonment: intrusive anxiety from the past. His story focuses upon an earlier event from his adult life, one that continues to trigger fear and anxiety and interferes in his current life.

As John's case unfolded, he addressed childhood losses.

When he was six, his father developed cancer and suffered a prolonged illness, forcing John's mother to work full time. Although his father's cancer eventually went into remission, the family business folded, and financial troubles forced them to move several times. There were numerous disappointments and broken connections for John along the way. John's childhood experiences made him especially sensitive to loss. As an adult, his strategy was to practice avoidance, to emotionally distance himself from his basic needs and feelings. He avoided relationships and the insecurities that went along with them.

There are many other patterns and behavior associated with a posttraumatic condition and many ways in which the fear or anxiety rising from your past separations may be interfering in your life today.

SIGNS AND SYMPTOMS OF POST-TRAUMATIC STRESS DISORDER OF ABANDONMENT

While not yet accepted into diagnostic literature, I propose the following list of symptoms for abandonment's posttrauma.

- An intense fear of abandonment (overwhelming insecurity) that tends to destabilize your primary relationships in adulthood

- A tendency to repeatedly subject yourself to people or experiences that lead to another loss and another trauma

- Intrusive reawakening of old losses

- Heightened memories of traumatic separations and other events

- Conversely, complete or partial memory blocks of earlier events

- Feelings of emotional detachment from past crises

- Conversely, difficulty letting go of the painful feelings of old rejections and losses, which generate ongoing emotional conflict with your parents or siblings

- Episodes of self-destructive behavior

- Difficulty withstanding the normal emotional ups and downs of an adult relationship

- Difficulty working through the normal levels of conflict and disappointment within a relationship

- Extreme sensitivity to rejection

- Tendency to emotionally or sexually shut down, but not be able to identify why

- Difficulty naming your feelings

- Difficulty feeling the affection and other physical comforts offered to you by a willing partner

- A pendulum swing between fear of engulfment and fear of annihilation

- A tendency to avoid close relationships altogether

- Conversely, a tendency to rush into relationships and clamp on too quickly

- Difficulty letting go because you have attached with emotional epoxy, even when your partner is unable to fulfill your needs

- An excessive need for control, whether you're controlling toward others or overly self-controlled; a need to have everything perfect and done your way

- Conversely, a tendency to create chaos by avoiding responsibility and procrastinating

- A tendency to act impulsively without being able to put the brakes on, even when you know there could be negative consequences

- A tendency toward unpredictable outbursts of anger

Not all of you who experienced traumatic losses during childhood were destined to develop these posttraumatic personality traits. There are many psychobiological factors involved in determining whether your earlier emotional traumas might lead to the development of a true clinical picture of post-traumatic stress disorder.

Many people who suffer from posttrauma of abandonment aren't able to identify any extreme abandonments in childhood. Instead, they came from relatively intact families with no known history of abuse. On the other hand, there are those who endured extreme childhood losses and yet appear relatively trauma-free as adults—able to weather rejection and loss without signs of posttraumatic stress. The reason for this apparent discrepancy might have to do with genetic endowment and other predisposing physiological and psychological factors. Researchers have speculated that some people are born with a tendency to produce higher concentrations of norepinephrine, a brain chemical involved in arousal of your body's self-defense response. This would mean that your threshold for becoming aroused is lowered, and you are more likely to become anxious when you encounter stresses in life that are reminiscent of childhood fears and experiences, hence more prone to becoming posttraumatic.

Whether or not you are a candidate for a diagnosis of posttraumatic stress disorder of abandonment, you may be experiencing some emotional overlay from your earlier losses. If so, this reexperiencing tends to intensify your loss.

TODAY'S TRAUMA

During the shattering stage, my clients almost universally respond to the word *trauma* and use it frequently, whether or not they consider themselves to be experiencing posttraumatic symptoms. In fact, the end of an important romantic relationship is in and of itself a trauma—not *post*trauma. It is a legitimate *initial* trauma.

Whether your abandonment grief is the result of a recent breakup or of cumulative wounds and whether your feelings stem from loss of a job, loss of a friend, or loss of a life partner, the experience feels traumatic.

> *"Having to move out of my house was the most traumatic experience of my life,"* said Carlyle.

> *"Travis put me through so much trauma."*

> *"Losing Lonny felt like I was traumatized for life!"* said Marie.

> *"I don't feel normal anymore,"* said Richard, *"all I feel is trauma."*

Depending upon the circumstances of your abandonment, your personal history and neurophysiological constitution, some of you may go on to develop posttraumatic symptoms from what's happening right now, while others won't. Naturally, this book is designed to help you temper the affects of the trauma.

SIGNS AND SYMPTOMS OF CURRENT TRAUMATIC STRESS

The following symptoms are commonly experienced by abandonment survivors:

Shock and Disorientation

In the wake of losing a beloved partner, people describe themselves as being in utter shock, disbelief, and bewilderment, unable to face the shattered reality of their lives.

There is a wealth of research suggesting that the brain's opioid system produces higher levels of morphinelike substances (one of which is called endorphin), during this early stage of grief. The opiates have a pain-reducing effect and may account for shock and numbing, as well as symptoms of withdrawal.

As you may recall from Belinda's story, she became numb to her surroundings after her fiancé announced he no longer wanted to marry her.

"Everything seemed strange," she said. "It felt as if my life had been a dream and that I had just awakened in a strange bed. I suddenly had no future. The day before, I had been picking out just the right shade of lipstick and remembering to buy extra film. The next day, nothing mattered except how to survive the pain.

"If the Eiffel Tower had fallen down right in front of me, I wouldn't have noticed it. I really didn't know which end was up. I didn't feel capable of buying a pack of cigarettes—and it wasn't until I got a hold of a cigarette that I remembered I had quit over five years ago."

Depersonalizing

Another feature of trauma is feeling depersonalized, alienated from your feelings and from your sense of yourself.

"I no longer felt like me," said Carlyle. "I couldn't find me. It was as if I had vacated. It was difficult to explain this feeling to anyone, so I just went through the motions. But I felt like a shell that had been abandoned or a river whose waters had run dry."

Unreality

In the wake of a severed relationship, nothing seems real.

"When Lonny broke up with me, it shattered my whole sense of reality," said Marie. "My friends just couldn't understand why I no longer cared about anything. They suddenly existed in a parallel world, a world that only carried the illusion of being in control, a world that no longer belonged to me. I had become a stranger in my own life."

Separation Anxiety

Also common is an undercurrent of anxiety that many have described as a *sinking feeling.* This free-floating anxiety stems from your sustained emotional crisis and the reawakening of old, emotionally charged experiences. We have already discussed the sympathetic nervous system arousal that underlies this discomfort. It induces a state of hypervigilance, which we experience as chronic anxiety and agitation, and a feeling of perpetual vulnerability.

"I went around with a sense of morbid dread," said Richard. "Like something terrible was about to happen. But what more could happen? The worst had already occurred. I just felt uncomfortable in my own skin."

Reality Distortion

Many people report perceptual illusions in which they keep seeing their lost partner in the street, in a crowd, going by on a bus or train. When they do chance to get close enough, they recognize their mistake.

While your mind continues *searching for your lost attachment,* your eyes scan the horizon, picking up visual signals. According to Candice Pert, the signals we pick up must make their way through five synapses within the brain—from the eye to the back of the brain (occipital cortex), and back to the front of your brain (frontal cortex). At each synapse, the image we see becomes progressively more detailed.

"I saw Lonny in every blue Volvo that drove by," said Marie. "No matter what make or model, I was sure it was him, right up until the moment the car got close enough for me to see that it was someone else."

Sometimes these illusions seem to come out of thin air. Roberta described seeing Travis's eyes looking down on her as she was about to go to sleep one night. She was very frightened. Michael thought he heard his lover call his name, though he knew he was alone in the room. Although these reality distortions are common to shattering and usually are temporary, they do confirm that you are indeed in the midst of an emotional crisis. If you begin to hear voices or have real hallucinations, you have a responsibility to reach out for professional guidance and support. There is no need to go through this crisis on your own when help is readily available.

Self-abuse

Another typical feature of trauma is a tendency toward self-abuse and self-destructive behavior. Your seething self-hatred may lead you to take risks with your life. People turn their rage about being rejected against themselves. They hold themselves to blame for their painful loss and want to punish or destroy the culprit—themselves. They might engage in unsafe sex, drive recklessly, overdose on medication, or even self-inflict injury. Mild to severe forms of self-mutilation range from pulling out hair and picking scabs, to creating real physical wounds.

"I am a diabetic, and I just stopped taking insulin," Sylvia reported. "I no longer cared."

Rather than bargain with your life, it is important to seek additional support as well as professional help during this crucial time.

Substance Abuse

We have already emphasized the discomfort generated by your body's self-defense system. Depending upon the level of traumatic stress, some seek desperate pain control measures: sleeping pills, street drugs, or excessive amounts of alcohol. Many report getting drunk frequently in the wake of rejection, even if they rarely drank before. Though your discomfort may be intense, using drugs and alcohol to get through your emotional crisis can lead to many risks, not the least of which is becoming addicted.

Many people in the addiction recovery programs report that they began abusing drugs or alcohol as a way of coping with an abandonment experience. Alcohol, heroin, and other drugs were the antidote for their wounds. The good news is that they recognized the problem and reached out for help, turning their situation into a positive one.

Spurts of Explosive Rage

Bouts of uncontrollable and unpredictable anger are typical of the shattering stage. We have already talked about how abandonment triggers the release of adrenaline and norepinephrine, whose surges activate your body's fight-or-flight response, supplying you with the energy required to run away or fight back. Even people who are normally placid can lose control and become enraged to the point of violence. This tendency for anger to flare up is especially pronounced when we use alcohol as self-medication. Alcohol and other drugs tend to release the inhibitions that control the expression of anger.

Anger that erupts unpredictably and spurts out of control is often intended for our lost partners, but regrettably we sometimes explode at close friends and innocent bystanders instead.

ABANDONMENT IS OFTEN NOT RECOGNIZED AS TRAUMA

During the shattering stage, abandonment survivors experience many of the same symptoms as victims of other types of trauma, such as rape or physical attack. The difference is that abandonment survivors are not often recognized as such. Yet the shock, numbing, disorientation, outbursts of anger, and tendency toward risk-taking are all symptoms of significant trauma.

We can see these symptoms in children who have been through abandonment experiences. Unlike adults, children do not have the tools with which to temper the impact. Their hurts and abandonments can leave a powerful imprint upon their developing brains and can effect their emotional responses throughout life.

REVERBERATIONS OF EARLIER SHATTERINGS

I am four years old, very close to my parents, an only child. My parents have dropped me off at the hospital. I am not prepared for this, for what is going to happen. I am left alone and I don't understand.

A doctor cuts my throat during an operation while I am under anesthesia. I wake up with a terrible pain in my throat. I do not understand that I have had my tonsils removed or why it hurts so much. I do not know where my parents are.

Somehow I think there has been a mistake. I am in a children's ward with many other children. There are rows and rows of cribs with children lying in them and nurses and parents hovering about. Every day, all day, parents visit the other children. But no one comes for me. I am all alone.

Many days later, my parents finally come. I am in a fetal position. I have to be massaged so that my arms and legs can relax enough to be moved, so that I can be taken home.

I have no recollection of this experience. My mother told me the details of this hospital stay.

SCENARIOS OF CHILDHOOD SHATTERING

My story is not unusual. Many childhood experiences create intense feelings of abandonment. A pet dies, or a grandmother leaves after a long visit, or your mother suddenly becomes busy with a new baby. You hear about someone else's mother dying and you begin to worry that such a terrible thing could happen to you. Your parents are late picking you up from school, or you see your parents having a serious fight, or you have learning problems in school. You have no one to play with on the playground, or you are yelled at by the teacher, or criticized by your father.

These are ordinary childhood experiences that can nonetheless arouse intense feelings of anxiety and despair. Children experience all loss, injury, and turmoil as abandonment. Their strongest attachment is to their primary caretakers. But they form other strong attachments to people, places, capabilities, ideals, and dreams. Any breach in those attachments creates fear—a feeling of being helpless, a feeling of being unable to hold on to what they hold most dear—in short, a heightened fear of abandonment. This is a fear that can live on indefinitely, often dissociated from your memory of the original events that caused it.

My mother noticed that as I went through elementary school, I had a very hard time whenever I had to wait for someone to pick me up from school or something to happen that was important to me. Even as I became a teenager, ordinary experiences like waiting for a date or anticipating a rejection could send me into apoplexy. It was especially noticeable as I waited for my date to pick me up for the prom. I began to fret and panic that he would *never* show up, that I would *never* know what had happened, that I would *always* be left alone. My mother felt it was important to tell me the hospital story.

"Susan, I think there is something you should know," my mother finally said. "It's about when you were four years old and had your tonsils out. Your father and I misunderstood the doctor at the hospital. We thought we were not allowed to visit. So, we went away for the weekend and didn't return until it was time to pick you up."

I told her of my only memory of the experience. *It is of my mother's and father's loving eyes looking down upon me in the hospital crib, spooning vanilla ice cream into my mouth. It was cold and made the pain in my throat feel better.*

"Yes," said my mother, "that all fits. After we saw what leaving you there did to you, we felt terrible. We hovered over you for hours trying to get you to relax enough to roll over and respond to us. We fed you ice cream until you were calm and then we brought you home."

Since then, I have tried every known technique—hypnotherapy, gestalt, psychodrama—to bring this memory back so that I might be able to release the anxiety still attached to it. But in spite of this and all of my years of training and practice in psychotherapy, nothing brings it back.

Needless to say, I have learned to avoid the type of people who would leave me waiting. Sometimes though, I do have to wait and under certain conditions I still feel anxiety grip my body, defying my rational mind's attempt to stay calm and relaxed.

I am not the only abandonment survivor of childhood to have posttraumatic symptoms from old emotional experiences. Nor am I the only one unable to remember the events that caused them. Many abandonment survivors continue to be flooded with fear, anxiety, insecurity, and maladaptive behavior patterns rising out of childhood experiences of which they have no conscious memory. They wonder how they managed to get stuck in the emotional past, why their earlier losses and abandonments still exert such an impact on their lives.

Many of my clients surmise that they must have repressed or suppressed their childhood experiences in their unconscious mind. These unconscious memories, they reason, continue to fester out of sight. They use the terms *suppression, repression,* and *unconscious* to suggest how they might have created these hidden memories. In using these terms, they are not trying to be scientists or psychotheoreticians; they are simply trying to make sense of the questions such as:

> *"How can my childhood have such an impact on me if I can't even remember it?"*
>
> *"Where do the memories go?"*
>
> *"If I am able to dredge up my past, will I be able to free my life of the insecurity, anxiety, and fear?"*

The field of brain science sheds some new light on these post-traumatic conundrums. Thanks to the pioneer work of Joseph LeDoux, we know a great deal about the *amygdala,* an almond-shaped structure located deep within your emotional (or mammalian) brain.

A MINI LESSON ON THE EMOTIONAL BRAIN

The amygdala plays a central role in the way you emotionally respond. It functions as the body's central alarm system, scanning for any possible threat, be it emotional or physical, but especially for anything that recalls a previous fear-laden experience. If the amygdala detects a problem, it declares a state of emotional emergency.

Imprinted in the amygdala are memories of how you have responded to fear and other perceived threats since infancy. These emotional memories help you detect dangers that you have learned about from previous experience, both as a species (don't step over the edge of a cliff) and individually (don't go near Uncle Charlie). It is believed to contain traces of your prenatal and birth experience as well.

The amygdala continues to gather emotional memories as you grow. Once it has been conditioned to an emotional response (i.e., feeling anxious when a loved one threatens separation), its learning is nearly indelible. In other words, when it comes to emotional memory, the slate never gets completely wiped clean.

We've already seen how a threat to an important emotional bond is perceived by the sympathetic branch of your autonomic nervous system as a threat to survival. Your pounding heart, the queasy feeling in your stomach, and the rush of adrenaline are signs that your body's self-defense has kicked in.

Children have these same fight-or-flight responses when they perceive a threat to their primary attachments. Depending upon the degree of fear involved, these experiences become imprinted in the amygdala's emotional memory. These emotional memories are reactivated when you perceive similar threats of loss in adulthood.

Emotional learning is similar to Pavlovian conditioning. In Pavlov's experiment with dogs, the bell and the meal that usually followed became a paired association—the dogs were conditioned to salivate every time they heard the bell. To illustrate how we learn emotional responses, let's look at battle trauma. In the heat of battle, the amygdala is fully involved. It incorporates into its emotional memory banks not just pain and fear but the sights, smells, and sounds of the battle. These become powerful paired associations of the battle trauma. Even years later, similar sights, sounds, or smells can activate the powerful amygdala circuits; veterans can reexperience a full-blown emotional flashback at the sound of a thunder clap.

Similarly, the sensations associated with separation from a loved one can be seen as an emotional trigger. Sensations reminiscent of the original trauma activate the amygdala's circuits, and you experience the fears and needs from that earlier loss all over again.

The amygdala receives input about perceived threats directly from your sensory organs (including your eyes and ears), without first having to go through your cerebral cortex. In other words, you can react to something that your eye detects *before* you know that you have seen it. Messages traveling along these subcortical routes move faster than those traveling along the circuits leading to and from your cerebral cortex, where your rational thought takes place.

The automatic nature of your response is a highly adaptive one in terms of survival. If you had to stop and reason out the best course of action, you might lose valuable time in the event of a life-threatening emergency. Your amygdala activates your freeze, fight, or flight response before your thinking brain has a chance to intercede. The amygdala also responds to thoughts or ideas formed within your neocortex. A fear-provoking thought can trigger an immediate panic response. Before you have a chance to reason it through more carefully, your body has been thrown into self-defense mode.

Responding quickly and automatically is imperative when we need to dart out of the way of a falling tree or react to the attack of grizzly bear, but it gets in our way if the perceived threat is the beginning of a relationship. The urge to fight, flee, or freeze can be quite an impediment on the second date. Many of us do freeze up, become agitated, or break into a cold sweat during romantic rough spots. Who invited our autonomic nervous systems to the movie, anyway? Nature did. We evolved that way to ensure our survival.

If losses from childhood or adolescence are capable of conditioning a fear response, then the amygdala is the part of the brain implicated in fear of abandonment, a fear common to all of us.

The arousal of learned emotional responses helps to explain the needy feelings of the shattering stage. Old, outdated symbiotic needs of early childhood flood your adult brain, and you're overwhelmed by feelings of desperation and helplessness. You can't, you think, even survive without your mate. In fact, if you point the finger at this emotional memory system, then you can think of your overefficient amygdala as an overprotective parent who doesn't want to see you get hurt.

The question remains though: How is it that you experience primitive feelings stemming from old traumas, and yet you can't

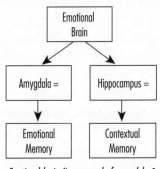

Emotional brain (is composed of amygdala & hippocampus)

remember the events that created them? Why do so many abandonment survivors have large gaps in their childhood memories?

The answer to these questions lies in the *hippocampus*, another structure of your emotional brain. The seahorse-shaped hippocampus is responsible for recording not the feelings but the *facts* surrounding emotionally charged events, such as where the event occurred, who was involved, and what actually happened.

The clincher is that, depending upon how intense or prolonged the event, the release of stress hormones can *impair* the hippocampus's memory function. You witnessed and may even have *participated* in what transpired, but you may not be able to retrieve the memory later on because it never got stored in the first place. The emotional memory is there, but there is no context memory to accompany it.

Other biochemical reactions to stress can have the opposite effect on hippocampal memory. The production of adrenaline has been found in some cases to *enhance* hippocampal memory. This may explain flashbulb memories typical of trauma in which you remember an intensely emotional event in vivid detail. We are going to learn more about the impact of the stress hormones on memory as well as other psychobiological functions in the next chapter dealing with the withdrawal stage.

In the meantime, we need to steer clear of the idea that our bodies are somehow programmed to keep us miserable. Neurobiology does not dictate destiny. No two brains or people are alike. Our psychobiological systems are not fixed but constantly changing. Our brains, like our personalities, are unique and multidimensional. The amygdala and hippocampus are not separate little kingdoms. They interact with our rational minds in ways that are unique to the moment and to each of us.

Enlightened by the information about the neurobiology of your experience, my hope is that you are better able to accept your emotional responses and avoid condemning yourself for not being able to carefully control your feelings in every situation. Instead, you can focus your energy on what you can control, on what you can change. Ultimately, you can master your own destiny.

THE SHATTERED PERSONALITY PROFILE: POSSIBLE PRECURSORS TO PTSD OF ABANDONMENT

You may find that you struggle more during one stage of the abandonment process than another. Abandonment survivors who tend to have the most difficulty during the *shattering stage* are those who suffered devastating repetitive losses, personal disappointments, and upheavals in childhood. These might include:

- Death of a parent

- Physical abandonment by a parent

- Being in the middle of your parents' custody or divorce battle

- Prolonged emotional distance from your caretakers

- Physical or sexual abuse

- Being sent to a foster home

Many of you may be the products of relatively intact families, but you experienced feelings of prolonged deprivation due to:

- Injustices within the sibling pecking order

- Chaos and conflict in family structure

- Emotional messages that left you in a double-bind situation where you couldn't win, no matter how you played it

- Rejection or exclusion from a peer group

- Prolonged childhood injury or illness

- Traumatic adolescent heartbreaks

- Significant disappointments (working hard toward something and failing to get the reward)

The shards and fragments of these and other traumas are reactivated when you go through similar upheavals and losses later in life.

For many abandonment survivors, this means intermittent emotional turmoil and chronic uncertainty about yourself and your relationships. As new experiences trigger the old emotionally charged memories, your self-defense system kicks in, releasing adrenaline and other stress hormones. The process leaves many feeling on edge and suddenly uncomfortable in their own skins.

When people who are prone to anxiety or those with traumatic childhood histories encounter a new crisis, the old shatterings can be truly overwhelming. Without an understanding of what causes the intense anxiety or how to cope with it, some desperate folks self-medicate with drugs and alcohol. If you feel overwhelmed, please seek professional help. Support and guidance is available; in some cases, medication may be appropriate.

It is not through any weakness on your part that you cannot by an act of conscious will rid yourself of the anxiety, pain, and fear. These intense emotions spring from the psychobiological nature of your crisis.

Shattering is a time of trauma, but it can lead to a new level of self-acceptance and understanding of life if we choose to learn from its wisdom.

THE BENEFITS OF SHATTERING

The secret gift of abandonment is that it has helped you find your way to old wounds from traumatic events you may not even recall. Finally you can address unresolved feelings. Shattering has accomplished what many psychoanalysts strive for in years of therapy—bringing you to the seat of your unconscious conflicts.

You are in a crucial period during which you must look to your own resources. You can no longer look to your lost partners for security and nurturance. Beyond the support of friends, family, and helping professionals, you spend most of your time with yourself; you are in an optimal position to look inside for strength.

Though your own parents may have tried, they were not able to sufficiently assuage your abandonment fears when you were children. As an adult, you face this challenge alone. First you must be in touch with your fears. Listen to what they are telling you about your emotional needs.

Shattering has been a *journey to the center of the self*, preparing you for deep healing, for the opportunity to shape your life from the inside out. It challenges you with critical questions designed to help you find the point from which you can begin again.

Can you accept your own separateness?

Can you face the ever-changing world around you?

Can you take responsibility to direct it?

Can you acknowledge that you are capable of benefitting from your abandonment?

Can you accept that you are able to stand on your own two feet?

Recognize that you have already gained something from your experience. The casts and crutches of your former life have been broken; you've awakened from a trance. You have been jolted out of complacency, thrown out of equilibrium, and forced to find a new way back. Carlyle put it this way:

"For me, shattering was an awakening. It helped me to change the direction of my life. I know I have a lot of work to do, but I finally know what's important. It took losing my wife to finally shatter my illusion of permanence, of being one with someone, of being in control. For the first time in my life, I realized how alone I was, how alone we all are.

"From somewhere in the abyss I was in, missing my kids and feeling lost, I was able to look up and be astounded at how painful loss is. Not just mine. All loss. I started to think about the millions of people who've suffered this experience before me and the millions to come. I was on intimate terms with human pain. My touch plate of feeling was alive as never before. And I knew I was forever changed by this knowledge. Painful as this was, it was a gift I would never give away. It made me intensely human."

Shattering has laid down its challenge to you. Through it you can achieve greater emotional independence, an undertaking that may be long overdue. Being emotionally independent does not mean accepting that you are condemned to live your life alone, but that you are able to reach for love and connectedness with self-reliance and emotional wisdom.

RECOVERY FROM SHATTERING

AKERU EXERCISES

Akeru has many meanings—to end, pierce, make a hole in, begin, expire, empty, make room for, unwrap, start, turn over, open—and all relate to the abandonment process. *Akeru*'s multiple meanings refer to processes that stem from the same underlying energy.

When I speak about energy, I am not referring to a New Age concept or a quantifiable scientific phenomenon. Energy, force, drive, instinct, and impetus all describe the direction and intensity of the grief cycle as we move through its stages. The energy involved in shattering is the life force, the inborn need for attachment. When that energy is thwarted, grief is the result. Its pain is our psychobiological reaction to being suddenly cut off, held back from the relationship we so desire. This powerful impetus to attach is ever present. It can be the source of pain, but if redirected, it can be the first step toward healing.

Akeru describes the empty space that is created when someone leaves. Your task is to work within that space to create new life. This may sound at first like a message of hearts and flowers, but the Akeru concept does not gloss over pain. It allows me to speak to the center of the pain without getting mired in it. It has helped my clients understand how to use its energy to their benefit.

Akeru allows me to talk about adversity and motivation as one. Adversity is the force that drives us to summon our greatest gifts of imagination and personal strength. Without guidance, our tendency is to fight against that pain. Once enlightened, we work with it.

I've included at the end of Chapters 2 through 6 a sequence of exercises—one for each of the stages—I use in my practice to facilitate real change.

Akeru has come to represent the method for abandonment recovery. It helps my clients conceptualize the fact that true recovery is the abandonment grief process turned around. By redirecting its energy, we can enhance our lives and increase our capacity for love.

The site of the greatest wound is the site of the greatest healing. Akeru.

UNITY OF OPPOSITES

Begin

End

Make Room For

Pierce

Unwrap

Turn Over

To Make a Hole In

To Expire

To Start

Akeru (multiple meanings)

Akeru embraces both an end and a beginning. For each sign or symptom associated with the end of a relationship, we can make a beginning. For **shattering**, there is reassembling; for **shock**, there is clarity and focus; for **severing**, there is wholeness; for **separation anxiety**, there is serenity; for **substance abuse**, there is sobriety; for **symbiotic regression**, there is self-reliance; for **reality distortion**, there is accepting reality; for **split thinking**, there is rational self-assurance; for **shame**, there is genuine humility and dignity; for **self-deprecation**, there is self-assurance; for **somatic breakdown**, there is revitalizing; for **suicidal feelings**, there is aliveness; for **self-abuse**, there is self-care; for **self-destructiveness**, there is self-building; for **self-hatred**, there is self-acceptance; for **self-absorption**, there is capacity to love.

Without guidance, this unity of opposites may not seem apparent, especially while people are in the midst of the shattering pain, but enlightened or not, the dual force of this transition is there. Abandonment and recovery are different aspects of the same energy waiting to be recognized: *Akeru*.

AKERU EXERCISE ONE: STAYING IN THE MOMENT

This is the first of five Akeru exercises designed to access the energy within the pain you're feeling. Exercise One, *Staying in the Moment,* offers a beacon to guide you through this momentary period of stark separation.

This exercise is effective for pain management but has other benefits as well. It uses the shattering energy—that raw sensation of separateness—to facilitate change. It serves as a foundation for the rest of your abandonment recovery program. Every time you accomplish *staying in the moment,* even for minutes at a time, you rediscover your personal power and build self-reliance.

Staying in the moment provides an alternative to drowning your feelings in alcohol, abusing drugs, or acting out in self-destructive ways. It allows you to stay with your feelings, to let them wash over you like waves. You will emerge from the storm. You can bear the very worst of these feelings because you know that they are normal and temporary, part of life's unpredictability and impermanence. As you continue practicing this exercise, you learn to take refuge in life around you.

The wisdom behind the Alcoholics Anonymous maxim, "One day at a time," is based upon the experience of hundreds and thousands of people who discovered redemption and personal salvation after hitting bottom. Coming up from the abyss, they discovered that the way to celebrate life and deal with its challenges is to live *in the moment, one day at a time.*

Abandonment survivors hit an emotional bottom; you, too, can take comfort in the healing potential of the moment, of today. There is a proviso: During the shattering stage, fear and grief can be so intense that thinking about how you will get through a whole day is often overwhelming. One day is too big a chunk of time to grapple with all at once. So your task is to get into this very moment. Focus upon the sensory information coming through your eyes and ears and nose and skin *right now.*

The moment is not a time for thinking, it is a time for *experiencing.* When you allow your thinking to take over, you are prone to thoughts about the future where you face the unknown, or you get pulled back into the past where you are confronted with your grief and loss. In the moment, neither future nor past have any relevance.

GENERAL SUGGESTIONS FOR STAYING IN THE MOMENT

It is better to think of staying in the moment as a way to experience life in general, rather than an exercise to be segregated from the rest of your waking hours. Much of the time, getting into the moment simply means tuning in to your environment and focusing on your senses, rather than your worries and grief. Staying in the moment isn't just an exercise, it's a way of being.

At times of greatest anguish, many find it is difficult to stay in the moment for more than a few seconds at a time. Fear has a tendency steer your thoughts, shuttling them back and forth between the past and future—between sorrow and dread. Intense anxiety challenges your ability to stay in the moment. This level of intensity is a hallmark of the shattering stage. When you experience these difficulties, your task is to simply keep returning to the moment.

When your stress is at its greatest peak, it is often difficult to *find* the moment. Sometimes listening to the radio to get your mind off your troubles isn't enough. You still can't keep those painful thoughts at bay. When this happens, it is time to turn off the radio and tune into the background noises, the subtle textures of sound that require more focused listening. Concentrating helps to bring you out of your painful thoughts.

Likewise, simply looking out the window isn't a compelling enough sensory experience to draw you out of the pain. Better to close your eyes and concentrate upon the galaxies of light that play on the back of your eyelids. This more disciplined approach will help draw your thoughts away from the pain and suffering and toward life around you.

Your senses are always there to draw your mind away from painful self-reflection, but at the most painful moments, this exercise requires a deliberate effort, a conscious act of will. Each time you lose the moment, find it again; use it as a mantra to take you through the whole day, one moment at a time.

"I found the only way to escape my pain," said Carlyle, "was to shut everything out and really concentrate until I was able to hear the faraway train whistles, the distant rustling in the trees outside my window. Then I knew I was in an oasis."

"When things got really bad," said Roberta, "I got in my car, rolled the window down, and concentrated on the feeling of the wind against my face, the roar of the car's engine, the pulse of blood in my stomach. It gave me a respite, made me feel strong."

What follows are instructions to guide you through the process of staying in the moment. As you practice these steps, let the sights, sounds, and sensations in your immediate environment guide you, rather than following the instructions by rote. They are meant only to stimulate your own imagination. Your goal is to incorporate the moment into the way you live your life every day.

STEP-BY-STEP INSTRUCTIONS FOR STAYING IN THE MOMENT

Preparing Yourself for the Moment

Begin right where you are. Just stop whatever you are doing and take in your immediate surroundings. Is there natural light or lamplight? Is the room sparse or cluttered with many things?

Take it all in: the sights, the sounds, the feeling of the room.

Listening to Background Noises

Is it quiet, or do you hear the blaring noise of a radio or television? If you can, turn them off. Your goal is to remove any sounds that can drown out subtle background noises. Listening for faint background noises is one of the most effective ways to get into the moment.

Close your eyes and focus your attention on the sounds you hear.

At first, the loudest noises command your attention. You may hear someone's voice in the background or people moving around in other rooms or a truck driving by.

Try to identify all of the sounds you hear.

Now listen more closely. Can you hear the distant sounds of birds? Can you hear cars on faraway streets? Can you hear the hum of an appliance in another room—the refrigerator or a ceiling fan? Keep going, listening for the faintest of sounds, as long as you can.

You have used your sense of hearing to momentarily come out of your thoughts and enter the peace and calm of the moment. Your task is as simple as this.

Use Your Sense of Touch to Bring in the Moment

Use your sense of touch in a deliberate, self-disciplined way. Close your eyes. Is there any movement of air in the room? Can you feel it against your face, neck, or hands? It may require deep concentration to tune in to this sensation.

What else do you feel? How do your clothes feel in contact with your skin? Can you feel their weight on your shoulders or their texture against your legs? Can you feel the weight of a watch or bracelet on your wrist, the weight of the shoes on your feet?

Think about everything in contact with your skin, beginning with your feet. Do you feel a breeze against bare skin? Pressure of warm socks? Are they too tight? Or do you feel only the pressure of sheets across your bare feet?

Next, think about the skin on your legs, then your torso and arms, as you slowly move up your body.

Pay close attention to your hands. They are very sensitive and can pick up the slightest movements of air. Reach out with your hands and feel the texture of things around you. What does the chair you're sitting on feel like? The sheets on your bed?

Your face is also sensitive to air currents and temperature. What do you feel? The weight of your hair across your scalp? Tingling?

As you take in these sensations, you have entered the moment. You are delivered from your painful thoughts.

Sense of Taste and Smell

I don't mean for you to practice this exercise at meals. In fact, you will gain the most benefit by trying to discern very subtle tastes and smells.

Concentrate on what the inside of your mouth tastes like. Is it a neutral taste? Minty? Smoky? As you inhale, do you notice any changes? Upon *in*haling, can you detect the scent of wood? Of dirt? Of cleaning agents? Of fruit? Use your senses of taste and smell to bring you out of your thoughts and into the moment.

Focus on Your Breathing

Feel your chest rise and fall, the air filling your lungs, your diaphragm expanding, then release it all. Can you feel the air as it exits your nostrils? Concentrate on the muscles that work to draw your every breath, on the air moving in and out of your lungs.

Most people are able to hold the moment very briefly when they are feeling intense grief and loss. The natural tendency is to slip back into obsessive thoughts. Staying in the moment is a skill requiring concentration and effort. Try to extend these brief interludes as long as you can and start again each time you recognize that the moment has slipped away. Try seeking out the most beautiful place you can find and drink it in with your ears, your eyes, your skin, and your nose. Listen to your favorite music. Keep good reading material on hand, books that will hold your interest and inspire you. Two I recommend are *Silences* by Hannah Merker, and *Full Catastrophe Living*, by Jon Kabat-Zinn. Writing (diary, journal, free writing) helps you concentrate on the present and is an excellent way to focus your thoughts, create an action plan for the day, or even plan your new life.

The more you practice this exercise, the better you become at accepting reality. It is a state of being that Zen Buddhists and other spiritual orders have aspired to for centuries. To learn to live your life with this kind of mindfulness is to accept change and participate in the joy, love, and bounty of life around and within you. Each time you use the moment as nature's greatest refuge from pain, you strengthen your ability to accept life on life's terms.

SUMMARY OF SHATTERING

The severing has cut through the dense tissues of attachment, right through to the molten core of self. Like it or not, you are in touch with your deepest needs and feelings. This is where a whole new life can start. The pain of shattering is an epiphany.

Abandonment cuts so deep it feels like a mortal wound, but as you have seen, it arouses your instinct for survival. Cut off and alone, you cry out. You feel primal need and fear. These are the most valuable and important feelings you have. They represent your most elemental needs that have been with you since birth. As you learn to manage the pain, it is important to listen to your fears. They tell you what you need. When you dare to accept these feelings, you are ready to begin to heal.

Akeru allows you to transform the piercing pain of abandonment into an opening. It offers an invitation to experience life in the moment. You become more present and accessible to others, to life, and to the child within. This child is free to experience sensations, its eyes and ears and skin not yet so well-defended against life experience. For the adult as well as the child, all the sensations of life are most intensely felt in the moment. It is this reawakened self that you bring into the moment with you—along with the openness, wonder, and discovery of the child.

As you emerge from the shattering state, you have taken significant steps in the direction of emotional self-reliance. You have learned to: step one, understand the depth and nature of your abandonment wound; step two, acknowledge its pain; step three, avoid shame by accepting your feelings as natural; step four, affirm your strength—you can *stand alone; and step five, manage your feelings by getting into the moment.*

Shattering is a rite of passage similar to the initiation rights of the shaman who journeys to the spiritual world and wrestles with demons before he can own his power. Some of best healers in our society are those who have been through overwhelming trauma, because they have worked through their shattering.

Chapter Three

Stage Two: Withdrawal

WHAT IS WITHDRAWAL?

The withdrawal stage is like being in withdrawal from an addiction. It is when you crave the other person after the initial shock of separation has worn off. Mediated by the brain's own opioid system, what you feel is similar to what addicts feel when they can't get a fix.

During the worst of it, you can't get away from your conviction that without your lost loved one, your life is over. This belief comes from the child within you. The child keeps telling you that you must get your loved one to come back at all costs, or you'll die. A primary relationship is a matter of survival for a child; no infant can exist without its nurturer.

Urged by the child, you may try to reconnect with your lost partner many times. Even if you don't take action, you fantasize about it. You keep going back because you're still not convinced that the one who's left is no good for you. You keep getting bruised, but the child inside believes that this time will be dif-

ferent. You're like the alcoholic who thinks next time he drinks, he won't get drunk.

You may get angry with others who try to nurture you. You may, for instance, lash out at your therapist, especially if she is encouraging you to stay away from your old partner. You may have agreed to leave the relationship behind, but the child may act out by missing sessions, switching sponsors, or changing recovery groups. You're angry at your therapist and others because they speak against the wishes of the child. The child fears that unless its urgent pleas are heard, its life is in peril.

The child within clings to false hope to ward off feelings of isolation, banishment, and loss. Without hope, you stay buried in despair, and these feelings evolve into profound grief, creating a bottomless well of tears.

But with the tears something else is released. Making its way to your consciousness, through memories of the times you were left unprotected and rejected, is your right to be loved.

Withdrawal is the stage when you listen to the child's cries. You recognize that her needs are your needs; that you must nurture your most important feelings.

There are those who try to bypass the withdrawal stage with a replacement for their lost love. But withdrawal is not the time for replacement—that will come soon enough—it is the time to accept yourself and your needs.

THE SECOND STAGE OF ABANDONMENT: WITHDRAWAL

KEATON'S WITHDRAWAL

It had been six weeks since Gabby packed up and left Keaton—suddenly and without warning. Six weeks since that evening he found a lengthy good-bye note on the just-emptied dresser.

He woke up in the dark, as he had each morning since she left, wishing he could go back to sleep but knowing that the adrenaline coursing through his body would not let him. It was 3 A.M. Instantly, he was flooded with panic. He had been through this before, more times than he wished to remember. He just couldn't seem to get a relationship to last. It always ended the same way—eventually she broke up with him. But he didn't expect it with Gabby. He had felt so sure of her.

Here he was again, writhing in his bed, drenched in anxiety, tormented by loneliness, discarded by somebody he'd loved. How would he ever get through this?

As he tossed and turned, Gabby inhabited every corner of Keaton's mind. The craving, longing, and yearning for her was unbearable. Finally, early-morning light began to creep into his room. Getting ready for work helped to push her out of his mind.

Today, he thought, he would get to work on time. He would go through the motions as best he could, focus, function, and act as normal as possible.

Everyone at work knew Gabby had left him. They knew why he'd lost weight and looked so down. He knew what they thought: "It's been six weeks, Keaton. Get it together, already. Snap out of it!"

Keaton was in *withdrawal*. The more time that passes, the longer your needs go unmet, the more your body and mind ache for all that you've lost. No matter how hard people try to hold themselves together, a profound sense of loss intrudes on every waking moment.

The effects of withdrawal are cumulative and wavelike. They often have to get worse before they can get better, a point lost on friends who expect to see your desperation dissipate, not mount day after day.

Keaton tried to tough it out as best he could, but he suc-cumbed to frequent bouts of crying and found it unbearable to be alone. Friends and family tried to keep him company and offer support in the beginning, but they grew frustrated when they saw that he wasn't moving forward or able to pick himself up by his own bootstraps after a few weeks. At least that's how he imagined they saw it.

The fact is, love-withdrawal doesn't operate on a schedule; it varies from person to person, situation to situation.

Keaton's abandonment legacy began in early childhood. His father was highly critical, berating him for every mistake and shortcoming. No matter how hard Keaton tried, it was never enough to please his father. He learned to feel disappointed in himself for not doing better in school, sports, or anything else. Whenever his father blew up at him, Keaton felt rejected. He blamed himself for not being good enough.

As a teenager, Keaton didn't shake the feeling that he needed to prove himself. He was extremely sensitive to rejection.

When his first girlfriend broke up with him at seventeen, he'd become severely depressed. The romantic rejection brought up all of the old feelings of inadequacy, confirming his deeply held belief that he was unworthy of anyone's love.

Overwhelmed with confusion and pain, he drowned his feelings in alcohol. What followed was a chain of relationships gone bad from which he emerged an alcoholic.

At the time Gabby had left him, Keaton had been in Alcoholics Anonymous for over five years. In spite of being sober, he still suffered the scourge of romantic rejection.

"I had already been through too many abandonments," said Keaton. "It felt like I was in advanced relationship failure—like I had a progressive disease—called rejection. My future seemed hopeless. I couldn't stop beating myself up for all the mistakes I made in my relationship with Gabby, damning myself for being such a failure with her, with everybody else, with my life."

Withdrawal is the second stage of abandonment. The word describes the pain and longing you feel now that you have separated from the one you loved. Withdrawal can set in immediately, or you may not feel its pull until the numbness and shock of shattering has worn off. As you saw with Keaton, withdrawal overlaps into the next stage, *internalizing*, in which you take your frustrations out on yourself. As you swirl through the abandonment cycle, you may revisit the symptoms of withdrawal many times.

I am going to share some of my own experiences with the withdrawal stage, and take you on a journey through the feelings and situations you'll encounter, providing information along the way that will help you understand the process and how to cope with it. I will explain how love withdrawal is a legitimate form of addiction withdrawal and discuss some of the posttraumatic aspects of withdrawal. Hopefully, you'll be able to identify unfinished business left over from your earlier experiences with love withdrawal. Finally, I'll show you how to maximize the growth potential of the withdrawal stage, introducing you to the second Akeru exercise designed to help you to recover from withdrawal feelings, both old and new.

JOURNEY THROUGH THE
WITHDRAWAL SYMPTOMS

Withdrawal is life without the medication of your lost relationship. You are coming down from the sedation of security to face reality.

Symptoms of withdrawal are intense. Many abandonment survivors are prepared to bargain, petition, beg, manipulate, do anything to get their loved one to come back. During this stage you are like the addict desperate for the love fix you can't get. What are these intense feelings of yearning, agonizing, and craving about?

Relationships are, in fact, mediated by the brain's own opioid system. Most people are familiar with the opiate drugs, *narcotics* like morphine, heroin, and opium. Our brains produce their own morphinelike substances, including endorphin. Both narcotics and the brain's own natural opiates help to block pain.

According to researcher Jaak Panksepp, when you build a close relationship, your brain produces more opioids. Conversely, when a relationship ends, the production of certain opioids decreases, and your body goes through physical withdrawal.

Biochemically speaking, then, your closest relationships are a form of endorphin addiction. What you feel during abandonment withdrawal—the *craving, yearning, waiting, and wanting* of your lost loved one—is psychobiologically akin to withdrawal from heroin or morphine. The difference is that when you are in love withdrawal, you associate your symptoms with your emotional loss rather than with a narcotic. In other words, the difference is the *context*—how you *interpret* the withdrawal symptoms—not the physical symptoms themselves.

What are some of these withdrawal symptoms?

WRENCHING APART

Even if your relationship is completely over and you have already been through the devastating breakup, you still face the process of *wrenching apart*. You are wrenching apart from the need for that person, from the presence of that person in your thoughts, hopes, and dreams.

"During withdrawal, it felt like I had been amputated from my Siamese twin," said Marie. "Shattering was the surgery without anesthesia. I was in the recovery room, bleeding to death, crying out in pain for my other half."

You'll alternate between moments when you think you might survive without your lost love and moments of total despair.

Even if the relationship had only been a date or two, your hopes for the future and your need for love were invested in that person. When hopes don't materialize, your disappointment can be profound; it puts you right back where you were before: *alone*. Your sense of loss may be no less painful than if you had been married for many years.

Human beings are social creatures. We all need to feel we belong. Building a relationship is one way in which we fulfill that need. You may have taken it for granted, but belonging to someone was essential to your sense of well-being. It felt good to know that you were an important part of his or her life—that someone loved and cherished you.

Even if you had just begun to date the person, the prospect of life without that relationship is fraught with desperation and loss.

"I thought I had finally found someone," explained John. "But she never returned my phone call. It turned out to be just a reminder of how alone I was, how empty my life really was, how much I needed to have love in my life. Just one date and it threw my whole life into emotional crisis."

WITHOUT

Being in withdrawal is being without—without the security and nurturance that you counted on or hoped for.

"I had no idea how much my wife meant to me until she left," said Richard. "Our relationship had been in the doldrums for a long time. We bickered constantly. There was always tension in the air. But when she said she needed space, and then actually got an attorney, I felt as if the bottom dropped out of my life and I couldn't find any reason to live anymore."

The irony is that people can be as devastated by the loss of a bad relationship as they are by the loss of a good one. Exploring why that is so is central to understanding the abandonment experience. Why is the loss of a primary relationship so awful? How did we become so dependent on another person?

Why do we feel incomplete now that they're gone from our lives?

The answer to that question is never simple. The fact is, mates and lovers fulfill a whole variety of complex needs; they are much more than companions or lovers or sexual partners. One of those most important roles they play is acting as *background object*.

Background Object

Our mothers or primary caretakers became background objects for us when we were two or three years old and began exploring the world beyond their embrace. We were content to roam freely so long as we knew Mommy's lap was just a call away. As adults, having someone in the background fulfills a similar need. A background object is the person from whom we derive our primary sense of connectedness, belonging, and security.

If your lost relationship was like most, having your mates in the background meant that even when you weren't physically together, you enjoyed the security of knowing they were there. They were someone to come home to at the end of a long day or to lie down next to at night or just to think about. It is a feeling that is very easy to take for granted—that sense of belonging and security. It's also inextricably entwined with our most basic needs.

"Redington traveled between England and Brazil," said Hope. "We spoke on the phone about twice a week—just to call each other special pet names and say our I-love-you's. And then each of us went back to our separate lives, perfectly content, knowing we belonged to each other."

Many people function as well as they do precisely because they feel so secure in their primary relationships. They are self-confident, self-directed, and content because they know someone is there for them. The fact that we tend to take our loved ones for granted isn't a character flaw. The element of security they

| Wrenching Apart |
| Without a Background Object |
| Will to Run Riot |
| Sexual Withdrawal |
| Weight Loss |
| Waiting and Watching |
| Wakefulness |
| Washed Out and Depressed |

Withdrawal symptoms

provide is the very thing that enables us to tolerate separation from them as we make strides in our careers and other pursuits.

One mark of a mature relationship is when each partner is able to give the other person space. They allow each other to function as background objects. These folks recognize that their significant others are part of their lives, important, but not their whole life.

When the honeymoon is over, many couples often settle into a period of complacency. Perhaps one or both will even gain weight as the adrenaline and urgency to bond abate and the relationship becomes more secure. This state of relaxation involves the parasympathetic branch of the autonomic nervous system that works to rebalance the body when the sympathetic nervous system has been aroused. The parasympathetic system helps to get your blood pressure and stress hormone levels back to baseline and turns other life-sustaining systems, like your appetite, back on. Ideally, this sustained period of complacency allows the couple to become industrious as they prepare for the future: start a family, build their careers. Each will operate in his or her own sphere yet bring something from that sphere to the relationship, too.

As we become secure enough in a relationship to take our partner's presence for granted, we may even indulge in fantasies about being with someone else. Such fantasies are not always a sign of trouble. They can add an element of excitement to a relationship in the doldrums. They are fantasies, after all. The reality of a lost partner is very different.

To better understand why background objects are so important, let's look at how children learn to function independently. As a young child, you needed to *connect* in order to move forward. As an infant, you depended on your mother to give the nurturance you needed, and your attention focused almost exclusively on that relationship. When you were a toddler, she became a background object as you began to develop and function more independently. You progressed from needing your Mommy figure in your sights at every moment to a stage where you could play by yourself for hours, alone or with other children, as long as you could reassure yourself that Mommy was still around—somewhere *in the background*. If something interfered with that development—if Mommy had to go to the hospital for a long stay—your ability to function independently may have been delayed.

Most of us trusted that our mothers were there to support us. That trust is what enabled us to withstand separation from her. Eventually, you built up enough trust to be able to endure the stress of being away from her long enough to go to school. The key to taking that step was to trust that your caretaker was at home waiting for your return.

Children occasionally question that trust and cry out for reassurance. A child with a stomachache may want to go home to be with Mommy. As adults, we're capable of regression, too. On some level we all need to be reassured of connections to our loved ones. Sometimes that takes the form of phone calls; other times you need their arms around you.

You may not have realized just how much you depended on these reassurances until the relationship is over. You may have downplayed how much you needed your partner, preferring to think of yourself as emotionally self-reliant. The fact is, expressing need and vulnerability are as essential to your psychological functioning as independence. Vulnerability awakened by abandonment is not a weakness; it is part of what it is to be human.

"I didn't realize how important Redington's weekly phone calls had been," said Hope, "until he called me the last time from Brazil to say that he had met someone. Then I found my

independent life suddenly didn't work for me. I needed him to be right there with me like I never needed him before. But he was gone, and I was totally lost and insecure. My life was suddenly an empty existence."

It's easy for us to *under*estimate our basic human need for connection. We live in relative isolation from one another, often far from extended family. When we lose our primary relationship, we are not cushioned by the support of a close-knit society as our ancestors were. The sense of deprivation is nearly total because so many of our needs were vested in that one person. Try as we might, we cannot will those needy feelings away.

WILL TO RUN RIOT

Abandonment is a form of *involuntary separation*. The fact that you did not choose to be alone arouses intense feelings of anger, frustration, and resentment. Your partner has upset your emotional balance, and as a result of his or her default, you are alone.

Remember that you're not railing against aloneness itself; the circumstances surrounding your sudden isolation are what cause your *will to run riot*. You are unable and un*willing* to accept the conditions of your imposed isolation. You have no control over it, at least for the time being.

During the withdrawal stage, you are feeling your partner's absence on many levels. You have emotionally lost the person you loved; you are physically apart, and perhaps worst of all, you are left to contemplate your future alone.

Being alone is not a disease or a social problem. It is a life-style preferred by many. In fact, more and more people are choosing to remain single, preferring to create composite lives out of career, friends, pets, clubs, and other interests. Over the ages, spiritual orders around the globe attest to the benefits of solitary living and even celibacy. They provide inspiration for those whose life energy is no longer invested in a primary relationship. But for those of you in the withdrawal stage, being alone is *unfamiliar* and *unwelcome*; you are not emotionally prepared to appreciate its benefits.

Choosing to be alone is by no means something I recommend as a goal to my clients. Yet once you are able to resolve the battle with your will—once you are able to get past your angry protest—you may come to look upon being alone with a more positive attitude. As you resolve the anger about being left, you begin to take advantage of what your temporary aloneness has to offer. This can be a time of healing solitude, a time to restore your emotional reserves, and a time of personal reflection. Perhaps it is time to question the complacency of your former life, to decide what is truly important to you.

The fear that you have been condemned to a solitary existence may be holding you back. You grieve over your lost love so keenly during this stage that it is hard to imagine becoming attached to anyone or anything else in life that will make you feel whole again. The sense that you will always be alone is one of abandonment's most potent feelings. But remember, it is a feeling, not a prophecy or a fact.

The truth is, very few people going through abandonment are destined to be alone for very long. As my clients begin to heal, I encourage them to make new connections as soon as possible, to go outside their usual social circles and widen their scope of activities, to reach out to new people and share their growing self-awareness. I'll discuss making connections in greater depth in Chapter 7.

In the meantime, it is important to realize that only when you stop fighting the fact that you're alone can you recognize its purpose in your emotional recovery. First you must work your way through your feelings of outrage, shock, and betrayal. Slowly you tap inner strength to get through the isolation. You truly stand on your own two feet.

The concept of *Akeru* is there to remind you that "to empty, to make a hole in" is also to create a new beginning. Being alone forces you to become more self-reliant. In the end, you count your time alone as an accomplishment that bolsters self-esteem.

"At first I thought I would die of loneliness," said Marie. "But now that I have gotten over the initial shock, I realize that my life is exactly where it needs to be right now to allow me to work on the things about myself that I need to. For whatever reason I'm alone right now, I've decided to make it for a good reason. I am able to find the good in it."

SEXUAL WITHDRAWAL

Another commonly reported symptom of this stage is sexual withdrawal.

When your body's self-defense system is activated, a number of body functions are shut down. Your energy is reserved for self-preservation. In crises, one of the areas to shut down is your reproductive system, a system that normally consumes a great deal of your body's energy. Your sexual drive usually decreases: females are less likely to ovulate; males may have trouble with erections and secrete less testosterone.

Yet abandonment survivors commonly report a heightened craving for sex, particularly for sex with their lost love. They may have more sexual fantasies, pursue sexual activity with substitute partners, or masturbate more often as a way of soothing withdrawal symptoms. Many make repeated sexual overtures to their old partners in the hope of seducing them back into the relationship.

"After Lonny was gone for a few weeks," said Marie, "pandemonium set in. I went into sexual withdrawal—a whole new torture to deal with. Suddenly I had the urge to make love to Lonny like never before.

"I had sexual dreams that were so powerful and agonizing that they woke me up, and I wouldn't be able to get back to

sleep. I went shopping for lingerie just in case I got the chance to seduce him. The desire was unbearable."

The component of sexual fantasy is only one aspect of the larger issue of physical withdrawal. Abandonment survivors are often embarrassed by their heightened sexual cravings and don't mention them to friends or therapists. Also, these extremely personal feelings may not seem relevant in the face of the other overriding issues they are being bombarded with on a day-by-day basis. Generally, heightened sexual needs tend to taper off as you make your way through the withdrawal stage.

WEIGHT LOSS

Many lose weight immediately after a breakup and continue to drop pounds or establish a lower then normal set point. Your general lack of appetite is interspersed with sudden bouts of ravenous hunger which help make up for the meals you've missed. Soon after, the butterflies and queasy feeling return and you lose interest in food again.

"I wouldn't feel like eating all day," said Roberta. "And then I'd have a craving for spareribs, something I ordinarily wouldn't touch with a ten-foot pole. But I'd devour them like an animal, grabbing meat off the bone with my teeth as grease poured down my fingers and face."

There's a biological explanation for why some people go on feeding frenzies while others seem to be on hunger strikes.

Your abandonment crisis boosts production of significant stress hormones. According to physiologist Robert Sapolsky, CRF (corticotropin releasing factor) and ACTH (adrenocorticotropic hormone) prepare your fight-or-flight response by shutting down your appetite and other digestive processes. Your salivary glands stop secreting, and your stomach goes to sleep. You notice a dry mouth and queasy stomach. This shutdown helps to divert energy to your major muscles—the ones that enable you to sprint across the savannah to escape a predator, or engage in battle, if need be.

Glucocorticoids, another group of stress hormones, are also involved in your self-defense response. These hormones appear to stimulate appetite rather than suppress it. Sapolsky's tests showed this effect in laboratory rats, but the effect is probably the same for humans. When your amygdala detects a crisis, CRF and ACTH are released first, preparing you to act quickly, if necessary. Next, levels of glucocorticoids begin to build. Glucocorticoids also increase your appetite, encouraging you to rebuild your energy stores in the event that an attacker poses an ongoing threat.

Timing helps to explain why some lose their appetites while others can't stop eating. Here's how it works: When your amygdala declares a state of emergency, it leads to a burst of the stress hormones CRF and ACTH. Their effects last for ten to twelve minutes, and it takes only seconds for them to clear the system once the crisis is over. At this point, your appetite shuts off. But in the meantime, your glucocorticoid levels are building, reaching maximum levels in about a half hour. They remain in your system for many hours.

What happens when both groups of stress hormones are present? CRF and ACTH override the appetite-stimulating effect of the glucocorticoids. In other words, during a sustained crisis, you appetite shuts off and stays off.

But if there's a break in the crisis (maybe your partner moves back in for a while), then you are not releasing constant surges of CRF and ACTH. Glucocorticoids lingering in the system urge you to eat, and in short order, you've got the munchies.

According to Sapolsky scientists could probably understand a great deal about your emotional state by analyzing the stress hormone levels in your blood. High levels of glucocorticoids in the bloodstream with only traces of CRF and ACTH indicate that things in your life have calmed down for a while. You've more than likely regained your appetite. (Biochemically, you're driven to stockpile energy for the next battle.) On the other hand, significant levels of CRF and ACTH in your blood along with the glucocorticoids indicate that you are still in the midst of an emotional crisis.

WAKEFULNESS

Because your breakup is an ongoing emotional emergency, most people continue to have trouble sleeping during the withdrawal stage. They report feeling anxious when they wake, and they tend to get up earlier than normal. Others stay in bed later (though they don't sleep well) and are drowsy later in the day when they are normally most active.

"I just couldn't face the day," said Roberta. "I'd still be in bed at three in the afternoon on weekends, and only got up because my lower back would start aching from lying around. Anyway, I was probably wiped out, because I was still waking up in the middle of the night, drenched in those cold sweats of panic, from all the bad dreams."

These interruptions in your normal sleep patterns are explained by the same processes that affect your appetite. Your body continues to secrete stress hormones that keep you awake and 'action-ready,' even at night. You're alert and prepared as though a predator is still lurking about.

WAITING AND WATCHING

One of the hallmarks of withdrawal is *waiting* for the lost loved one to return. This expectant feeling is common to all types of grief. Even when a loved one has died and there is no chance he or she will return, the mourner goes through a period of hopeful anticipation of the return of the departed.

This aspect of grief has been studied extensively by pioneers in the field—Elisabeth Kubler Ross, John Bowlbe, Mary Ainsworth, and others—and is often referred to as *"searching for the lost object."* From a biochemical standpoint, searching and yearning are the emotional expressions of opiate withdrawal.

What accounts for this deeply entrenched pattern? Forming attachments, as I explained in Chapter 2, is a powerful biological mandate. When your loved one is torn away, you feel the loss immediately and deeply. During withdrawal, your mind automatically seeks an emotional bond it can no longer find. This seeking is your emotional brain (your mammalian or limbic brain) trying to capture what it is conditioned to believe is necessary for your survival.

Try as you might to control this, you are usually unable to stop the futile search for the person whom your rational mind knows is no longer there. In spite of your efforts to regain your composure, your mind goes right on searching for your lost partner. It is as if your loss were an amputation of a limb, and you are suffering the effects of intense phantom pain.

The waiting and watching for your lost loved one is the result of your amygdala preparing you for hypervigilance—to be alert and on the lookout for any signs of your old partner. Your body prepares you for this sustained vigil. Your pupils involuntarily dilate so you can better see the object of your concern. Your hearing and other senses are more acute as well, hence the tendency to jump at the slightest noise. Your conscious mind is preoccupied with all matters pertaining to the missing person, assisting your emotional brain in its search. You look through photos and gifts that remind you of your time together, perhaps retracing the last moments of contact, hoping to discover clues to why it had to end. You may even feel compelled to go to the actual places where you met. These visits evoke memories that provide fresh clues for your relentless search.

"At the beginning," said Marie, "I just had a need to drive past Lonny's apartment at night, to see if his car was there. Somehow, I felt less anxious if I could at least keep track of his whereabouts. If his light was on, he was found. I knew where

he was. If not, he was lost, and I'd become frantic. Where could he be? He was out there lost somewhere."

Your tendency to mistake others for your lost partner can reach an all-time high. You imagine that you *see your* lost loved one at a distance, in a crowd. As you approach, of course, it turns out to have been an illusion.

Accepting loss is a slow and painful process, and you spend a great deal of time and emotional energy before your intense searching effort gives way to reality, and your mind's waiting game is finally over. You must accept the reality of your loss not just rationally (usually easy enough) but on psychobiological levels—including those beneath your conscious awareness—before this vigilant state begins to subside.

WASHED OUT, MISERABLE, AND DEPRESSED

Withdrawal symptoms represent stage two of your separation trauma, a continuation of your psychobiological distress that began with shattering. Withdrawal takes its toll over time, wearing you down, depleting your energy supplies.

"I had trouble dragging myself to work," said Roberta. "I had this horrible vulnerable feeling all of the time like something bad was set to happen any minute. I was stressed out and ready to drop. I even thought I might have mono or chronic fatigue syndrome or some other mysterious ailment. But my blood tests came back negative."

The continued loss of appetite, intermittent wakefulness, hypervigilance, relentless, and searching for your lost partner are all signs of posttraumatic stress. Many also report having intense dreams that leave them flooded with anxiety or profound desolation upon awakening. Experiencing one or all of these symptoms doesn't mean you are going to develop a full-blown case of *post-traumatic stress disorder.* Your body is endowed with self-corrective mechanisms, and many of these symptoms will subside. In the meantime, the experience can be overwhelming.

WITHDRAWAL STAGE IS POSTTRAUMA

Abandonment isn't like an automobile accident from which you immediately begin to recover. It is more like spending weeks or months on a battlefield, constantly under attack. You feel the painful repercussions of your loss again and again each time your ever-wary amygdala triggers the release of stress hormones.

Abandonment poses an additional complication: reopening of old wounds. For those who lived through some kind of childhood separation, going through the withdrawal stage means dealing with the emotional reverberations of the recent and past wounds simultaneously. They merge together into one prolonged state of emotional emergency, a tumultuous and intense time of great stress.

As Richard put it, "We are surrounded with the blood, gore, death, and dismemberment of our whole lives."

Upon hearing this, Keaton joked, "Don't you think, Richard, that that's a bit understated?"

Your lost relationship helped to regulate many psychobiological functions. It is almost impossible to say how many aspects of your emotional and hormonal health were dependent on it, since so much of it happened beneath your conscious awareness. But in fact, you had become entwined with that person in complex ways.

The relationship met countless needs that helped to maintain your state of equilibrium. You incorporated your loved one into your thoughts and plans and made countless adjustments in your behavior in order to acheive a balanced relationship.

As your attachment formed over time, you achieved what

researchers call a state of attunement. Being attuned means that you and your partner's pupils dilated in synchrony, you echoed each other's speech patterns, movements, and even cardiac and EEG rhythms. As a couple, you functioned like a mutual bio-feedback system, stimulating and modulating each other's bio-rhythms.

You had even grown accustomed to one another's *phero-mones,* chemicals that human beings (as well as other animals) emit into the air. A small organ within the human nose (the vomeronasal organ) detects their presence. This organ is distinct from the olfactory organ for smell. The detection of one an-other's pheromones represents a sixth sense that has been found to regulate menstral cycles and play a role in human attraction. Needless to say, your relationship maintained your social, emo-tional, and *physical* well-being on all different levels.

Now that the relationship is over, the many processes that it helped regulate are in disarray. It is during withdrawal that the effects begin to express themselves cumulatively, creating a mounting feeling of agitation.

It is difficult to isolate how a single body system is affected, since the body's systems interact to form a complex web. I've tried to do so with the brain's opioid system (separation distress has been found to lead to a reduction in the opioids, and to symptoms of withdrawal akin to heroin withdrawal) and with the stress hormones (which effect appetite, sleep, and other states of alertness and action-readiness). But in fact, stress hor-mones influence many other functions as well, including the im-mune system, the growth process, aging, memory, energy levels, and moods. Sustained arousal of the body's fight-or-flight re-sponse is associated with anxiety. Increased levels of glucocor-ticoid and CRF stress hormones are found in people diagnosed with depression.

Hormonal, neurotransmitter, opioid, and other biochemical levels usually return to baseline as you progress through the stages of recovery. In the meantime, you are left to contend with your body's sustained state of arousal, along with the practical challenges you face. It is no small wonder that you are temporarily washed out, stressed out, miserable, and depressed.

During withdrawal, you are fighting an enormous aggressive mental battle, exerting as much energy as if you were actually wrestling with a powerful enemy.

UNFINISHED BUSINESS FROM THE PAST

THE ABANDONED CHILD WITHIN

When I was going through my own withdrawal, I discovered that none of the professional and self-help literature I read over the years described the emotional intensity of my experience. I realized that I would have to write my own account to plumb the depths of this unique emotional crisis. What came out of my efforts was a story entitled "Black Swan." This adult fable describes a child who has been left on a rock. It represents my abandonment, as well as echoes from all of my past losses. It is imbued with all I learned through years of working with children in the throes of abandonment, as well as the emotional truths shared by the many adult abandonment survivors I have worked with and known.

The fable represents a composite of those experiences and contains twelve lessons of abandonment recovery. I began to share this personal story with my adult clients and found that it resonated with them. It soon became a staple in my work. (The following is a synopsis of "Black Swan." For the complete story and its twelve recovery lessons please contact the author at the address on p. 341 or call 1 800 247 6553.)

A child goes on a walk deep into the woods with her father. They come upon a huge rock perched on a small island in a brook. The father lifts the little girl high on the rock, promising that he will pick them some huckleberries for lunch. "Don't be long," begs the little girl, as she watches her father disappear into the woods. After a while, the child grows frightened and frantically calls out to him, but he doesn't come back, and she spends the night on top of the rock, huddled in terror.

She waits for first morning light, then finds her way down from the rock and sets out into the dense forest to search for her father.

Storytelling appeals to the imagination, creativity, and healing powers contained within us all. Each of us has been that child on the rock. The circumstances of your childhood may not have been as dramatic as the little girl's, but your feelings may have been similarly intense. All of us have had to climb down to find our own way out of the woods.

Holding the image of the abandoned child in our minds helps to reclaim the needy, helpless, frightened part of us and acknowledge feelings we may have all but forgotten or denied.

Alma's Withdrawal

"*I wasn't aware of it at the time, but I went through withdrawal as a kid,*" said Alma. "*My mother went back to work full-time after my father died. Her employer knew she had a kid, but they kept her working long hours anyway. She would come home exhausted and I'd be hungry, lonely, and bored waiting for her.*

"*When my father was still alive, we used to spend time together, going places. I was the center of attention. But all of that ended. The loss wore on me in ways I had no clue about. I was just a kid trying to fill up time waiting for some human contact, for someone to take the emptiness away. My mother would come home from work with that scowl on her face, bringing pizza or putting out a bowl of cereal for dinner. Then she'd go to bed, and I'd go to my room and stare at the walls.*

"*Eventually, my mother remarried, and a lot changed, but being alone, waiting for her—those are the memories that come back to me now that my Jacob is gone.*"

Like Alma, many of you may find yourselves reexperiencing feelings of loneliness, frustration, and emotional hunger stemming from earlier times of loss.

I described in the last chapter childhood events that sometimes create wounds that reopen during the shattering stage. What follows are childhood losses that are more likely to resurface during withdrawal. Most of them describe times when the people you counted on for love, attention, guidance, and nurturance were emotionally or physically inaccessible.

CHILDHOOD SCENARIOS OF WITHDRAWAL

- Illness of one of your parents

- Death of a close family member, one you counted on for attention and emotional support

- Loss of a beloved grandparent

- Parents preoccupied with fighting, bickering, or their divorce

- An earthquake in your family structure—your father or mother moving out

- Older sibling leaving home—one who had been your champion, role model, or supporter

- Workaholism in one or both parents

- Alcoholism in the family system

- Chaotic family—sometimes when you most needed them, one or both of your parents weren't available

- Moving—breaking social ties, being new kid on the block over and over

- Parents dealing with prolonged conflict or grief; they emotionally withdrew from you

- Depression, mental illness in the family

- Birth of other siblings, relegating you to an emotional back burner

- Death or illness of a sibling, which absorbed your parents' full attention

- Parents whose behavior is defined as self centered, narcissistic, or insensitive

These and other events may have left you feeling deprived of the attention and nurturance you needed. Some of them may have left an imprint deep in your emotional memory.

Researchers have found that separating newborn animals from their mothers even for a brief period of time creates biochemical changes that have lifelong effects on the animal's brain. Infants separated from their mothers show significant changes in the structure and function of the *locus ceruleus,* a structure also found in the human brain. When these animals reach adulthood, the organ is underdeveloped and produces less norepinephrine. Norepinephrine is one of the chemical messengers (neurotransmitters) that helps to regulate the brain's state of hyperalertness during a perceived threat. It also plays a role in anxiety and depression.

One study followed a group of infant macaque monkeys who were separated from their mothers on an intermittent, unpredictable basis over a period of months. As adults, they responded to novel situations with behaviors closely resembling human anxiety and depression. Researcher Myron Hofer describes them clasping their hands and sitting in passive hunched positions. They created an atmosphere of tension within the group and were disinterested in exploring their surroundings.

By contrast, monkeys in the control group (who were separated from their mothers on a rhythmic, predictable basis—in other words, they knew what to expect), did not exhibit anxious or depressed behaviors in novel environments as adults. Hofer's work supports the extensive anecdotal studies on humans that show that childhood separation traumas often lead to lasting changes. These children grow into adults who tend to be unusually anxious in new situations and have trouble forming secure attachments.

POSTTRAUMATIC REPERCUSSIONS

It may not be clear exactly *how* your earlier experiences of loss and separation have been stored in your brain and affect the way you cope as an adult. Even if you don't have vivid memories of these losses, you may have developed a pattern of behaviors designed to cope with them.

In the previous chapter on shattering, we looked at behavior patterns that indicated posttrauma from childhood abandonments. Now we are going to zero in on patterns in your adult life that may have emerged from times when you felt deprived of important needs.

ADULT PATTERNS OF WITHDRAWAL

Dependency and Codependency Issues

For some of you, childhood withdrawal affected the way you related to the people you looked to for emotional support, the types of dependencies you formed, and the quality of your relationships. You may have looked to others to fill your emotional void, to assuage your feelings of loneliness and frustration. Many of you report feeling a chronic emptiness.

"It was only my mother and me," explained Richard. "My father left before I was born; I never met him. I hung on to my mother, did everything I could to keep her constant attention. The more she tried to ignore me, the more I tried to get her attention. She was always trying to get me to go out and play, to get me out of her hair. 'Go get a life,' she'd tell me.

"But even though I was good at sports and there were lots

of kids on the block to play with, I would come right back in the house to be wherever my mother was.

"I never recognized that this was a problem until my mother and I were called to the school counselor. I had become a behavior problem in school, not focusing on my work, getting easily distracted, not following directions, that sort of thing. Finally, the counselor pointed out that I was lonely in school— that I had trouble being away from my mother. 'I am? I do?' I responded. I had no idea.

"I think being around my mother and driving her crazy was really all I had in the way of security, of family, of an emotional life. So I was always wanting—in withdrawal—too strung out to concentrate in school or focus my energy anywhere else."

The Need to Self-Medicate

Many abandonment survivors who went through times of childhood withdrawal developed a need to find self-soothing behaviors. These patterns led to overeating, overdrinking, over-shopping, overworking, over-people-pleasing, and other forms of self-gratification designed to quench their emotional hunger.

"As a teenager," reports Barbara, "I couldn't get enough of anything—friends, boyfriends, shoes, clothes, earrings, partying, talking, sex, ice cream sodas. I was a major consumer of everything that wasn't nailed down. In college, I went into serious debt charging merchandise at Macy's. I think I'm still paying that bill. But when I married Howard, I was finally motivated to put a lid on it. It was time to get in control.

"But now, I feel those old feelings of isolation and loneliness again—the ones that I used to try to fill up with all of that stuff."

Setting Yourself up for Reabandonment

Much as you might consciously try to avoid it, you may be setting yourself up for relationships that echo those of your childhood. This is what Freud called a repetition compulsion.

Many abandonment survivors have learned to accept as normal those relationships that will never provide the support they need. Some of you may have settled for a life partner who offers you very little in the way of emotional gratification. You do most of the giving and tolerating and get very little in return, beyond criticism and emotional distance.

The old familiar feelings that it just isn't enough persist. You've unwittingly re-created your childhood scenarios. The dynamics are the same, even some of your behaviors are the same; only the props and players have changed.

Patricia provides a fairly typical example. As a child, her mother was diagnosed with multiple sclerosis and confined to her bedroom most of the time—not so much because of physical debilitation but because she was so severely depressed by her chronic illness. Although she could still get around, she missed Patricia's school plays, concerts, and graduation exercises. As the MS progressed, Patricia gradually took over more and more of her mother's care and spent less and less time with friends or participating in school activities.

Patricia's father had left the family years before her mother's diagnosis and had long since reestablished himself in a new community. He even had a new family. When Patricia reached out to him for emotional support, she went away feeling like one of the leftovers—as if she had imposed on his time.

Patricia continued to take care of her mother and never went to college in spite of excellent grades. At eighteen, she got a job working for an insurance company, and at nineteen, after her mother died, she married Barry, who had been her romantic idol throughout high school. Barry was a popular star athlete and a heavy partier. Ten years into the marriage, Barry was an alcoholic who barely held down a job.

"After we were married for a while," says Patricia, "I realized that his drinking was out of control. He began coming in late, drunk, and acting obnoxious. It got so that all I had to do

was see him picking up a drink, and I'd feel betrayed and aban-doned all over again."

As his alcoholism progressed, Barry became a phantom who aroused Patricia's deepest needs for love and closeness but couldn't satisfy them. (This is an example of the symbiotic par-adox I discussed in Chapter 2; Patricia felt most dependent at the very moment Barry pushed her away.)

"The pathetic part of this," says Patricia, "is that I let this pattern go on. I finally started going to Alanon, which helped. I learned to deal with some of it and make some changes. But the old feelings of abandonment were still there—a constant, nagging grief. It wasn't until I started abandonment recovery that I began to come out of love withdrawal and learn what my real needs were and how to take care of them."

Memory Gaps

Many of you are able to see the blueprint of earlier experi-ences behind your behavior. But when you try to remember what led to them, you come upon big gaps in your memory. Why do we seem to forget some of the most traumatic times of our childhood?

"My girlfriend broke up with me over a month ago," says Banford, "and I'm really having trouble coping. This with-drawal feels like old stuff, like something putrid that's been rotting inside of me for years. I'm sure it must go back to the fact that my mother died when I was three, but I don't remem-ber anything about it.

My grandmother told me that my mother was totally devoted to me. Supposedly, I'd scream every time my mother tried to leave me with a baby-sitter. I guess I hated being separated. It must have been pretty traumatic when she died, but I don't remember it—or her—except for her picture.

My father took care of me after she died and by all reports he was out of it for a long time. Apparently he had to hire a

*series of baby-sitters, because I went through them like crazy.
I guess I was difficult to manage, taking it out on everybody.*

*"I must have been freaked out that my mother was no longer
there, but I don't remember any of it."*

Difficulty remembering the past is an enormous frustration.
Familiar feelings of emptiness, anxiety, fear, and panic bring an
emotional intensity to bear that seems all out of proportion to
what's recently happened. Yet you can't recall any earlier, de-
fining event. You want to make sense of the intrusion of panic
and gain mastery over your emotions. "I feel as if big chunks
of my childhood memories have been amputated," said Banford.

What accounts for these periods of childhood memory black-
out?

Mini Lesson on Memory Recent studies have shown that stress
hormones play an important role in forming memories and
lapses in them.

First a review of our mini science lesson on the emotional
brain. Remember the *hippocampus,* the small seahorse-shaped
structure within your emotional brain? Unlike its companion,
the amygdala, which controls the way we form emotional responses, the *hippocampus* records memory details of the actual
event—the fact that you were in a car, that the car crashed, that
someone was hurt, that an ambulance arrived at the scene, etc.
The hippocampus then relays the facts to other parts of the
brain for long-term memory storage.

Why are the earliest childhood experiences the hardest to
recall?

The answer has to do with the fact that the hippocampus
completes its development later in childhood than does the
amygdala. In adulthood, when you experience an emotional
emergency like an abandonment, it triggers fragments of emotional memory from, for example, your birth. But because your
hippocampus is not yet developed at birth, you have no corre-

sponding memory of the actual event—no context in which to place the memory you do have of the way you felt.

Stress Hormones and Lost Memories What about gaps in memory that occur *after* the hippocampus has been developed? This is where stress hormones come in. Depending upon the type, intensity, and duration of the crisis, stress hormones can either heighten memory or impair it.

We have already seen how stress (such as the stress of childhood or adulthood abandonments) triggers the release of stress hormones CRF (corticotropin releasing factor) and ACTH (adrenocorticotropic hormone). They in turn lead to the production of the glucocorticoids. Depending upon the magnitude of and intensity of the stress, these hormones have been found to *impede* hippocampal memory function. Joseph LeDoux explains that the same stress hormones *intensify* the imprinting of your amygdalal emotional memory, indelibly inscribing the event in the deep structure of the brain.

The upshot is that you pick up emotional baggage but not the details of where or how you acquired it.

So you try psychotherapy, hypnosis, dream interpretation, primal screaming, and past life regression. But some experiences simply can't be retrieved. Thanks to stress hormones, your hippocampal memory function was impaired, and the details of the event were never recorded in the first place. You are left to grapple with intrusive anxiety that floats free from its context. This free-floating anxiety is one of the posttraumatic symptoms of childhood abandonment.

The exact opposite phenomenon—heightened memory—is also explained by stress. Adrenaline, another hormone involved in the stress response, is found to *heighten* hippocampal memory.

"I keep going over in my mind the exact moment when Gabby said she wasn't coming back," says Keaton. "It's like it happened yesterday. Every detail is still etched in my mind. It

keeps coming back in living color whether I want to think about it or not."

We have all heard people say that they can remember exactly where they were when President Kennedy was shot—not just the feelings, but the *details* of the context. This is an example of flashbulb memory, possibly due to the adrenaline that coursed through their bodies when they first learned about the assassination.

This adrenaline factor may help to explain another commonly reported symptom—the need to give a blow-by-blow account of the traumatic event. Screening out the less relevant details seems beyond the teller's control.

"When I have to explain to one of our old friends where Lonny is," explains Marie, "I try to just give the outline: 'We broke up. He left me.' But before I know it, I am going into details that I hadn't planned to talk about. I can see that the other person is becoming uncomfortable. But I can't seem to stop myself, I become so involved in the story. It's like I can't press the pause button. I'm forced to recount the details all over again."

Could heightened memory serve a purpose in your recovery? Mentally reviewing what happened is one of the ways we try to make sense of things that frighten or deeply upset us. We revisit details in order to fit the event into our perspective of reality, to gain some mastery over the emotional impact it has on us. By going over the pivotal point of loss, you remind yourself *why* you feel so out of control, that something traumatic *really did* happen. Typically, people have both gaps and intensely detailed memories. You might have a heightened memory of the recent abandonment and free-floating emotional intrusion from an earlier loss.

These intrusive old feelings serve a purpose in your recovery. As old wounds reopen, you are finally able to address the needs, longings, frustrations, and broken promises that you have carried with you. This is one of the hidden gifts of the withdrawal stage—being able to make contact with your most basic needs and feelings.

Many who have been abandoned believe (as many therapists do) that unless you are able to remember your past, you will be stuck with the feelings of your past traumas forever. Though a widely professed view, it simply is not true. You may *not* have a working memory of your past—and the lack of it may be frustrating to your rational mind, to be sure—but you do have an emotional memory, and that is all you need to make contact with your abandoned child and benefit from the Ak<u>e</u>ru exercise to follow.

AK<u>E</u>RU RECOVERY FROM WITHDRAWAL

LEARNING TO *GO WITH* THE ENERGY OF WITHDRAWAL

"I had a constant pulling in my gut, this aching for Gabby, said Keaton. "I suppose if I was still drinking, I would've tried to medicate it with alcohol, just to calm down. But I needed to find a less destructive way to put out this torch."

The withdrawal stage is driven by attachment energy, the impulse to bond. Just because the object of your attachment is no longer available to you does not mean that your need to bond goes away. On the contrary, it pulls with all of its might to regain what it has lost.

During withdrawal, you feel the potency of this instinct most keenly because it is being thwarted. In fact, at no time is this force more apparent than when you are in acute love withdrawal. As painful as it may be, you need this *pull*. It provides the impetus for your recovery, once you learn to redirect it.

When your need for attachment is being satisfied—when it has found an object—it blends once again into the background of your emotional awareness. Its energy is working for you, but you can no longer hear the hum of its engine. When this energy is thwarted, the urgency will not abate until it finds something else attach to, until it reinvests itself elsewhere.

"It wasn't until I became really good friends with someone I had gone out with in the past," said Keaton, "that the wrenching feeling in my gut gave me a breather. She and I were both going through the same thing, and we started spending a lot of time together. Being able to connect with her helped a little bit, it took some of that feeling away. But we were just friends, and it wasn't the same as finding the person."

We are always searching for an ideal partner who will meet our greatest needs. This search brings us to the second Ak̲eru exercise, which is designed to help you find that ideal someone. To begin with, that someone is you. Forming a significant relationship with your*self* helps you take another step in the direction of self-reliance and serves as the basis for a new level of connectedness to others.

Remember that one of *ak̲eru*'s meanings refers to the empty space created when someone has left. This empty space creates pain, to be sure, but when you know how to direct its energy, it becomes a reservoir of new life. Your task is to use the attachment energy to address your innermost needs—the feelings rising out of your abandonment wounds old and new.

No one expects you to do this by osmosis. The process involves a hands-on exercise that, by steady increments, creates a vehicle for emotional healing. The technique is easy. The results are remarkable.

The good news is that making a connection to your core feelings does not rely upon crystalline memories of your childhood. Given the pitfalls of memory we have discussed, trying to reconstruct childhood memories often proves to be a waste of time, effort, and money for even the most determined souls.

The only thing you need to bring to this exercise are your feelings. And thanks to your amygdala, most of your primal of helplessness, dependency, grief, fear, and hope are still there, stored within the circuitry of your emotional brain. For better and for worse, many of them have been reawakened.

The urgency you feel comes from your most primitive self, which is frightened, alone, and desperately trying to make its presence known. Your task is to *adopt* this abandoned child, to lift it from the rock.

THE SECOND AKERU EXERCISE

The second Akeru exercise involves a technique called separation therapy. Paradoxically, separation begins the process that leads to forming a significant relationship with your emotional core. The idea is to separate the abandoned child from your adult self.

You'll do this by starting and maintaining an *ongoing dialogue* with your inner self. My clients all report remarkable emotional and behavioral changes as a result, so bear with me if any part of this sounds embarrassing or awkward. I will walk you through the process step by step. Your aim is to establish a new relationship between your conscious adult self and your emotional core.

This exercise was developed by psychoanalyst Dr. Richard Robertiello and his colleague Grace Kirsten. It is described in detail in their groundbreaking book, *Big You Little You: Separation Therapy*. The book discusses the theoretical basis for the separation technique I'm about to describe and provides clear, easy, and thorough instructions for its use. What follows is a greatly abbreviated version of Robertiello and Kirsten's exercise. I encourage you to read the book to maximize the potential benefits of their work.

Dialogue with Inner Self

Step one: Your first task is to create a vivid picture of your abandoned child, that newly awakened part of yourself. Recall yourself as a very young child (of about four) and use that image to personify your emotional core. Imagine that you, the adult, can stand back and observe this child, as if she or he is a separate being, standing outside of you. This helps to cognitively draw the needy feelings this child represents out from where they are hidden within your limbic brain. Robertiello and Kirsten recommend that you picture this child standing five feet away from you on your weaker side. If you are right-handed, that means on your left side. The idea is to remind you that your child self is in fact more vulnerable and dependent than your adult self.

The child has long been within you, making its needs known, trying to control and interfere in your adult life. When you feel insecure, for instance, it is the child within you who is insecure, the child who feels desperate for acceptance and approval. It is also the child who is afraid to take risks and the child who sabotages your attempts to form new relationships. Rather than forsake these feelings, your task is to accept and care for this long-abandoned part of yourself.

Step two: Now visualize your adult self. Form a picture in your head of the person you wish to become.

"I had a hard time visualizing my adult self," said Keaton. "I wasn't too comfortable with him. In fact, I didn't even like him. He had let me down too many times."

Keaton's difficulty is common. Many struggle at first when they try to see themselves as strong, capable adults. Try picturing your adult self doing something you know you are reasonably good at. Keaton was able to overcome his difficulties by visualizing himself playing poker. He focused on one night in particular when he played a winning hand for all it was worth. Marie saw herself making lasagna, her specialty, and confidently serving it to a room full of friends. Think of the times you knew you were at your best, most competent, and independent. From these positive recollections, form a composite image that includes all the best of you.

Step three: Now you're ready to start a dialogue between the adult image of yourself and the child—between big you and little you.

By creating an image of your child self and potential adult self, you have created a triangle. You, the individual, are at the top of the triangle. The child is on the bottom left, the adult on the bottom right. You are going to remain at the top as an objective observer, where you can mediate the dialogue between these two figures, between your most urgent needs and the capable adult you know you can become.

The role for the adult self: Your adult self's job is to provide the child with all that he or she needs: a sense of belonging and love, to be admired and listened to, to be relieved of guilt and burden. Your adult self should act like a good parent toward a cherished child.

The role of the child self: In turn, the child will express its feelings and look to your adult self for help. As you begin to see your child self as a separate figure, he or she reveals its most basic needs, fears, hopes, and dreams. Many of these things have been buried for a long time. This exercise is designed to bring them out in the open.

The role of the individual: As the mediator of the dialogue, you will be conducting a kind of one-person role-play. You, of course, give voice to both your child self and adult self. When you are speaking for the child, you take on the language and attitude of a child. When you are speaking for the adult, you take on the body language of a strong and sensible adult whose main goal is to help the child.

Your task is to become more aware of what you are feeling. Attribute these feelings to the child. You are also supporting the adult who is striving to be strong and emotionally self-nurturing.

To gain maximum benefit from this exercise, practice it daily, preferably at a fixed time and in the same place. Your adult self opens the dialogue by greeting the child and asking about its

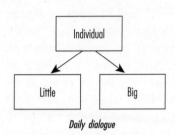

Daily dialogue

feelings. Big you draws out what is really bothering little you by asking questions and demonstrating a sincere interest in understanding and helping.

At first, the dialogues can be long. The child often has a great deal to say. Later, the dialogues become more focused and direct. Your overall approach is to reassure the child that everything will be all right. This also helps to reinforce the strength and confidence of your adult self. Your goal is to put your child in a good mood if at all possible. Getting the child to express its feelings is the most effective way to lift its mood (and yours).

Here is an encapsulated version of one of Roberta's first dialogues:

BIG: *What's the matter, Little?*

LITTLE: *I'm sad.*

BIG: *Tell me what's bothering you. I'll help you.*

LITTLE: *I think you made a mistake yesterday at work, and I'm afraid your boss will be angry with me. I don't like being yelled at. I'm scared.*

BIG: *I understand how you feel. You don't need to be afraid. If my boss yells, I will handle it. I'll take care of you no matter what happens. Besides, he's usually very nice. He doesn't expect me to be perfect. Anyway, this is not your problem. It's mine. Don't worry about it. I'll make sure he doesn't hurt you.*

Roberta was able to keep her adult self and child self separated into distinct roles, functioning as two separate figures. The child's feelings have been validated and acknowledged by the adult, who gains confidence along the way.

"Doing this exercise surprised me," said Roberta. "I had no idea my situation with my boss was stirring up these feelings inside. Just hearing Little come out with her feelings helped me to feel very connected—and somehow stronger. Nothing got resolved from doing the exercise—at least not in terms of the way I was going to handle my boss. But I knew something nice was happening inside. I felt Little's presence all day and found myself to be self-protective—more self-possessed—when I finally did approach my boss."

This exercise does not guarantee that you will walk away from the dialogue with all of your conflicts neatly resolved. Establishing a *dialogue with your inner self* is no different from opening any other type of dialogue; it is an ongoing process whose outcome is far from predetermined.

Working with the child within is really nurturing the growth of the adult. By administering to the child, your adult self becomes free of the child's destructive, negative influence and functions on a more mature level. In fact, when you find yourself handling stressful situations poorly, it is because you have allowed the child to slip back inside. Your goal is to make sure that your child and adult selves remain in their separate roles.

Many report that at first their adult selves don't know what to do.

"My child was so difficult, my adult was completely stumped," said Jill. Here is one of her early dialogues:

LITTLE: *I feel fat and ugly and its all your fault, Big!*

BIG: *I'm sorry, Little. But I really do know how you feel.*

LITTLE: *Don't hand that "I know how you feel" crap to me, Big. You're the one doing all of the eating. I'm the one doing all of the suffering. I want to look nice, and you won't let me.*

BIG: *That must make you feel sad and lonely.*

LITTLE: *Well, do something about it, Big. Go on a diet and stick to it, so I don't have to feel so terrible and ugly.*

BIG: *I'll try, Little. I know how you feel.*

LITTLE: *Never mind* try. *That just means nothing will happen. You always let me down.*

BIG: *It's not all my fault, Little. You're the one who loves sugar.*

LITTLE: *Don't blame me, Big. You always go ahead and eat too much, and I'm the one who has to pay for it. I hate you for making me fat!*

In this instance, Jill is having trouble keeping her roles for Big and Little separate—they are beginning to become reversed. Big is beginning to act like an angry sibling rather than a protective adult, and Little is reacting to this.

It is common to let the lines between these roles blur when you're getting the hang of this exercise. If the dialogue becomes upsetting or unproductive, it is up to you, the mediator, to put a stop to it. Review the roles of adult and child, and pick up the unresolved issue later, perhaps taking a different tack with Little's feelings.

"I didn't know how to handle Little," explained Jill. "Every time I approached her, she was hostile and extremely demanding. But at least I found out that I had a lot of anger inside— anger toward myself! I knew that the only thing to do was continue the dialogue every day. Little didn't change her tune at all, but my adult self kept getting stronger and stronger."

As Jill continued her daily dialogues, her ability to remain in the adult role in response to Little's attitude showed steady improvement. With a bit of practice, her adult self took on a more effective role.

Here is an example:

BIG: *I want to be thin too, Little. But I am going to need you to talk to me every time you feel needy or hungry.*

LITTLE: *What does that have to do with it?*

BIG: *I care about your feelings, Little.*

LITTLE: *All I care about is for you to get thin and pretty so I don't have to feel so fat and ugly.*

BIG: *Exactly, Little. And I care about those feelings, too. It helps when you remind me of them. In the meantime, I am going to get some help losing weight.*

LITTLE: *It's about time you admitted you can't do it by yourself. You're too weak.*

BIG: *For your sake as well as mine, I'm getting stronger.*

You'll get the best results if you begin by writing the dialogue. Writing helps you, the individual, to keep Big's and Little's roles clearly defined and keeps you on task. Writing is a form of *taking action;* it involves you more deeply in the exercise, just as taking notes helps you focus on a lecture.

In spite of the aversion many people have to writing, the results are almost always worth it. The kind of writing you are doing is very different from preparing a report or lodging a formal complaint with a credit agency. Anyone can do it. It goes fast because the idea is not to give critical thought to what is going down on the page but simply to record the conversation. No one is ever going to read your dialogue unless you want them to; it does not need to be legible or coherent. As you write, your feelings will carry your pen swiftly across the page.

As you become more practiced at this exercise and your child and adult are well-defined, you can speak the dialogue aloud instead of writing it all down. Some people who have been doing the exercise for a number of years, report they are able to perform the dialogue silently, inside their heads.

Whether you are writing, speaking, or thinking the dialogue, the important thing is to keep the needs and feelings of the child from slipping back inside your head where they can subvert your efforts to become the strong and capable adult you know you can be.

When you can't get in touch with the child, go back to step one and create a distinct visual image of the child. Imagine it outside of yourself, and then begin writing dialogue to draw the feelings out. The process sometimes takes a great deal of effort. As any parent knows, finding ways to relate to a needy child is a real challenge. You may have to summon all of your patience, but keep gently pushing, keep asking questions.

Remember that Little can easily feel abandoned. She needs to feel taken care of all the time. That means talking to Little at least once a day.

"I found that my child self was too angry to share his feelings," said Keaton. *"He'd been neglected for too long. But I kept nudging him. Finally, Little exploded:*

LITTLE: *Why should I tell you anything! You don't care about me. You haven't paid me any attention in my whole life! So don't pretend now that you care about my feelings. You'll just forget about me all over again and pretend I don't exist!*

BIG: *I'm sorry that I neglected you for so long. But I genuinely want to know what you're feeling. I want to comfort you. I really do care. I won't neglect you this time.*

LITTLE: *It's too little too late. I'll never speak to you.*

"Of course that was just lip," Keaton told the group, *"Now I can't get Little to shut up."*

Marie's Little expressed similar anger for being abandoned.

LITTLE: *I feel so upset, Big. You let Lonny leave! How could you lose him! It's even worse than when Mom died. I'm lonely all over again.*

BIG: *I know how hurt you are, Little. But even though Lonny left, I will always be with you. I would never leave you.*

LITTLE: *But I miss Lonny.*

BIG: *I know you do, Little, and so do I. But at least you know that I love you and always will.*

Remember that the purpose of the dialogue is not to wrap up a problem in a two-minute conversation. It is to create open channels of communication that lead to change over the course of time.

"After doing this exercise a few times, I became more and more in touch with myself," said Marie. *"I won't call it a love affair exactly, but I feel very caring toward myself and stronger as an adult, too.*

"There were times when Little became really impossible— demanding, inconsolable—and that's when I knew I was onto something really important."

In fact, many clients report that the child makes unreasonable demands. He or she is, after all, only a child, frightened of being alone and full of needs. It is up to Big to parent the demands of Little and gently but firmly explain to Little why some things can't happen. Let's look at Marie's ongoing dialogue.

BIG: *What's the matter, Little?*

LITTLE: *I don't trust you, Big.*

BIG: *Why not?*

LITTLE: *Because you put me through too many horrible things. I want you to promise that nothing bad will ever happen again.*

BIG: *I can promise that I will never let anything come between you and me ever again.*

LITTLE: *No, Big, I want you to promise that nobody will ever leave me again. I want you to promise that you will find someone who will always love me, so that I never have to go through this again.*

BIG: *I can't make promises that I may not be able to keep, Little. If I could control these things, I would. But the truth is that there are no guarantees in life when it comes to other people's feelings or behavior.*

LITTLE: *But I want you to protect me from being hurt again.*

BIG: *One thing I can guarantee is that I will do my best to find somebody who is loyal and devoted, to help you feel more safe and secure.*

LITTLE: *I want you to promise.*

BIG: *I can promise that no matter what happens with the other people my life, I will always love you. I will never leave you.*

Some people report that Little tries to get them to do things that their child selves want much more than their adult selves. It becomes a power struggle.

"Little Keaton was really angry at me because I wouldn't let him get a dog," explained Keaton. "Of course I couldn't tell anyone else about this because I'd sound like someone with a multiple personality disorder. But we were having a fight, Little Keaton and I. I had to tell Little over and over that my landlord

didn't allow pets. It took a lot of writing and many sheets of paper to convince Little, to get him to calm down.

"Of course, Little got me to promise that I'd do other things to make it up to him. And I'd damn well better carry them out, or he would be on by case all day. Little has become so real that I can't imagine turning my back on him again—I'm afraid he'd kill me."

After doing the exercise for a while, the child self begins to feel like a real presence, with its own personality. Some like to remind themselves that Big and Little are simply images, others prefer to think of them as real people. Some of my clients christen Little with names of their own, including *inner child, inner self, core feelings, primal self,* or *emotional core.* Regardless of how they refer to these figures, after doing the exercise a few times, profound changes begin to take shape.

Marylou became involved in abandonment recovery in order to deal with her old abandonment wounds. She was plagued by childhood demons, as she called them, stemming from the fact that her father had been sexually and physically abusive, and her mother cold, distant, and severely punitive. So Marylou began doing the exercise with great hopes and expectations for relief. Things turned out very differently from what she expected. About three weeks into it, her Little asked her to go to her grandmother's grave.

BIG: *It's four hundred miles away, Little.*

LITTLE: *But I want to go. She is the only one who ever loved us.*

BIG: *But I have to work, Little.*

LITTLE: *I want you to take time off and drive me there.*

BIG: *Maybe when my vacation comes up, I'll take you.*

LITTLE: *I can't wait that long, Big. I want to go now. I want to remember what it felt like to have Grandma's love, to talk to her. I want to get her love back.*

BIG: *How about if I read to you tonight, Little, or do something else you like? Then you'll know how much I care about you. That's what really counts.*

LITTLE: *No, I want to visit Grandma. I miss her, and I want to be near so I can talk to her.*

BIG: *But I don't really want to drive to Massachusetts just to talk to Grandma, Little.*

LITTLE: *I want you to. If you care about me, you will.*

Marylou described how Little nagged her on a daily basis until she finally agreed to make the long trip to visit Grandma's grave. As she made plans for the trip, it occurred to her that an old high school friend still lived in Massachusetts, so she looked her up and they talked about old times. They made plans to meet for dinner.

So off Marylou went to Massachusetts. During the car ride, she was urged to listen to Little once more. Little asked her to buy something to plant at Grandma's grave site. Marylou went along with this, hoping that this would be enough to satisfy Little.

At the grave site, Marylou had a very emotional experience. Little reminded her of the times when she was nestled in her grandmother's lap, feeling cherished and at peace with the world.

Marylou went off feeling drained but with sense of emotional relief and looking forward to meeting with her old friend. Together, they planned a trip to Norway—Marylou's first trip abroad—to visit the homeland of both their families.

To be effective, the dialogue needs to be an ongoing part of your life. As you continue practicing, you will be able to gradually resolve unfinished business—injuries from earlier losses and abandonments, as well as any current crises, all the while helping your adult self become stronger and more effective.

This Akeru exercise doesn't attempt to sidestep the grief. It works *with* it, using withdrawal's powerful drive toward attachment to form a bond between your adult self and your child self. Rather than distracting you from these feelings, this exercise uses them as fuel for growth. As you strengthen your adult self and address the needs of your child, you have taken a giant step in the direction of becoming emotionally self-reliant.

Separation therapy works. It is not hard to learn, and along the way you become your own therapist and mentor. And it works for everyone. We all have a child who sometimes needs help.

SUMMARY OF WITHDRAWAL

Withdrawal is when all of the connections with our lost love are torn. We try to move forward with loose wires hanging out, exposed and sparking. We were so medicated by the relationship, we didn't realize how intricate our connections had become. Only now can we distinguish which of the wires are part of a healthy connection to our loved one and which were based on fear or the excessive need to please. As we heal, we test the loose wires through soul-searching, therapists, sponsors, friends, and trial encounters with new people. Eventually, we discover the connections to true nurturing and healthy relationships.

Our core feelings are awake and alive—the oldest, most enduring part of ourselves. All else is ripped away. The child on the rock cries out for what is lost. It is this child who feels the wrenching tear in the tissues of attachment, the frustration and intense need to reconnect. When we give the child a voice, we are finally able to administer to the needs, fears, and longings of our innermost self.

During withdrawal we are like the baby chick without its shell, still wet, facing the world without its protective cover. It is the ultimate trial of survival. We are free from the restrictive bonds of security. No longer sedated by our former relationships, we emerge stark and alive, our needs exposed, our feelings raw, to forge new connections.

Withdrawal is you becoming you for the first time.

It is individuation.

Chapter Four

Stage Three: Internalizing the Rejection

WHAT IS INTERNALIZING?

Internalizing means incorporating an emotional experience, making it a part of yourself, and letting it change your deepest beliefs. It is an insidious process. You don't realize how much it affects you.

Internalizing the rejection is how your body incorporates the wound of abandonment. You have taken it to heart. By internalizing rejection, you injure yourself.

During the internalizing stage, the self searches desperately for its lost love, then turns its rage and frustration against itself. The wound becomes a self-contained system where self-doubt incubates and fear becomes ingrown.

Internalizing is the most critical stage of the abandonment process, when your emotional wound is most susceptible to infection. If you don't tend to the wound, it can damage your self-esteem. It is a time to treat the virulent bacteria of rejection that have left you momentarily weakened.

As with shattering and withdrawal, during the internalizing process your old wounds reopen, spilling their toxins in the new sore. But therein lies its benefit. Abandonment is a cumulative wound—rejections past and present merge. It's a time to clean out the insecurities, feelings of worthlessness, and shame that have been festering since childhood.

Your task is to dredge up the bottom of the swamp and sift through the muck to salvage what's important. You begin to reconstruct.

THE THIRD STAGE OF ABANDONMENT: INTERNALIZING THE REJECTION

BARBARA'S INTERNALIZING

Barbara was a homemaker and mother of five children all under the age of ten when her husband left her for another woman, someone he'd met through his business.

"When I asked Howard to tell me about her," says Barbara, "he told me she was a colleague, *as if that was supposed to explain everything. 'What does that make me?' I asked him. But I already knew who I was. A dependent housewife with no identity outside of him or our family, that's who. We had been married for thirteen and a half years. It never occurred to me that Howard would want to leave. I just didn't have enough worldly sophistication to hold his interest. After all, I had been home with the kids all this time, while he was out making his mark. I must have been the picture of the homely housewife, knee-deep in laundry, soccer practices, and screaming kids.*

"I guess I was counting on those perfect pie crusts and that homemade jam to hold Howard's interest. I thought I was being the ideal wife by ironing his shirts and keeping his socks sorted. But I realize I made a big mistake allowing myself to become his servant. That must have been all I meant to him as a bed partner, too. All that lovemaking. It always meant a lot to me,

but to him it must have been about as meaningful as physical exercise. I had just been a receptacle.

"I know I sound bitter. That is something Howard used to catch me on—negativity. He didn't have that problem—he could let go of things easily. In fact, he never complained about the way I ran the house, though I know I probably could have done a better job. I don't think I yell at the kids more than any other mother, but Howard had no way of knowing that. He probably couldn't stand it, but he kept his mouth shut like the perfect gentleman he always was. If only I'd realized he would someday grow tired of the whole scene and of me, I would have done things differently.

"I was naive enough to believe that all he needed from me was to keep the home fires burning. But he was out in the world, constantly coming into contact with more interesting women. I should have known. He got tired of me, the one he domesticated. He obviously wanted a more equal partner. Actually, I thought I was his equal, but I can't compete with the type of career woman Howard is with now.

"When he calls, he first asks about the children, and then if I found a job. I know I need to work for all of us to be able to survive financially. But I am petrified that I won't be able to do anything. I'm sure my college degree is obsolete by now after all of these years. Who is going to hire me? You need work experience to get a decent job.

"I'm scared, and I know Howard must be right—I'm the one who dug myself into this corner, wanting all of those kids, hiding behind the needs of the family."

Barbara's own account includes many of the "I" words associated with the internalizing process: the self-indictment, the painful introspection, the insecurity about her role, the tendency to idealize the one who has left, her feelings of inadequacy and sexual invisibility, impotence over the circumstances of her life, and the inventory of choices she now regrets.

Not all of us make self-deprecating comments out loud the

way Barbara does, but many abandonment survivors report feelings similar to hers. In a way, Barbara is fortunate to be conscious of them. As she begins to work through her recovery, this awareness will help her to identify and challenge these negative thoughts. For most, the process of internalizing happens on a deeply personal level, in the privacy of your innermost thoughts. Self-doubt takes its toll silently and over an extended period of time. It becomes the invisible drain that leeches self-esteem from within. Your friends and family probably don't realize that you are going through the potentially most damaging part of the grieving process.

Internalizing the rejection is the third phase of abandonment, but its process is at work throughout the grief cycle. Internalizing occurs every time you become angry or frustrated with yourself over your loved one leaving you. And it is painful. Anger turned against yourself accounts for the intense depression associated with abandonment. It is one of the hallmarks of this part of the grief cycle.

I'd met Barbara about two months after my own abandonment experience. As I observed her progress, I found myself struggling in the same quicksand of worthless feelings and self-doubt. This internalizing muck can claim anyone's self-esteem, at least temporarily. I was determined that it was not going to get mine.

I tried to make my way through the quagmires of self-deprecation by rationalizing. I had nothing to feel ashamed of, I told myself. I was gainfully employed. My career was intact. I had successfully raised a family. In fact, my youngest child left for college the same month that my partner left me, and I managed to survive the sudden isolation. I tried to reassure myself that I was okay, but it was hard to be convincing. I found myself rambling around in an empty house that a month ago had been bustling with the activity of a loving family.

I knew I had done nothing wrong. I had loved and cared for this man in every way possible. I had upheld my end of things; I'd even maintained my ideal weight after all of those years. I'd paid special attention to my clothing, makeup, hair. In fact, I reassured myself looking in the mirror, I looked better now than I did before. Besides, I was wiser, more successful, more seasoned. So, why suddenly weren't my accomplishments enough? Didn't they mean anything?

But I was only too familiar with the toxic fumes that rise out of the abandonment wound. Those colorless and odorless gases can seep silently into your consciousness, even when you think you're keeping a positive outlook. As a therapist, I knew I had to break free from the miasma of self-doubt and find a way to resuscitate myself. I forced myself to try new things and break out of my familiar routines. I traveled and visited friends I hadn't seen in a long time. Ultimately, it did help restore my picture of myself. I found my roots and felt centered once again.

Amazed by the effort it took, I came to truly appreciate the power of the internalizing process. I learned for myself that affirmations were not enough to ward off the impact of the abandonment and its potential damage.

One of the primary tasks of abandonment recovery is to prevent feelings of self-doubt from adhering to your sense of self. I discovered it cannot be done with rational thoughts alone. Bolstering self-esteem requires a more dynamic approach. You need to go *with* rather than *against* the internal focus of this stage. If internalizing forces you to become introspective, then take advantage of its centripetal force to bring light and vision along with you. Your goal is to bring positive feelings *inward*.

I am going to take you on a journey through the internalizing process and guide you through the feelings and situations you're likely to encounter along the way. I will explain the significant ways abandonment grief differs from other types of grief, as well as some of the biochemical and hormonal changes that are taking place at this stage. I will also help you identify unfinished business left over from previous losses and outline some of the childhood scenarios that may have affected your self-esteem. Throughout, I will reinforce your central task: It is to use this time of inward focus to incorporate positive feelings and experiences into your sense of self. Finally, I am going to introduce you to the third Ak<u>e</u>ru exercise, which tackles injuries to self-esteem that have been holding you back. The goal is to emerge from this introspective time with a stronger sense of self, more capable of life and love than before.

ANATOMY OF ABANDONMENT GRIEF

Up till now, many of the emotions we've discussed—the devastation, shock, and feelings of withdrawal—are feelings we share with those mourning the death of a loved one. During this critical third phase, the special circumstances of abandonment become most apparent, setting it apart from other types of grief.

When we think of grieving, we think of a profoundly emotional experience universal to the human condition. The grieving process has been extensively studied and its stages clearly described and defined. It cuts across cultures, genders, ages, and social strata. We even see evidence of these grief stages in other members of the animal kingdom.

As a society we acknowledge grief over a death. But still largely unrecognized is grief over being left. When a friend's mother or husband dies, we expect an extended period of bereavement. We offer social and spiritual support to the mourner. There are no social rituals to comfort abandonment survivors. Your grief may be just as intense and enduring and as financially and emotionally debilitating. Imagine the woman with one bottle of milk left in the refrigerator, three hungry children, no means of supporting them, and a husband who has just flown the coop for another woman. Her concerns go beyond the practical; she is experiencing a complicated grief mixed with rage, a sense of betrayal, and the stigma of being left.

In truth, abandonment grief is not yet recognized as a legitimate form of grief. Unlike grief over death which has received serious attention from professionals, abandonment is psychology's neglected stepchild.

Yet like any grief involving loss of a loved one, abandonment is a process that follows its own path. Because it so often goes unrecognized, sufferers often hide it, storing their feelings deep within where they silently eat away at them, unbeknownst to friends and family, and sometimes even themselves. Many report how isolated they feel, how difficult it is to make others understand what they're going through. Yet this grief can give birth to fear and sadness and diminish self-esteem and life energy for a long time. Unresolved abandonment grief can interfere with future relationships.

"I find it hard to imagine that something that happened ten years ago could still be bothering me," said John. *"But after my fiancée broke off our engagement, I didn't know what to do with all of the pain. I guess it stayed with me.*

"At the time, it was hard being alone, dangerous even [he had suicidal thoughts], *but I hated depending on my friends back then. I got tired playing the victim, so I learned to keep what I was going through to myself. I did what all the self-help books said to do: I tried to let go and move forward, and find happiness from within. I got so good at acting as if everything was okay, that I thought I was past it. Just to make sure I would be okay, I avoided relationships so I wouldn't have to be reminded of the feelings. I had no idea that I was grieving. What could I do but try to ignore it? That's why it's come to haunt me now after ten years—because I'm finally trying to find someone to be with."*

By hiding his grief, John had become one of abandonment's many walking wounded. He had no obvious injury, but his unrecognized grief silently burdened him for a decade.

To better understand what you're going through, it is important to recognize the special features of abandonment grief.

WHAT MAKES ABANDONMENT GRIEF DIFFERENT?

Personal Injury

The crux of the difference between bereavement and abandonment grief has to do with the fact that someone you love has not died but instead has chosen to end your relationship. Your loss is experienced as an affront to your personal worth, rather than an act of nature.

When we are rejected by someone important to us, our whole sense of value as a person is thrown into question. Being discarded and disrespected creates a narcissistic injury. A narcissistic injury is a slap in the face, an affront to our pride, to our most personal sense of self, a stinging wound that can leave a deep imprint. Sometimes even apparently insignificant losses such as being overlooked for a promotion or being rejected by a friend raise questions about our self-worth. When abandonment involves losing the most important person in our lives, the impact can be devastating.

"After Lonny left," said Marie, "not only did I miss him and miss our lives together, but I missed feeling good about me. I suddenly regretted being me. I felt my confidence go right down the drain."

Marie is describing that invisible self-esteem drain that is the hallmark of this phase. Silently, insidiously, self-doubt leeches your sense of worth from within. Unconsciously you begin to interpret new experiences as evidence of your personal inadequacy.

The injury to your sense of self is what sets abandonment grief apart from all others.

Grief's Pain

One of the most common misconceptions that abandonment survivors face in the throes of their grief is that their feelings are unjustified, that grieving a death is somehow worse. Abandonment and death affect us in different ways, but it's impossible to say that one is more painful than the other. The intensity and longevity of your grief is related to the nature of your relationship, the circumstances of the loss, and your emotional and constitutional makeup.

"I went to the funeral for the husband of a friend," said Barbara. "I realized as I watched everyone gather around her, that I was in as much grief as she was. But there was no dignity about my grief. I had to keep it hidden, all the while participating in a public outpouring of support for her.

"It seems that only death qualifies a person to feel this much pain."

Loss

What both types of grief do have in common is *loss*. The stages of abandonment grief do, in fact, overlap with Kubler Ross's and Bowlbe's stages of grief. Regardless of whether your loss is caused by abandonment or death, losing a loved one disrupts your entire life. You may feel the loss in the middle of the night when you wake up alone, or when your car breaks down and there's no one to pick you up from the repair station. Losing your partner is like losing a part of yourself. It is like a psychic amputation; you feel intense phantom pain for what is lost. Both abandonment survivors and widows alike must grapple with the emotional and practical burdens of facing life alone.

Lack of Social Role and Recognitions

Society, unfortunately, does not assign bereavement roles when someone is abandoned. There is no funeral, there are no letters of sympathy. Rather, you are seen as someone who has been dumped.

Abandonment survivors are left to wonder if perhaps they caused their own problems. Maybe it was their fault the relationship ended, perhaps they shouldn't feel such pain, perhaps it's a sign of emotional weakness. These self-recriminations add another layer of shame, forcing us farther into emotional exile.

"When Lonny left, I felt completely isolated. He wasn't lost to friends or family," says Marie, *"he was lost only to me. I was alone in my grief. If he had died instead, then everyone would have lost him. Family and friends would be grieving all over the place. My phone would have been ringing off the hook. People would have been staked out at my house. Everyone would be gathering to give each other support and to support me. After all, I would be the* bereaved, *the honored one who gets to shut the coffin in the end. And then there would have been a funeral, a grave site, a ritual to mark how sad and tragic it all was.*

"Not to mention that the house would be full of sympathy cards and flowers from even our most distant acquaintances. But since Lonny didn't die, it was inappropriate for anyone other than my closest friends and family to acknowledge what I was going through. The rest of the world turned its back, kept a discreet distance. Maybe people didn't want to embarrass me, or maybe they were oblivious to what I was going through. It certainly was not a public matter—because there was no death."

Numbing and Shock

There are issues confronting the bereaved that are different from the ones confronting abandonment survivors. When a loved one dies, we are forced to face our own mortality. Death is absolute, irreversible, and final; the yearning to be reunited with our loved one is fraught with a sense of complete hopelessness and despair. We are so afraid of death, and the idea that we'll never see them again is so incomprehensible and terrible, that we initially go into shock. As discussed, the brain produces opioids (natural painkillers) which may account for the numbing that grievers report. This numbing helps the bereaved survive the initial trauma, and for some, can even create interludes of respite from intense pain.

Those who have been left by a loved one also report shock and numbing (as you read about in Chapter 2), but there are differences. Abandonment survivors are not confronted with mortality but rather with the anger and devastation of *being left*. While they are often numb to life going on around them, *they rarely report being numb to the pain of rejection*. Instead, they feel unremitting pain. This feeling apparently overrides the pain-numbing effect of the body's opioids.

Anger

Anger is common to both types of grief. Indeed, many experience the death of a loved one as a form of abandonment and openly express their anger over being left behind. Those who have been abandoned are also angry, but for many, the grievance is real. Your loved one voluntarily pulled away.

To compound matters, your lost partner may be oblivious to the pain you feel. Often while you are still suffering through the worst of it, your lost partner has already moved on to a new life or perhaps a new lover. So even though your relationship is lost to both of you, the one who *was left* carries a far greater burden of emotional pain than the one who *did the leaving*.

As Marie put it, "When Lonny left, I lost the one thing I treasured the most—him. He had all the gold, and I was left with nothing but loss."

Denial

When a loved one dies, the loss is absolutely final. Denial actually helps to ease the person into acceptance. But with abandonment, denial is more complicated. Since your loved one is still alive, you can make contact. In some cases, there might be the possibility for reconciliation. Abandonment survivors' denial, then, can be fueled by realistic possibility. This creates a more active and tenacious kind of searching for the lost object (a stage common to all forms of bereavement that I discussed in Chapter 2).

This difference does not make abandonment more or less painful than other types of grief, but it means that abandonment survivors may remain in denial and postpone closure, sometimes indefinitely.

Closure

You can attempt what the widow cannot—to get your lost partner to return. The bereaved can only hope to rejoin their loved one on a spiritual plane. Accepting that their loved one is physically gone is a terrible challenge. Many grievers seek out spiritual mediums in an attempt to visit the other side, where they hope to make contact.

For abandonment survivors, the process of closure—of *letting go* of a relationship—when your lost partner is still alive is that much more difficult.

Love Loss

In grieving over a death, the mourner gets to keep the love of the person who has died, cherishing it, perhaps even feeling comforted by it. In contrast, when a loved one chooses to end a relationship, the love we once felt has been love taken away— perhaps to be given to someone else. It is an ambiguous loss. Love loss and rejection are special kinds of pain that affect your core beliefs about yourself.

One of the goals of abandonment recovery is to recognize this process as a legitimate type of grief. It is a grief that has two faces. One is common to all grief; everyone feels *loss*. The other—the *narcissistic injury*—sets it apart.

There has of course been a great deal written about dealing with loss, and you can draw much value from the work of philosophers and healers.

General Grief Work: Accept the Pain of Loss   One of the primary tasks for all types of mourners is to *accept the pain of loss.* Even the bleakest moments of despair are a universal experience. We all have to come to terms with loss at one time or another. The death of a parent or a partner's decision to leave both remind us of life's impermanence. Nothing, after all, can stay the same forever. All human beings are part of this transience of life. In the end, you must let go of all attachments; everyone must pass on. Accepting necessary losses is an important, though difficult, part of life. Remember that the pain of loss is a natural part of what it means to be human. The real work of grief is to accept this pain.

Sogyal Rinpoche, in the *Tibetan Book of Living and Dying,* quotes Buddha as saying:

What is born will die
What has been gathered will be dispersed
What has been accumulated will be exhausted
What has been built up will collapse
And what has been high will be brought low.
The only thing we really have is nowness, now.

For many, recognizing the transience of all things helps them deal with their own loss. But for abandonment survivors, there is still that narcissistic injury to contend with—the invisible wound of self-injury.

Reversing the Injury to Self   The personal nature of your grief— the very thing that makes abandonment grief different from all others—provides you with a powerful incentive to begin the healing process. You will be motivated to find greater life and love than before, not in spite of the rejection you incurred but because of it. The special focus of the rest of this chapter is to help you *reverse the injury to self* that defines the internalizing.

*   *   *

What follows is an inventory of "I" wor/ abandonment's internalizing process, a quick gu.. recognize its characteristics and alert you to its pitfalls. ʌɔ , become more conscious of the ways in which abandonment can damage your sense of self, you will actively intercept and refute its negative messages and avoid internalizing them.

INVENTORY OF INTERNALIZING

Idealizing the Abandoner

Abandonment survivors tend to idealize the one who has left them, ultimately diminishing themselves. This is often the most difficult thing for friends and family to understand. For many, lost partners acquire power because of the pain they caused when they left. This pain becomes a power to fear, a force that intimidates you. It is easy to become confused by this fear and imagine that your abandoner is more powerful, more important than he or she really is.

"Everything in my life suddenly revolved around Howard," said Barbara. "The sun rose and set on whether he called. Look at the relief he could bring, the pleasure he could create—if only he came back! Look at the pain and agony he caused by going away! I felt utterly defeated by him. He became so powerful. How could I stop myself from being in awe of him for a while?"

Being left has temporarily placed you in a subordinate position. You're astounded by the power of their absence; you're emotionally overwhelmed by the strength of your attachment to them. Feeling at an emotional disadvantage, and powerless to change things, the natural tendency is to create a hierarchy in which you place the abandoner somewhere above you—on a pedestal.

What does self-subordination look like on a biological level?

Women with *premenstrual syndrome* understand the relationship between shifting hormone levels and feeling down about themselves. Scientists now understand a great deal about the role that serotonin (a chemical messenger in the brain) plays in the way people feel about themselves. Prozac and other serotonin-based antidepressants are widely prescribed as treatment for depression, feelings of low self-worth, and other emotional troubles.

But neuroscientific studies reveal relationships between hormones and mood that focus on the down-and-defeated feeling common to abandonment survivors. To understand this relationship, we look to the social world of baboons, our ancestral cousins, which were the subject of studies conducted by Robert Sapolsky. According to Sapolsky, who studied baboons in their natural habitat, "Baboons work perhaps four hours a day foraging. . . . That leaves them with eight hours a day to be vile to each other—social competition, coalitions forming to gang up on other animals, big males in bad moods beating up on someone smaller, snide gestures behind someone's back—just like us."

What do baboons have to do with feeling defeated? Social status in baboon society is based on a baboon's relative position of subordinance or dominance to others. Dominance among males is established by who regularly avoids eye contact with whom, who takes their aggressions out on another without fear of retaliation, and who wins a contested piece of food (or female)—in short, as Sapolsky puts it, by "who gets to give the ulcers, and who gets to receive them."

Sapolsky tested his subjects for levels of stress hormones and found that dominant males had the lowest levels of glucocorticoid stress hormones. Subordinate members—the ones who took all of the flak—accumulated the highest levels.

Under normal conditions, hierarchies remain stable, but when baboons experience grief—when a member of the troop dies or an important bond is broken—levels of stress hormone in the dominant males nearly double. This is accompanied by a sudden dramatic change in their behavior: dominant males stop dominating.

What follows is a shake-up in the hierarchy. Males of all different ranks begin jockeying for new positions. Stress hormone levels in individual baboons rise dramatically when they fight off the advances of *lower*-ranking males. Most intriguing is that stress hormone levels *do not increase at all* in males fighting to overtake those who are *above* them in the hierarchy.

This implies that baboons respond in different ways to stress depending upon whether they are trying to gain something, such as a higher social rank, or defending themselves from a potential loss, such as losing one's rank.

The human equivalent of a baboon's position in the social hierarchy is roughly translated as "status" within relationships or as how well you are able to assert your worth. Your ability to assert yourself is based primarily upon how confident you are, which in turn is based upon how you assess your own self-worth. The loss of your loved one is followed by an increase of stress hormones and represents at the biochemical level what you experience subjectively: a temporary reduction in your sense of confidence. You feel powerless, subordinated to the one who has left, and down about yourself.

Sapolsky's research suggests that our best recourse in the face of rejection and defeat is to fight for greater gain rather than to be caught up in defensive behaviors, to move forward rather than hold on to the past.

Whatever biochemical shifts may be taking place, your task is to stay on top of this powerful process. You may feel your power has been overthrown by your lost love because you cannot control them or make them come back. However, you can control your actions and set new goals for yourself.

Why do we tend to idealize the one who has left? For many it serves a purpose. It may help you to believe that you have lost someone so special, so unique, so superlative, that you can't help but fall apart now that they're gone. You elevate their status and power as a way of justifying why you feel so devastated. You convince yourself that the reason you feel helpless and dependent is because you have lost someone who was completely indispensable and irreplaceable.

To reverse this self-defeating way of thinking, it helps to remember that this state is *temporary*, that these feelings are natural to the process, and that, if you choose, you will indeed find a replacement who has just as much if not more to offer. You will vindicate the loss.

Barbara's tendency to idealize others was part of a pattern that began in childhood.

"I've always had a tendency to put people I love on pedestals," said Barbara, *"and put myself beneath them. I took Howard's leaving as a sign that I wasn't good enough for him.*

"It was hard to fight this power he had over me. I'd keep telling myself that I was better off without him. I'd enumerate his faults and mentally list my own attributes. But it was hard to let go of the idea that he was irreplaceable.

"I finally came around to realizing that I was the one who bestowed this power on him to begin with. Therefore, whose power was it? Mine. My job was to overthrow his power and give it back to myself. If I can create it, I can own it."

Following Barbara's example, your task is to follow the inward direction of the internalizing energy to the seat of your own power. As you catch yourself idealizing your lost mate, remember that you are strong. You are surviving the assault to your sense of self. Make a list of your own strengths to idealize.

Impotent Rage

Rage is the subject of the next chapter, but the internalizing stage of abandonment has its own type of anger. Your anger at this stage is victim rage: that useless flailing into space, those ineffective assaults upon pillows, dishes, and figurines. These behaviors indicate that you have become the object of your own rage. Your rage is a form of frustration. You are frustrated by pain and loss and frustrated with yourself for feeling so helpless.

Idealize the Abandoner
Impotent Rage
Isolation and Shame
Indictment
Identity Crisis
Keeping up the Fight

Inventory of internalizing

"Every night, thinking of Travis, I stabbed my pillows to death," said Roberta. "I would wear myself out, punching and stabbing. How else was I supposed to release the pain? I felt so dismissed, so powerless, so insignificant in his eyes."

Abandonment survivors often have trouble controlling their aggression during this stage. It is as if the child within has taken over. Sometimes it comes out in tears. Other times you simply explode—usually when you least expect it, and often at people who aren't at all to blame.

You may also find yourself making unrealistic emotional demands upon others. You expect the others in your life to compensate for the nurturing and love you so sorely miss. You expect them to accomplish the impossible.

"A close friend and I spent the day together a few weeks after Travis left," said Roberta. "I told her my life was over. She said I was being too negative, too pessimistic, that I shouldn't feel so hopeless. It felt like she was denying my feelings. It was easy for her to dismiss how seriously devastated I felt—it wasn't her life going down the tubes. But did this give me a right to start screaming at her in the middle of a restaurant? My friend tried to quiet me down. 'I was only trying to help you,' she said. But that only got me screaming again. I felt totally justified at the time, but in hindsight I know I was just feeling helpless and taking it out on her."

Many take their anger out on others, pillows, or themselves, all because they don't feel strong enough to direct it at their lost love. They have become gun-shy of rejection, more easily intimidated, and afraid of backlash and another abandonment. They don't want to risk further pain or injury. Ultimately, they are afraid of forfeiting their chances, however slim, of getting their lost partners to return.

"I was afraid to get angry at Howard because I couldn't stand to lose one more drop of love. I was groveling for crumbs of approval."

Remember the baboons who had *lower* stress levels when they were fighting to gain from upheaval? Think of them and try to take an active rather than passive role in your own healing. Avoid submissive posturing, and and resist the tendency to diminish yourself. Instead, stand up and assert your self-worth.

Isolation and Shame

At the center of the emotional wound created when a loved one leaves is *shame*—the terrible shame of being thrown away. Shame is what drives you to keep silent about your feelings. *Loss* can be worked through, it can be mitigated, it can be displaced, it can be projected, channeled, medicated, lessened. But the shame of abandonment evades almost all remedies.

Roberta said, "I had no trouble going places by myself before Travis left me. But afterward, I wouldn't be caught dead going to a concert by myself or sitting alone in a restaurant. I was too ashamed."

Almost all of us have felt the tidal wave of shame that washes over us when we have been left—the condemning silence and crushing isolation. Don't let this feeling overwhelm you. Instead, name what you're feeling, lift it out of isolation. This helps to dissolve the shame.

At first, when your world seemed to shatter, being alone was a shock, devastating. During withdrawal, being alone was an unwelcome condition that intensified your grief. But during the internalizing stage, you see being alone as evidence that you are unworthy of love. It is at this point that being alone is transformed into self-deprecation. In isolation, your shame can incubate, creating the invisible wound of abandonment.

At the very heart of the shame is the belief that you are undeserving of love, a crucial and potentially dangerous belief. Remember, this is a feeling, one commonly experienced by abandonment survivors. But as potent as it is, it is only a feeling, not a fact. You are deserving of love, as we all are.

Indictment

One of shame's chief reinforcers is self-indictment. The question most people can't help but ask during this stage, no matter how strong their self-esteem, is: What did I do to deserve this?

Self-doubts and recriminations are usually potent enough to override affirmations you may be using to keep your self-esteem afloat: *"Yeah, I'm beautiful; yeah, I'm wonderful. In fact, I do everything right. So what! What's wrong with me that somebody wanted to dump me? How did I wind up alone?"*

We naturally question our beliefs about life and ourselves when we grapple with loss. It is a normal part of the grieving process. But when abandonment is involved, this introspection can develop into a scathing internal dialogue.

"When Gabby moved out," said Keaton during the course of one support group, "being alone felt like a punishment—as if I was guilty of something. I felt so demoralized that I wanted it to happen to everybody—so that I wouldn't have to be the only person who was dumped. That's one of the reasons I came here—so I wouldn't have to feel like the only loser.

"Seriously, I felt singled out. Like there really must be something wrong with me. How come other people have control over their lives, keep their relationships going, and I can't?"

Introspection can become obsessive during the internalizing stage.

"I stayed up in the middle of the night," reported Roberta, *"examining every word, every gesture I could remember, looking for clues as to where I went wrong with Travis. I wished I were a different person; I wished I could do it all over."*

Why do we indict ourselves? As painful and potentially destructive as these thoughts are, they serve a temporary purpose. They provide a sense of control over what has happened. By holding ourselves culpable, we feel we have the power to change the things that brought the relationship to an end. All we have to do, we reason, is correct our faults, and we can get our lost partners back. Even if they don't come back, at least we can learn what to do (or what not to do) for the next time.

But accepting all of the responsibility for the failure of your relationship can lead to further self-injury. As you look inside for *deficiencies* to correct, you may come to believe that there is something *inherently* unacceptable about you. Be on the lookout for this noxious idea, which is an erroneous and a *temporary* by-product of your loss.

Many feelings described above belong to the child within, not to your adult self. It is important to reassure your child self that being alone is *temporary*. If you choose to be in another relationship, you shall be. Your isolation does not mean that you are unworthy, but that you are in a period of transition and profound personal growth.

Identity Crisis

"I was always part of a relationship," said Barbara. *"Now who am I?"*

A breakup often prompts this question, and many feel as if "being dumped" has branded them. You may begin to worry about how others see you. Do they think there's something wrong with you, that you carry a defective gene that makes you unlovable? Some start to worry that these imaginary deficiencies show on the outside.

"I have to go to a wedding," said Holly when she first came to see me, "and I have no one to go with. I feel like I'll be wearing a neon sign that reads, Nobody Wants Me. Everyone else can tell what's wrong with me, can see why I'm alone all the time, except me."

Your concerns about how others perceive you can range from mild self-consciousness to paranoia.

Holly's history had been one of repeated rejection. As an adolescent, she began to believe that people were talking about her behind her back. While she outgrew the pervasive feeling she had as a teen, it did creep up on her from time to time.
"Sometimes when I heard whispering or laughter on a bus or in an elevator, I thought it was about me. I guess that sounds pretty paranoid, but I'd been hurt and let down so many times, I really thought that there was something conspicuously wrong with me that made other people not want to be with me."

Invisibility
Paradoxically, my clients also report feeling invisible—sexually and romantically. Roberta did.

"First I thought I was going to die unless I could have sex with someone, anyone I could find. I would have gladly made love to a tree. Then I went to the opposite extreme. I felt completely sexless. I was convinced that I lacked sex appeal, charm, charisma, whatever it took to get someone to be with me. My sexual self-esteem was in a free fall. I felt like, when Travis left, he sexually disqualified me."

When someone chooses to break off a relationship, you may well question your ability to attract the love you so desperately need. The child within says, "Nobody loves me, I'm not good enough. I'm not special enough."

These feelings may harken back to the times you had trouble winning your parents' love or attention. You may have taken these experiences to heart, developing ingrained doubts about whether you could attract and hold the love and attention of another. This left you vulnerable to romantic rejection later on.

One psychoanalyst refers to this as having a "limited capacity to *perform the work of conquest*" the work "necessary to transform an indifferent object into a participating partner." That's a very clinical way of saying that you feel you're not desirable enough to win someone's love and loyalty.

When a loved one leaves, this belief about your "limited capacity" comes to the fore. It is as if the breakup has confirmed what your child within has believed all along—that you are unworthy.

It is important to surround yourself with caring, nurturing, and affectionate friends and to seek out positive, life-affirming activities. You might choose to join a self-help group, become involved in an exercise regimen, or seek out the guidance of a therapist. This is where abandonment recovery workshops can provide a lot of positive feedback and support. (For information about developing abandonment recovery workshops, see my address and website at the end of this book.)

At this point you are probably not emotionally ready to become deeply involved in a new relationship. But as you continue to reach out, you will soon discover that you have not lost your appeal as a person or as a sexual being. No matter how invisible and diminished you feel right now, you will live to love again.

Keeping up the Fight

Your abandonment experience may have temporarily humbled you and brought you to your knees, but it has not vanquished you.

If Sapolosky's research with baboons wasn't enough to convince you to stand up and fight, consider Maier, Watkins, and Flesner's work with laboratory rats.

According to these researchers, when a group of male rats live within a single cage, one will become dominant—the alpha rat. When the experimenter introduces a stranger rat, the alpha rat will attack him. The intruder initially fights back but eventually displays a posture of defeat. When the alpha rat sees these outward signs of submission, he no longer considers the new rat a threat, and he leaves the intruder alone.

The researchers looked to see what effect being attacked and defeated had upon the intruder rat's immune system. They learned that in the weeks following the ordeal, the production of antibodies (the good immune cells) was greatly reduced. In other words, the rat's immune system response was weakened.

The researchers also examined whether this reduction in antibodies was an effect of the physical assault (being bitten and pushed) or the result of being psychologically defeated. They carefully studied a group of rats who, when placed in the intruder role, did not adopt submissive postures, but instead continued to fight back. Their remarkable finding was that even though the feistier rats were repeatedly bitten and otherwise abused, their antibody levels were unaffected.

This study supports data that has been gathered from human health care professionals—that people who don't fight back, who are passive during a crisis, are more likely to develop cancer and other illness.

The message reads very clearly: You can and should fight the thought that you are somehow unworthy. Take this time alone to examine your life and vindicate your loss by taking positive action.

UNFINISHED BUSINESS FROM THE INTERNALIZING STAGE

As I struggled with self-doubts after my longtime partner left me, old feelings began to emerge from a painful and difficult period of my childhood. It started about the time my mother was pregnant with her third child. I was the oldest, and at age seven was starting to get fat.

With the arrival of a new baby brother, I was probably feeling emotionally relegated to a back burner. I'm not sure if there was a physiological or genetic component to my weight gain. It could have been due to the buildup of glucocorticoids I described in Chapter 3. Was I feeding my emotional hunger with one too many chocolate chip cookies? I can't know for sure, but regardless of the cause, by the time my new baby brother was a year old, I had become an extremely obese child.

This was out of the ordinary for my family. We were a picture postcard family, thin and beautiful, except for me. I felt like an eyesore. Years later, my mother told me that she had also gone through a fat stage as a child. She'd been terribly ashamed of herself and felt shunned by her own family and the world. I must have been a vivid reminder of a painful time in her own childhood, and I wonder if that was why she seemed to detach from me.

To make matters worse, my relatively small mouth couldn't accommodate my adult teeth. One eye tooth, not knowing where else to go, grew straight out. With my now erect tooth and double chins, I wanted to hide. My mother came to the rescue and gave me a home perm to perk me up. It didn't work. My hair fell out in clumps. What was left were pathetic frizzled tufts. I was convinced my hair would never grow back and that I would be hideous, an eternal blight on the family portrait. I tried to act like none of it bothered me. I didn't want other kids to see how much their taunts hurt.

The summer before sixth grade, I surprised everyone by going on a strict diet. I lost all the extra weight, my hair grew back, my eye tooth straightened itself out, and I entered the sixth grade slim and attractive. Slowly, my self-image began to improve, but it took a lot of doing. As I learned how to pick myself up, I tried to help my friends feel better about themselves, too. An emotional healer was born.

But despite all the reconstruction I did then and since, a lot of the old fat feelings came to the surface when my mate of twenty years left me. Deep down I harbored a self-hatred that was waiting for the right moment to reassert itself. The breakup was the tripwire that did it.

"Mine wasn't about my appearance, it was about health," said Pamela. "I had heart problems as a kid. I spent half of my childhood going back and forth to the hospital for operations. Then I'd have months to recuperate. I would look out my bedroom window and watch the other kids playing, wondering why I was the one who had to be sick.

"I believed I was marked by fate, like the other kids were better than I was. I felt shy and awkward when they'd come over. I reasoned that I wasn't as strong and healthy as they were, and that made them better than me."

Children can feel diminished by almost any kind of loss: a death in the family, divorce, having to share mom's love with a new sibling, health problems, losing a friend or a dream. In each of these losses, the child feels the shame of abandonment. Children naturally see the world from their own limited, self-oriented perspective, so they experience every loss as a slight to their personal worth. Their intellectual abilities aren't developed enough to distinguish a purely impersonal situation from one that involves a failure on their part. So they take almost all losses personally. Though these disappointments, slights, and indignities may have happened decades ago, they can be reawakened when their loved one abandons them.

Childhood Scenarios of Internalizing

What childhood experiences contribute to low self-esteem? People in my support groups frequently mention parents who:

- put you down, criticized, and rejected you

- yelled at you, told you you were bad, ridiculed you, or humiliated you in public

- showed favoritism to another sibling or compared you unfavorably to a sibling

- withheld affection as punishment

- blamed you for their moods and frustrations

- singled you out as the focus of the family problems

- labeled you irresponsible, lazy, stubborn, selfish, or disorganized

- worried about you so much that they undermined your self-confidence

- treated you like a baby, failing to recognize your maturity and independence

- failed to give you responsibilities (you didn't feel you had an integral role in the family)

- gave you too much responsibility—you were everyone else's servant, not important enough in your own right

- expressed disappointment in your achievements

- set expectations that were too high

- set expectations that were too low

- directed the brunt of their anger at you

Or perhaps you had:

- trouble achieving in school

- physical problems or physical differences that led to pervasive prejudice

- difficulty making friends

- an overachieving sibling you compared yourself unfavorably with

- a sibling with a greater sense of entitlement than you

- bad experiences with teachers

The good news is that as the insecurities stemming from these and other childhood situations surface, you are in a position to address them as a rational adult. Now is the time to rethink some of the beliefs you've held about yourself since childhood, to resolve self-doubts you don't need to carry around anymore.

Up to this point, these experiences have deeply affected the decisions you've made and the quality of your relationships. But they don't need to anymore.

Holly's Internalizing

Holly, a single woman and accountant for a legal firm, described herself as "the poster child for the invisible wound." Holly made this statement during our first meeting. She was responding to my description of the internalizing process of abandonment, but as her story unfolded, her self-doubts were in sharp contrast to her striking appearance. She had a slight scar near her upper lip, but it only highlighted her dazzling smile.

"It's been the story of my life—not being able to find someone. At this point, I feel romantically invisible. In fact, I'm the original invisible woman. You've heard of The Invisible Man. Well, that's another type of abandonment, being abandoned by a whole people. I don't know which kind is worse, I only know what it feels like to be left out and disregarded."

Holly was full of intelligence, beauty, and life, apparently capable of giving a great deal of love. Yet, like so many abandonment survivors, her invisible wound had become a barrier to relationships.

As she went on to tell her story, the effect her personal his-

tory had on the here and now became clear. She had been abandoned at birth by her mother, moved from a foundling hospital to a foster home, then to another foster home. She was finally adopted at the age of three by wealthy, well-educated parents. The scar on her lip was courtesy of her alcoholic adoptive mother.

"My father hoped that adopting me would get Mother to sober up. Well, I didn't help. In fact, I became the person she blamed for her problems."

When Holly was six, her mother became pregnant with the baby she had been trying to have for fifteen years. From the start, James was the center of the family's life, casting Holly, now a nuisance, into shadow. He was an extraordinary achiever and eventually became a urologist. For Holly, the emotional upheaval of being displaced by her brother and her mother's drinking interfered with school. She barely made it to college, and then only lasted two years before she dropped out to follow a band on tour through California.

She returned covered in bruises—the physical evidence of bad relationships and hard living. She was heavily addicted to cocaine and alcohol. Her parents were disgusted with her. It was nothing new, but this time they cut her off financially. She was abandoned again in a real sense—too old to be a foundling, but not too old to feel very, very alone.

Fortunately, the bottom she hit had some give to it. Like a trampoline, it propelled her upward. She entered a twelve step program. By the time I had met her, she had been off drugs and on program for over ten years. She'd completed her college degree, was gainfully employed, and also volunteered for a suicide hot line. On weekends, she worked as a hostess at a restaurant. Despite her busy schedule, there was time to sink into the funk of being alone in the world.

She had never been in a long-term relationship and had no hope of finding one. "There's something about me that makes people keep throwing me away."

Although Holly's case is an extreme one, it illustrates how separation traumas can damage your self-image. If severe enough, the loss of self-esteem can become a barrier to love and intimacy. No matter what Holly tried to do to feel better about herself, memories of being abandoned worked from within to drain her self-esteem away. This invisible drain became a shield. It blocked Holly from recognizing her talents. It can hold you back from reaching your potential, too.

Very few of us experienced the kind of trauma Holly did, but most people do remember incidents that made them question their self-worth and that still affect them today. Most people recognize signs of low self-esteem in themselves and others. They include:

- Difficulty asserting yourself

- Feeling inhibited in certain situations

- Indecisiveness

- Excessive need for approval

- Difficulty tolerating imperfection in yourself or others

- Feeling inadequate, not good enough, not up to par

- Becoming intimidated around those who seem to have a stronger ego

- Comparing yourself to other people, feeling they have what you don't

- Being oversensitive to criticism

- Avoiding competition for fear of failure

- Fear of performing—you're convinced you'll make a fool of yourself

- Fear of succeeding—you don't want to make others envious of you

- Letting performance anxiety hold you back professionally
- Ruminating about how you behaved during a stressful social encounter
- Worrying about how others perceive you
- Letting insecurities interfere with your relationships
- Avoiding the spotlight but resenting the lack of recognition you receive
- Difficulty expressing anger or negative feelings directly
- Difficulty asking for what you want, especially if it is emotionally important to you
- Difficulty accepting compliments
- Wanting power and authority but having difficulty marking your territory
- Feeling small, weak, easily taken advantage of
- Putting yourself down before others have a chance to

Some of us are all too familiar with this list. A great deal has been written about these indicators, and most require very little explanation. But I've left something off this list, something rarely recognized as related to self-esteem, yet it is a cornerstone of low self-esteem. It is the need for **immediate gratification.**

Do you have trouble sticking to a diet? Do you quit early because you can't resist eating that piece of chocolate cake? Do you buy things you can't afford, take that second or third drink, or grab for a host of other quick fixes that you've already decided aren't good for you in the long run?

Difficulty delaying gratification is common among abandonment survivors of childhood. It becomes an internal saboteur, interfering with your ability to achieve long-range goals, like Holly's feeling that she could have become a doctor like her brother.

"I had as much on the ball as my brother. But I didn't want to do all of that studying, go through all those years with little money and less sleep. I felt miserable enough and was down about myself. I needed something to make me feel good—right away. That's why I went to California. The band made me feel like a queen, for a while anyway."

Those who can wait for gratification are usually those whose self-esteem is in good supply. Where did they get it? They may well have inborn talent and reaped the success that stemmed from it. But behind the scenes, there was often a loved one encouraging them, reminding them of their inherent worth. Their families bolstered their confidence, made them feel deserving of success and capable of achieving it.

The truth is that many who have difficulty delaying gratification long enough to reach a long-range goal, are often as intelligent and talented as those who can. Some do have success when they apply their skills and gifts. The difference is that they feel an urgency rising out of their self-doubt and emotional hunger. It says, "I need a fix now."

Why do they need immediate gratification? And how does it relate to self-esteem?

In Chapter 3 we talked about the fact that many abandonment survivors endured prolonged periods during childhood in which their parents were either physically or emotionally unavailable. You may recall that empty feeling—those times that you felt you needed something you couldn't get—when you waited for something that never arrived. You couldn't force your parents to take better care of you. So what happened to that emotional hunger, those feelings of frustration?

Chances are, you internalized them.

You turned the frustration on yourself. You despaired of getting Daddy's attention or becoming Mommy's favorite again. You believed yourself unworthy or inadequate in some important way. As your needs became more and more urgent, you learned there were ways to temporarily put them off. You grabbed for the quickest, easiest fix you could find—food, television, masturbating, compulsive exercising—anything to stifle those unsettling feelings.

Sometimes children who internalize emotional hunger carry those frustrated feelings into adulthood. They become adults whose need for immediate gratification interferes with major life goals. They find themselves stuck on the bottom rung of the ladder of success and blame themselves for it.

While some abandonment survivors of childhood are under-achievers, others are overachievers, constantly striving to compensate for what they firmly believe are flaws. They're always working, denying themselves rewards. Both over- and underachievers are caught in a vicious cycle of self-deprecation that is at the heart of these extremes.

Many massage their uncomfortable feelings with self-medication of all kinds. They turn to drugs and activities to take the edge off the urgency rising out of a growing stockpile of unmet needs. Be it food, drink, exercise, work, or other people, they become dependent on anything or anyone capable of soothing, numbing, or distracting them from their emotional hunger.

The antidote to these self-reinforcing patterns of dependency and codependent relationships is to dare to name your goals, to pursue your abandoned dreams, and to strive for real emotional fulfillment. The third Akeru exercise is designed to facilitate this process. It will help you to open new windows of opportunity, make new decisions, and work toward reaching your true potential.

THIRD AKERU EXERCISE: BUILDING A DREAM HOUSE

The third exercise involves working *with* the energy involved in the internalizing process. It taps into one of your most powerful resources, your imagination. You can practice this exercise any time—while driving your car, on the treadmill at the gym—whenever you have a few minutes to focus your thoughts.

The first two Akeru exercises laid the groundwork for this one. *Staying in the moment* helped you to use the moment as a way of dealing with pain and intensified your experience of the world around you. The *daily dialogue* put you in touch with your most basic feelings and needs. You learned to nurture yourself.

This third exercise, a visualization exercise, takes you one step farther. It strengthens and enhances your new relationship with yourself. If internalizing is a time of interior focus, you can use its energy to help rebuild your inner core and create positive change in your life.

Through guided visualization, you are to focus your energy on goals, dreams, and ideals, laying a foundation upon which you will build a new self. The process introduces a set of principles that I call the four cornerstones of self.

It is during the internalizing stage described in this chapter that the injury you've suffered in the wake of a breakup can burrow into your self-image. Unfortunately, many people try to fight this injury playing by its rules; they fight narcissistic injury with narcissistic defenses. They tell themselves, I *am* important. I *am* sexy. I *am* worth more than he is. I *am* successful. These affirmations place all of the emphasis upon your attributes— upon how beautiful or talented you are.

But the *four cornerstones of self* are not based upon your unique talents. The point is not to enumerate your physical attributes, skills, or professional accomplishments. The cornerstones are more basic, addressing the intrinsic, universal aspects of what it means to be a human being. They are inalienable. Neither age nor disability nor even being abandoned can diminish them. These are invincible principles of self that no one can take from you.

The Four Cornerstones of Self

1. **Facing, accepting, and ultimately celebrating your separateness as a person.** We are, each of us, a wholly separate

human being, whether we are in a relationship or have just ended one. We enter the world and depart from it on our own.

2. **Celebrating the importance of your own existence.** You are not more or less important than anyone else. Every person's existence is important, and it is up to you to value and respect your own. Regardless of your age, attributes, or physical capacities, each person's existence is important. Life is a fleeting, precious gift that must be realized in the moment.

3. **Facing and accepting your reality.** No matter how difficult things may be for you at this moment, it is the only reality you

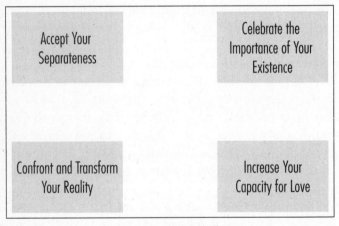

Four cornerstones of self

have. Remember that it is always changing and that you are the force that moves it forward. You may not have chosen the challenges you now face, and chances are you are not to blame for the things that have gone wrong. But the situation is yours to deal with. You can choose to rail against it, or you can make the best of it. The responsibility for owning it and changing it belongs to you.

4. **Enhancing your capacity to love.** I believe that most people use only about 5 percent of their capacity to love. Love is

one of the most compelling powers we possess as human beings. You cannot control the love of another, but you can increase your own capacity to give and receive love and all of the benefits that flow from it.

Building a Dream House

This exercise provides the vehicle through which to incorporate these four principles into your thinking and into your core of beliefs. It involves building a dream house out of your imagination. You construct the dream house based upon the *four cornerstones.*

All it takes is a few minutes. The exercise brings about rapid results, but it is hard to explain how or why it works. Your goal in abandonment recovery is not to simply read about and intellectually understand the cornerstones but to adopt them and be changed by them. In this way you are using the internalizing process to your advantage.

Through visualization, you override the limitations of purely cognitive learning. How many smokers could recite a list of the damages of smoking but are unable to use it in a way that helps them quit? This visualization is a way of getting past the skepticism and complacency. By using your imagination and making time to contemplate your dreams, you are able to ride in on the internalizing energy and bring your visionary powers to bear upon your gravest self-doubts.

While I can't fully explain why the process works, the clinical evidence of its effectiveness comes from many sources: my own clients, other clinicians, abandonment survivors, and professionals from a variety of fields. All report that this exercise produces remarkable results. Within the dream houses we create, we forge our new selves, ones that are able to steer our lives in new directions.

My clients often initially resist this technique because visualization requires you to let go of logic and suspend your need to understand. For now, forget about how it works. Try it and then decide whether to continue based on the changes you notice in the way you think and behave.

You will only have to be guided through the visualization once. Afterward, you will be able to conjure it in a matter of seconds. Some find it helpful to tape themselves reading the instructions below. Alternatively, a friend can read the instructions as you close your eyes and follow along. (*For a copy of the author's audiotape of this exercise, please refer to my address and website information at the end of the book.*)

Building a Self Begin by closing your eyes and imagining that you have unlimited financial resources—billions of dollars at your disposal. Perhaps you've won the power ball lottery. You can't bring people back from the dead or control other people's behavior, but you can accomplish plenty with enough money.

Imagine the ideal environment for the ultimate dream house, the house of *your* dreams. Imagine that your house is so satisfying in every way that you could happily live in it alone if you had to.

What climate would suit you best? Does it snow there in the winter months? Or is it tropical? Is the perfect setting for you a mountaintop? Does it overlook an ocean, a river, a lake, a valley? Is it on a sandy beach? In a dense forest? In a rural farming area? In the city? Is it blissfully remote, or are you surrounded by other people? Is it a cozy neighborhood? Is it an apartment with glorious views? Is it in a planned community with all the amenities? Is it near where you live now or in another state? Another country? (Pause, taking time to visualize)

Now that you've decided on the ideal location, start thinking about the house itself.

Remember that money is no object. If small and cozy suits you, so be it. If a mansion is what you have in mind, go for it. The idea is to create a place so ideally suited to your needs that within it you are able to *celebrate your separateness* as a human being. You and Little will be content to spend your time alone, at peace and happy in this house of your imagination. The house has everything to satisfy your adult self as well as your child self. If moats or iron fences are what it takes to make you and Little feel secure, include them in your plans. You can shape and embellish the property to suit your whims. You can landscape it any way you want. You may choose to have vast property with its own private road or perch your house right on the main street of your favorite town. (Pause)

Now think about the interior. How much room will you need? Where is the kitchen? The living space? Do you need a library, office, observatory? Deck, porch, dining room? What about balconies, skylights, stairways, nooks and crannies? Take a few minutes to think about the quality of the space you'd like in this dream house.

Which room is your favorite? Where will you spend most of your time? Imagine yourself in that room. (Pause)

To design this room, imagine that this spot is the very heart and soul of the house. All of the other rooms fan out from this one. Is your favorite room the kitchen? Are you sitting at a counter looking out the window at your favorite view? Or are you in the living room, sitting in the most comfortable chair in the world next to a huge stone fireplace? Are you lounging outside on the deck? Decide on your favorite spot within this room and sit yourself down. (Pause)

Imagine that you are extremely comfortable in your favorite spot. What can you see from where you are sitting? Picture a captivating view—one that gives you enormous pleasure and makes you feel totally alive. Looking at this view, you appreciate the *importance of your own existence*. What is it that draws your attention and enthralls you? Is it a brook? A waterfall? A mountain? The woods? A sandy beach? Imagine a view that puts you in touch with life itself and helps you truly live in the moment. (Pause)

What does your room look like? Is it filled with space and light? Does it offer complete privacy? Or is open to the rest of the house? What other things are in this room? An old potbellied stove? Oriental rugs? Wood floors? A piano? Imagine the comforts and pleasures surrounding you. Your surroundings should be so complete that this room becomes the one place where you would be able to *accept any reality* you might be faced with, no matter how difficult, even the one you're dealing with right now. What things in this room draw your attention in a pleasurable way, away from painful thoughts? A bird outside the window? A beautiful bouquet of flowers? The sound of the ocean? A special photograph? A painting? The room contains these special items, and the view beyond encompasses wondrous elements of nature. All of it helps you to accept your reality, no matter how challenging. (Pause)

Imagine yourself two years from now. What are you doing in your new life within your dream house? What meaningful activity occupies most of your time? Are you enjoying a life of leisure or an exciting new job? Are you traveling? Writing? Painting? Cooking? Arranging family gatherings? Are you getting a degree? Building a new career? What career? Are you physically training to prepare for a mountain climbing trip? Or are you at rest? Do you spend a lot of time out of doors? Visiting others? Imagine what you are doing in your new life that gives you joy and satisfaction. (Pause)

What friends and family would you like to include in your world? A new relationship, perhaps? Are you with children? Living alone? Does anyone share any part of the house with you? Where do they stay? In which rooms do you interact with them? (Pause)

Imagine that your *capacity for love* increases every day. All people in your life feel your love. It has warmed a special place within each of them, connecting you with them in deep and meaningful ways. You feel this connection to those in the next room and with those far away. This new generosity of spirit has grown out of your acceptance of your *separateness* as a person. It's because you can appreciate the *importance* of your own existence and embrace your *reality* that you have increased your capacity for *love*. Where are these people now? Can you hear them upstairs? Is a car pulling up the driveway at this minute? (Pause)

Now conjure up the whole house, the people in the back-ground, your new occupation or activity (or delicious lack of one), the surroundings, and the climate. Gather up as much of it as you can into a single image. This house is you—the you that you are becoming. Its architecture and embellishments represent your substance, your physical and emotional needs as a human being, your most deeply felt dreams and goals. It is the direction your life is taking. (Pause)

To maximize the benefits of this exercise, practice it consistently and frequently. Because there is no need to rebuild the house every time you conjure up the image, it only takes seconds. You don't need to recite the four cornerstones. Just make sure that the way you've imagined the house takes each of them into account. You should be able to *celebrate your separateness,* the *importance of your existence,* your ability to *accept reality,* and your *love capacity* just by being in the house. You have only to conjure up the image of the house to reinforce these principles because they have been built into its structure.

I recommend you perform this exercise no less than three times a day for a few seconds or minutes at a time. There is no need to close your eyes. You can revisit the image on the train or standing in line at the post office.

As you identify new goals, renovate your dream house accordingly, so that it keeps up with (or stays ahead of) your hopes and dreams. You're developing as a person; your needs are changing. You're fine-tuning your goals. You may decide to move your dream house to another location or make it smaller or larger. You may decide you need to add a room or tear one down. You may change your favorite spot from one room to another.

As you continue, you become a virtual architect, learning to solve practical problems, like figuring out the best place for a closet or staircase. The more vivid the image you have of your dream house, the greater the benefit.

Get out paper and make a floor plan. Many of my clients

carry a diagram of the house with them. The important thing is to return to your dream house at least three times a day.

This visualization technique taps into one of your most powerful resources—your imagination. Through it you become the engineer and architect of your own life. As the master designer, you create an internal space to suit your greatest needs, goals, and desires. The house represents your true self and at the same time gives it a place to grow.

What part of our minds does the building, designing, and problem solving involved in this exercise? My guess is that our wellspring of hope does the work of the visualization. This wellspring wants us to break free from self-doubt and people-pleasing. In our imagination, we are freed to discover a higher power within.

Where has this self been all of these years? As toddlers, when we were just beginning to discover the use of our limbs, we used them to venture away from our mothers and explore the world around us. Visualizing an incipient part of us strengthens that part of us that wants to explore, exercise its autonomy, experience freedom from the constraints of old relationships, and celebrate the future.

SUMMARY OF INTERNALIZING THE REJECTION

During the internalizing stage, we are in the heart of the self-injury process. We internalize feelings of rejection and anxiety about being alone.

The internalizing energy is powerful. It acts like a centripetal force, pulling the feelings of rejection and desertion toward our centers, where our core beliefs are forged, where we silently judge ourselves unworthy or unlovable.

When we were children and felt abandoned, we were less able to fight off self-doubts and anxieties, less emotionally resilient, and more easily wounded. We internalized feelings of rejection. We became afraid of being left alone.

As children, we erected makeshift barriers. We created inter-

nal gatekeepers to prevent hurt and fear from burrowing so deep.

As adults, losing our love attachment wakes up the internal gatekeepers who have been secretly trying to keep life out all along. We feel everything keenly once again. But now we no longer choose to doubt or devalue ourselves.

It is time to internalize good feelings, to celebrate the importance of our own unique existence. Abandonment recovery beholds a vision that allows us to bypass the gatekeepers and rebuild with dreams, goals, acceptance, and love.

Internalizing brings us to a place deep within, where we wrestle the demons of doubt and fear. It is the soul's Gethsemane from which we emerge with humility, strength, and vision.

Chapter Five

Stage Four: Rage

WHAT IS RAGE?

Rage is a protest against pain. It is how we fight back, a refusal to be victimized by someone leaving us, the way we reverse the rejection.

Those who know abandonment's rage know that its wound is tender, hot, and sore during this pivotal point of the healing process. We're agitated by nagging pain as we fight off toxins in the wound.

Mending tissues are raw and taut. If anything comes near them, we cry out in anger. We are prepared for any threat, ready to defend against the subtlest criticism.

Others may not realize the scope and depth of our wound. They brush up against it with no inkling of the pain they cause. We stand guard, protector of our emerging selves.

We defend ourselves against further injury with the outer child. The outer child is the part of us that acts out our inner child's fear and rage. The outer child pretends to be our ally, our foot soldier, but it is really our gatekeeper. Its mission is to fight change and defend against feeling.

It is during this fourth stage of abandonment that our defenses can become calcified. People think they are strong again, but this outward show of strength is only the outer child becoming more firmly entrenched than before.

Controlling the impulses of our outer child is the key to true recovery. Learn to recognize its traits, and we can begin to dismantle our unhealthy defenses. Until now we have been doing the groundwork of healing; outer child work is the next task of recovery: We're changing our behavior.

We all know that rage burns. It seethes and boils in the molten core of self. It also awakens the outer child—draws its maneuvering out in the open. Exposing the outer child is the turning point in the recovery process, the bridge to lasting change.

THE FOURTH STAGE OF ABANDONMENT: RAGE

Roberta's Rage

Roberta vividly remembers the night she first noticed her mood turn from isolation to anger.

She was getting ready to go to the symphony. She hadn't been inside a concert hall since she had caught Travis, the great maestro himself, with that other woman. She wished she had hit him harder, knocked him down with her bag and broken his nose. As far as she was concerned, he got off far too easily.

But that was six months ago. Why should she be feeling so riled up about going to a concert now? She had learned the role Travis demanded of her and performed it for years: Be there at the concert to witness the accolades and afterward, lavish him with praise. How had she put up with it so long? Now she was on her way to the symphony again, this time, in the anonymous role of spectator.

Not that she had ever been more than a spectator in Travis'

life—he just needed her to keep his voracious ego fed. He certainly never gave anything back to her. Instead, he had taken
the last four years of her life, her best years, and she had nothing
to show for them. She spent the last six months in pure hell
trying to get over it. It was time to wash the whole miserable
mess out of her hair. How did he create such turmoil in her life,
anyway?

She said all of this to herself, standing in front of her mirror.
She really shouldn't have agreed to go, but John had an extra
ticket, and in a weak moment, the part of her that loved music
had told John he couldn't let it go to waste. She agreed to go,
thinking it was long overdue. But suddenly the thought of walking into the concert hall was definitely not something she rel-
ished. She hadn't been out with anyone for so long. Well, this
wasn't a date. It was only John, a friend, someone she'd begun
talking to after the abandonment recovery groups. John was no
Travis. Not that he wasn't pleasant-looking, but he was definitely not her type—just too basic, missing that . . . she couldn't
quite put her finger on what. John better not have any ideas.
No, she hadn't given him any mixed signals. They were just
friends.

Then came the knock. "Flowers," she almost shouted as she
saw John's offering. "Get them out of here." John stood blankly
in the doorway. Roberta grabbed the flowers from his hands
and stuffed them upside down in the wastebasket by the door.

"Roberta," said John.

"I'm just not ready for that," she said, surprised at herself
for such a display of anger. She wasn't expecting to show this
side of herself to John. She tried to regain control. "I'm just not
in the mood. You should know that, John. Doesn't anybody
understand?" She held her head in her hands.

John stood still in the door frame. "Oh, just come in," she
said. "You'll have to ignore me. I have no idea why I'm reacting
like this." But they both knew what it was about. She had told
John all about Travis, many times.

John reached in his pocket and handed the suddenly teary

*Roberta a tissue. "How's my eye makeup?" she asked, blotting
her face, trying to regain her composure.*

"You look good," said John.

*"That's not what I mean," she said, angrily. "Are my eyes
smudged? Do you want me to go to a concert looking like a
basket case?"*

*He handed her another tissue. "Roberta, if you don't like . . .
we don't have to go," he said.*

*"No, let's go," she snapped, and grabbing up her purse, she
slammed the door behind them.*

The fourth stage of abandonment, rage, is the most volatile.
The night she went to the concert with John, Roberta's anger
spilled over the edges of her wound. She had not yet learned
how to harness her anger. In her case, it's easy to sense the grief
and loneliness lurking just behind her anger. Notice that her
anger is directed outward, rather than at her*self*. This represents
progress from the victim rage that we saw during the internalizing process. Roberta feels a more effective, self-empowering
type of anger that we begin to feel during this fourth stage. In
Roberta's case, the transition from victim rage is not yet complete. She has not yet learned to channel the anger in a positive
direction, and she displaces it upon an innocent bystander—
John.

Sometimes we cycle through the five stages of abandonment
so rapidly that we experience them almost simultaneously.
Sometimes the process takes just minutes, sometimes it stretches
over months. We know we're cycling through the rage process
when our anger takes on a momentum of its own.

Rage comes in emotional surges that leave us irritable and
edgy. Sometimes a surge is explosive. Losing our keys can send
us into a blind fury. In fact, any loss or personal slight, real or
imagined, can cause an unexpected eruption.

After the isolation of the internalizing process, the fact that
we can express anger is a good sign. It signifies active resistance
to the injury. Rage tells us that the beleaguered self, under siege

from self-recrimination, is ready to stand up and fight back. As the self is no longer willing to take all of the blame, our rage must find another release. Our anger begins as an impotent protest. We strike out at inanimate objects like pillows, but as we gain strength, it becomes more directed. We use its energy to break through the barriers of isolation. Rage insists upon righting the injustice and restoring your sense of self worth.

We can apply many of the "R" words characteristic of this turnaround to Roberta's scene with John. Through her anger she is starting to *reverse the rejection* and remove Travis from his pedestal. Her return to the concert scene is an attempt to reclaim her territory and relinquish her painful attachment. Difficult as it is, she's ready to make her reentry into the world.

Turning the energy behind your rage outward is not always a smooth process. It begins in fits and starts. Despite its turbulence, feeling and expressing rage is a necessary part of recovery. It is an active protest against injury that demands change. It helps us to start functioning again.

"I thought I was really losing it," said Marie. "I didn't know whether to cry or scream. I had trouble coping with everything. At work, I had a no patience at all. When teachers see students behaving the way I was, we call it 'low frustration tolerance.' Suddenly, the term applied to me. Everyone thought I had taken a turn for the worse. But it turned out that I was finally coming to terms with the changes in my life—and the hard work I had ahead of me to get back on track."

In its raw form, rage is unrefined aggression. We act without thinking, yet we feel justified. Rage maintains an internal dialogue that feeds on itself and fans its own flames. It becomes *defensive aggression* when we perceive a personal attack and use rage to protect ourselves. Rage becomes offensive aggression when it is used to perform destructive acts of retribution.

Rage can be both destructive and constructive. Your task is

to transform its energy into healthy self-assertiveness—that is, to take positive actions on your own behalf.

In the throes of rage, it was hard for me to believe that the turbulent mix of emotions I felt could possibly lead to peace or tranquillity. But I'd seen that this aggressive energy served a purpose in the lives of the abandonment survivors I'd worked with. I knew that the agitation I was feeling was life calling me out of my self-imposed isolation. It meant that relief was just around the corner.

This chapter will guide you through the forms that your anger can take during this stage. By the end, you'll be able to recognize anger's many functions and redirect its energy for your benefit. Later, I'll help you identify the unique characteristics of your outer child. Identifying outer-child behaviors focuses your attention on the impact of your old losses. Now is the time to address that unfinished business, focus on where you may be stuck in anger, and break patterns of behavior that hold you back.

THE ANGER FRAMEWORK

What follows are feelings and behaviors characteristic of the rage process.

READY TO EXPLODE

You're feeling irritable, consumed with angry thoughts, maybe even ready to explode. What's going on under the surface?

At a psychobiological level, *rage* represents one of your body's self-defense options. It's choosing to *fight* instead of *flee* or *freeze*.

According to Daniel Goleman, whose book *Emotional Intelligence* describes our emotional responses, anger is triggered by a sense that we are endangered. Physical threats as well as threats to our self-esteem or dignity—such as being treated unjustly or rudely—can both lead to rage. We are particularly vulnerable to this kind of threat when someone we love has left us.

It is possible for us to use our rational minds to temper the expression of our anger, but particular situations pose an overwhelming challenge. Remember that your emotional brain is also known as your mammalian brain. Its evolutionary design dictates that at crucial moments, we act first and reason later. Picture the squirrel darting off in a split second to avoid a pebble launched from a child's slingshot. Your own mammalian brain is primed to flinch, dart away, freeze in fear, or lash out when it detects imminent danger. In the wake of your breakup, just about any affront to your injured sense of self can be perceived as danger.

The amygdala's role in anger is pivotal. It acts as your brain's central alarm system. Like a well-trained watchdog, it relays urgent messages, alerting its master of any possible threat, and it prepares to launch a defense. It declares a state of emotional emergency when it senses the threat of another abandonment and calls for a fighting response. Working faster than conscious thought, the amygdala (depending upon the emotional lessons it has learned) responds automatically.

Ready to Explode
Reversing the Rejection
Renouncing the Abandoner
Reversing the Loss
Railing Against the Reality
Resentment
Rewriting the Closure
Revamping the Outside First
Revenge

Rage framework

Dolf Zillman explains that anger entails two waves of arousal. Having perceived a possible threat, your amygdala signals for the release of stress hormones that trigger immediate action and help to sustain your ability to react to further threats.

The first wave is an adrenaline rush (or catecholamine rush, which involves a release of both adrenaline and norepinephrine). We feel a quick surge of energy, in Zillman's words, enough for "one course of vigorous action." Depending upon the situation, this first wave of arousal dissipates within a few minutes.

The second wave involves the release of glucocorticoids which generate energy for hours and even days afterwards. This creates what Goleman calls a 'background tone of action-readiness.' This background tone creates a 'foundation on which subsequent reactions can build with particular quickness.' Goleman explains that, 'this why people are so much more prone to anger if they have already been provoked or slightly irritated by something else.'

"I was missing Gabby and feeling bad about myself. I was also ready to blow up at everything and everybody," said Keaton. "One day my sister didn't return my phone call. For all I knew, she was away for the weekend, but I didn't want to listen to explanations. I was just ready to explode."

Because his injury was still tender, Keaton was already in a heightened state of arousal—a state of action readiness. He perceived the silence from his sister as a rebuff and was flooded with a surge of anger that carried a physiologically driven urge to lash out.

"Finally, my sister called from the car phone on her way back from upstate. 'Just checking in,' she said. 'Wondering how you're doing.' Unfortunately, I had already left a belligerent message on her answering machine."

While you might be concentrating on something else, your ever-vigilant amygdala is busy scanning the horizon of your experience for emotional threats that bear any crude resemblance to your old traumas. As Goleman puts it, the amygdala plays a kind of "neural *Name That Tune*." It makes snap judgments based on just a few notes of the song, forming whole impressions from a few tentative signs. At times of extreme arousal, when your background tone has been set for action readiness, you can go off half-cocked, striking out at things that later prove to be innocuous.

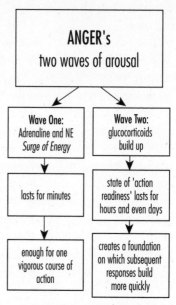

"*I was supposed to meet my closest friend for dinner on Saturday night,*" said Barbara, "*and she canceled because she had a date. I was so angry that I crashed into a tree backing out of the driveway. That made me even madder, so mad I got out and kicked the car, hurting my foot in the process. All of my neighbors were watching, probably trying not to laugh. I have no idea what came over me, but it turned out that I fractured my toe and had to wear a cast on my foot.*"

Anger's two waves of arousal

Why this hair trigger? Your brain has a special pathway that relays sights and sounds directly to your amygdala, altogether bypassing your neocortex, the part of your brain where conscious thinking takes place. In other words, your emotional brain reacts to a potential threat in milliseconds—well before your neocortex has a chance to receive and process sensory information. Your eyes sight the enemy, and your amygdala activates a *fight, freeze, or flight* response well *before* your reasoning mind has a chance to get involved.

While your emotional brain is thought of as the mammalian brain, your neocortex makes more refined and accurate appraisals of real or imagined threats. It is the seat of rational thinking. The circuits leading to and from your neocortex are more complex and have many more brain cells than the circuits to and from the amygdala. Neocortical circuits take about twice as long to process incoming information. Although slower, the outcome is more precise.

Once your rational mind has a chance to realize that a potential threat is innocuous, it relays an all-points-safe bulletin to your amygdala, signaling it to call off the dogs. However, by that time, the second wave of arousal is already under way, setting that background tone of fighting readiness.

Since this background tone functions subliminally, most of its effects evade conscious awareness. You are often unaware of your heightened state of arousal. When an apparently small irritation crops up, your overreaction can come as a complete surprise.

"One day I yelled at my seventh-period class—which I never do. I was completely shocked," said Marie. "I didn't feel it coming. Otherwise, I would have headed it off at the pass. First came the outburst, and then came the realization that I must be angry. I hadn't realized it until I'd blown my cool. I had to get on top of the rage. I didn't want to keep taking it out on my students."

Like Marie, we need to monitor our feelings, especially during this sustained emotional crisis. You can contain the impulses to lash out at those who aren't to blame.

Alcohol only makes controlling these impulses more difficult. It is a drug (ethanol) in liquid form that acts as a depressant on the central nervous system. It depresses the part of the brain that inhibits us from acting out our destructive impulses. Under the influence of alcohol, it's harder to control our anger.

"I met my friends for a drink one night, and one of them said, 'You seem so much better, Roberta.' Well, for some reason, that infuriated me. 'Don't you get it?' I exclaimed. 'I'm trying to go on with my life, but it's been pure hell. You just

want to believe I'm better because all of you are tired of looking at my sorry face. You don't want to hear it or see it. So I have to put on this big act just for you—to make everybody else happy.'

"When I got done with my tirade, they all just looked at me. Lashing out like that is not like me.

"The next day, it occurred to me that this was about how raw I was feeling and not about how insensitive they were. Only then did it dawn on me that maybe I had gone a little overboard."

The abandonment wound is still tender at this stage. Once your background emotional tone has been set on edge, it takes less and less (smaller and smaller provocations) to trigger a reaction. Almost any slight that carries a nuance of rejection can become the straw that breaks the camel's back. Caught off guard, you can easily find yourself striking out at innocent bystanders.

When someone neglects to give you the right of way on the road, you grip the steering wheel like a vise (as a substitute for the other driver's neck). Your threshold for anger is lower, and your amygdala has perceived this minor traffic incident as a form of dismissal. Given what alcohol does to aggravate the situation, avoid driving under the influence at all costs.

REVAMPING THE OUTSIDE FIRST

The state of action readiness can create a kind of nervous energy that leads to many types of actions, not all of them angry or aggressive. Many of my clients express their anger by making a major change in their physical appearance.

"I dyed my hair," said Marie. "No more salt-and-pepper look for me. I became a brunette again. In fact, I went beyond my natural dark brown, all the way to deep black. A few weeks later, I cut it short and bought an outrageous pair of earrings."

People often make external changes as they make other important transitions. Take pregnant women, for example. It's not unusual to hear of an expectant mother redecorating a room or revamping the entire house in preparation for the dramatic life change to come. A colleague was recently promoted to director of a psychiatric unit. Although his salary didn't increase substantially, it was a prestigious appointment, one that validated expertise and long years of professional dedication. He celebrated by buying a luxury car—a far cry from the old wreck he'd been driving since I'd known him. He felt good about himself and wanted to show that on the outside.

The need to express the changes you are going through in a tangible way is universal. Some try a different hairstyle or buy new clothes. Others concentrate on their homes or dedicate themselves to getting fit. As superficial as these changes may seem at first glance, they are a sign of taking action, of turning rage energy outward.

The alterations are often symbolic; they set the stage for change and prepare ourselves and others for what's to come. A whole new look tells the world, "Here I come. Get ready. Make room for a new me."

Family and friends may be confused by these changes, and you yourself may not be conscious of what's driving your sudden interest in makeup or sky diving. Ultimately, it's about the need to take control of the transition imposed on you when your partner left.

"I decided that if abandonment was going to change me," said Barbara, "I was going to make damn well sure that the change would be for the better. I began tearing my living room apart with a vengeance. Remember, I still had my foot in a cast. I redecorated my whole house with candles, old photographs of my family, and some of the paintings I made before I met Howard. Then I invited all of my friends for a party and served fondue, a dish Howard did not like."

Reversing the Rejection

One of the primary functions of the rage process is to help you *reverse the effects of the rejection.* Instead of being angry at yourself, you expel hurtful feelings and negative messages. Instead of beating yourself up and *internalizing* your doubts, you *externalize* these messages, turning them *outward.* Some have likened this process to an erupting volcano. You can only contain the hurt and injury for so long before the negative messages you've internalized have to find their way out.

"I just couldn't accept one more drop of blame," said Keaton. "I was filled to capacity, tired of holding the bag for everything that went wrong. I decided that some of the blame belonged to Gabby."

Anger is a sign that you're ready to stand on your own two feet again. Of course, not every expression of rage need be volcanic. You can use the energy of your anger to thoughtfully revise old beliefs and rebuild a healthy sense of yourself.

"It can't be all *my fault," Keaton continued. "It wasn't all because I wasn't worthy. In fact, it's an outright injustice that Gabby threw me away like that. I have a right to be angry!"*

Releasing the Regrets

The trick is to focus your regrets on the circumstances of your breakup and not on presumed inadequacies that you've been blaming for ending your relationship.

"At first I regretted being me—being someone Lonny could fall out of love with. But then I began regretting having ever met Lonny," said Marie, "having ever loved him. All those years of happy family life didn't seem worth the pain I went through when he left."

You can hear the plaintive tone expressed in Marie's regrets, but you also sense that she is beginning to turn her anger outward. Regret can last a long time when all of your hopes and dreams go down the tubes with a relationship. But as you begin to expel the self-deprecating assumptions you have made about yourself, you relieve yourself of the damages wrought by self-doubt and self-recrimination.

RENOUNCING THE AUTHORITY OF THE ABANDONER

Another way to reverse the impact of abandonment is to question the reliability of the source. It's time to revoke the power you have given to your abandoner, to look closely at his or her credibility.

"Who was he to dictate whether I was desirable or not?" declared Barbara. "I'm worth too much to let one person's dismissal of me count for anything! Even if it was Howard. In fact, Howard is a fool for discarding me."

Some describe difficulty making the transition from *idealizing* your lost loved one to *renouncing* their authority. It's hard to make a realistic appraisal of your own worth. You have so completely subjugated your own self-worth to theirs that you find it hard to believe that your life will be worth living without them. Your task is to name and revise your old assumptions.

"I had to throw my wife off her pedestal," admitted Richard, "but it wasn't easy. Her opinion had counted for so long. I finally listened to my friends. They kept telling me that just because she kicked me out of her life did not prove that I had done anything so terrible or that I was lacking in some essential quality."

Many of my clients report that their lost partners became extremely critical and hostile as they pulled away. To justify their desire to end the relationship, they blamed the breakup on the person they had left.

"Gabby must have felt really guilty for having to leave me," Keaton said, *"so she wrote me this long letter, telling me all of the things I did to drive her away, everything I ever did that she didn't like, all of the terrible things about me that made her want to leave.*

"At the time, I took all of this to heart, believing everything she said and beating myself up for it. But I'm beginning to see that her laundry list was a way of finding an excuse *for getting out of the relationship."*

You were naturally so hurt by your loved one's rejection, that you have a hard time finding the strength to fight those negative messages. The barrage of criticism weakened you, making it that much harder to dethrone your abandoner. If you're struggling with this issue, ask for help from friends, family, or professionals who can provide guidance. Or join a support group where you can fully express your feelings, get realistic feedback, and work on these issues. Abandonment recovery workshops can provide invaluable support. (For information on workshops, see my address and Web site, at the end of the book.)

"It took me a while to get in touch with my anger," said Marie. *"But I was tired of feeling hurt and dejected all the time. After listening to other people's stories, I began to see a pattern in Lonny's behavior—it was entirely selfish and irresponsible. How his self-centeredness managed to escape me while we were married, I don't know. I guess I'd idealized him right from the beginning.*

"But I was no longer blind. That Lonny walked away with so little explanation suggested that he lacked regard for me as a human being. How could he have left me out there to grapple with the broken pieces of our relationship all by myself?

"I was furious that I had been left with all the unanswered

questions. If Lonny really was the person I had always given him credit for being, he would at least have tried to warn me or explain things more carefully. Suddenly, he seemed like a cad."

REVERSING THE LOSS

"I didn't find it was necessary to rage against my wife's behavior," said Carlyle, "even though she was the one who left me. I was able to understand that she was just being herself, doing what she felt necessary at the time. Getting angry didn't change anything.

"Some of my friends insisted that I wouldn't be able to heal properly unless I got in touch with how angry I was at her. They were angry with her for what she did. But I was in my own rage—not about her but about life. In fact, I felt like an angry bear, growling and frothing at the mouth over all the work I had ahead of me to get a new life started for myself. Why make this rage all about her, when it was really all about me—the pain I was in, the isolation from my family, the loneliness? That's what I was agitating about, not who was wrong or who did what to whom, but how to turn it around."

Carlyle is not the only abandonment survivor who is able to bypass the need to get angry at his lost loved one and move directly toward rebuilding his life, but he is not in the majority. Most feel the need to direct their anger toward the one who left.

RAILING AGAINST THE REALITY

Many abandonment survivors have trouble moving forward because they feel a deep-seated need to rail against an unwanted reality. *Railing against reality* is a form of rage that postpones accepting your situation.

"I tried everything, and I still couldn't get out of my own way," said Jay. "I was locked into rage. I just couldn't get over what my wife did to me."

In Chapter 4, we talked about the importance of accepting reality. In the Akeru exercise for visualizing a dream house, you created a home in which to forge a new vision for your life. *Accepting reality* is one of the cornerstones of that vision.

The ability to accept and face reality on its own terms is crucial to abandonment recovery. For many, it is one of the greatest challenges. Some do anything to avoid accepting situations they don't want or like. They act as if by protesting it, they can make it go away. We all know people who rankle over something they can't control. They act as if keeping up the fight will wear reality down. They wear themselves out beating their heads against a stone wall and sometimes wear out their welcome with otherwise supportive friends.

Facing reality means accepting the loss and the grief that goes along with it. *Railing against* it is a futile attempt to fend off the loss. In the long run, this strategy can't work. There will always come a day of reckoning when you must take stock of what has happened and grieve your loss.

Indeed, abandonment has placed you at an important crossroads. You can chose to fight the things you don't like, or you can face facts. The reality you face today isn't permanent. Reality is constantly changing. But it is up to you to take charge of it and move it forward.

"I was having such a difficult time with all the pain and anger. Then one day I said, 'Face it, Marie: You don't have what you most want in your life. Lonny's not here. It hurts. Face it, accept it, and move on.' It may not have been a joyous beginning, but it was a beginning."

Christopher Reeves, the actor well-known for his role as Superman, is a dramatic example of someone who faced a loss with remarkable strength. His was a different type of loss—loss of a physical capacity. He suffered a serious spinal cord injury from a riding accident. Today, he's an inspiration to thousands with similar conditions and to us all.

For Christopher Reeves, *blame* is irrelevant. If he chose, he could torment himself, going over and over in his mind the exact point at which either he or his horse made the wrong move. More important, he acknowledged the fact that life as he had known it had changed and now held radically different challenges. He could not afford to expend his energy *railing against reality*. He had to recognize the futility of protesting what couldn't be changed and focus on the things he could control. Like many abandonment survivors, he had to face the fact that the life he once had was gone. The life he faced was not one he wanted, but it was the only one he had. Only he could choose to make the best of it. He could have chosen despair, but he chose life.

Fighting against reality, resisting its pain and losses, makes for our most difficult moments. Things get better when we are able to confront it and begin to see what we can do to make it better. Once we accept, we can focus on making our lives, from moment to moment, as meaningful as possible.

Christopher Reeves shows it is possible to go beyond accepting a difficult reality and even to celebrate it. Doing so reaches a higher level of human existence—a state called *amor fati* in Italian. Literally, it means *"love your fate."* A similar expression in English comes from twelve-step recovery programs: *Want what you have.* In order to make the psychic leap all the way from railing against reality to *amor fati,* you must do the hard work of acceptance. Let go and recognize the growth that your abandonment experience has brought you.

Unlike Christopher Reeves, abandonment survivors don't publicly share their wounds with an adoring public. We share our longings, rejection, and self-doubt only with our closest friends and family, if at all. In truth, physical injury evokes one set of social responses, the stigma of abandonment another. But what abandonees do have in common with Christopher Reeves is that they are faced with a situation not of their own choosing—one filled with loss, transition, and challenge. They both have an opportunity to refocus their energy, to enhance their capacity for life and love.

RESENTMENT

Resentment is low-grade anger that boils just beneath the surface. Even as you begin to get a handle on acute episodes of rage, resentments tend to build. Every day, you deal with repercussions of your loss, indignities of being left, like taking in the groceries by yourself or going to the movies alone.

The resentment you feel varies from situation to situation. You might resent explaining the absence of your ex every time you bump into a mutual acquaintance. Others feel resentment when friends try to set them up on blind dates or when they weather the ordeal of joining a dating service. Then there are all the mundane tasks you once shared: taking out the garbage and doing the laundry, not to mention covering the rent that the two of you used to share. There is resentment over the lonely Saturday nights and over the need to fill a weekend that stretches endlessly before you. And for some, there is the burning resentment when you happen to spot your lost partner with a new lover.

"Resentment? I've been left with two kids," said Margaret, "a low-paying job, and an attorney who wants $5,000 up front. I also have an invitation to my cousin's wedding, and no money for a dress and no one to go with. How much more resentment can I feel before I explode into dust?"

Although resentment is a natural and unavoidable aspect of the abandonment process, you can use its energy to make improvements. The challenge is to convert your resentment into healthy aggression by finding new activities that are enriching and enjoyable.

"I felt so much resentment that it even spilled out onto my kids," said Barbara. "I needed them more than ever before, now that I was feeling so alone. But coming home from my new full-time job, I found caring for them all by myself absolutely overwhelming.

"Something had to give. I didn't want to be eaten alive by my own resentment. I was going to have to change things. My first step was to get my kids in a program at the Y on weekends so that I could join the gym. It worked out pretty well because I wound up meeting someone there who invited me to join an abandonment support group.

"Slowly, my resentment began to subside—but it meant going out and getting myself a new life. For every bad thing, I was going to have to find a good thing to take its place."

REVENGE

Some deal with their mounting resentment by imagining scenarios of retribution against the one who's left. Others *act out* these scenarios. When divorce is involved, one partner may retaliate by imposing financial penalties on the other or by withholding visitation. These and other vindictive acts are, in part, an attempt to equalize the pain and hurt.

Revenge fantasies and retaliatory acts may help you feel less like a victim and more like a force to be reckoned with. Although this is an understandable and common defense, you may also squander a great deal of valuable energy in pursuit of revenge.

"When Carlotta decided to kick me out," said Jay, "all I could do at first was go crazy on her. I didn't know how else to feel but angry in those days. I didn't have a clue how to have any other feeling. I only knew rage. And I didn't know what

else to do with anger except take it out on her. I wasn't satisfied unless Carlotta was breaking out in hives. When I wasn't getting even, I was drinking myself into a stupor. Needless to say, that left me out of control. It got so bad that I even threatened her physically. One night, she actually called the police and managed to get me locked up. Sitting there in jail over the weekend, I was the one getting the hives."

It is an understatement to say that we often regret things we do in anger. When our emotional brain perceives a threat, we automatically have an impulse to take defensive action, which can take the form of aggression. Yet there are very few situations in modern society that justify striking out. You might feel justified at the moment, but 99% of the time, acting out physically is something you'll regret.

According to Goleman, "Unlike sadness, anger is energizing, even exhilarating. It is one of the most seductive of the negative emotions. The self-righteous inner monologue that propels it along fills the mind with the most convincing arguments for venting rage." When someone we love leaves us, our anger is fueled by a deep and personal wound. We have been wronged, forced into exile from human relationship. The case you build against your abandoner becomes a way of justifying almost any retaliatory action.

These thoughts are the domain of your neocortex—the domain of conscious thinking—which also contains neural pathways to and from the amygdala. As one grievance builds on another, the impact ripples through these neural pathways, activating your emotional brain for action readiness. So although your rational mind can calm your amygdala-driven reactions, its mounting resentments keeps your emotional fires stoked.

"When I got to see my kids on weekends," Jay continued, "I spent the whole time blasting their mother for everything she said or did. Sure enough, I made them cry. And then I'd feel more determined than ever to win them over to my side. I even

*decided to fight for custody. After spending $7,000 on attorney
fees, my kids told the judge that they didn't want to hurt my
feelings, but they'd rather stay with their mom.*

*"I wanted to get Carlotta bad for that—like it was her fault.
I punched holes in the walls and broke things. Needless to say,
I was so distraught going through all of this that I lost tons of
business. I was just too frenzied and hungover most of the time
to follow through with my clients.*

*"I really hit a low point when I found out that Carlotta was
seeing someone else. I had already fired at least three therapists
for suggesting that I shouldn't interfere, that I needed to back
off. Let go of Carlotta? I believed I owned her, that she was
my property, that she had no right to do what she was doing.
All I wanted to do was to win, to get even, to make her pay
for my pain and loneliness."*

Retaliation isn't the only way to reverse the rejection. As Jay
later discovered, there are alternatives that better serve personal
growth. When you learn to harness its energy, rage mobilizes
you to take positive action. But its higher purpose is difficult to
discern if you leave its power in the hands of your outer child.
The outer child represents the patterns of behavior that are
deeply entrenched. It shows its face when you act out or behave
in misguided ways to deal with your feelings.

*"It wasn't until I realized what my rage toward Carlotta was
doing to me," Jay continued, "that I was able to put the brakes
on. But first I had to do a lot of talking to myself—to turn
myself around. I must have a will of iron, because I'm completely off the booze now. Bumping into Keaton was a lucky
break for me. He took me to a couple of meetings and that got
me started. Now I am on a major improvement plan to put
Humpty Dumpty back together again."*

The good news is that rage, once redirected, gives you the
energy to do the work of rehabilitation. Your anger shows

you've chosen to defend yourself rather than to *flee* or *freeze*. Your energy can be focused on fighting to retake your life. Use this time of surging energy, riveted attention, and acute sensory awareness to take on the challenge of rebuilding your life. Rage, a process of becoming action-ready, can lead to *pro*action.

REWRITING THE CLOSURE

One of the most vexing problems for many abandonment survivors is closure. Often there is too little closure, and most find themselves left with agonizing questions that won't go away. An ongoing search to understand what went wrong feeds the insidious process of self-injury. You do not need to remain in suspended animation, struggling to put the broken pieces of your former life back together again. Now that your anger has reached critical mass, it is time to take back control.

Your task is to rewrite the story of your broken relationship on your own terms, from a position of greater strength, wisdom, and objectivity. Rather than being the one who's been left, *you* get to decide how to end things on your own emotional terms. You are not the victim anymore. Put your aggressive energy to work and create your own ending.

Most abandonment survivors begin by imagining a few different scenarios. They rehearse conversations with their lost partners, giving voice to things they never got the chance to say. These trial runs help you come to terms with facets of the relationship you may have overlooked and things that may help you put it behind you.

Practice these scenarios in whatever way you feel most comfortable. You can talk to yourself, write letters to your lost mate, or go over what you'd like to say with a friend, therapist, or sponsor. The important thing is to consider all the issues that need to be addressed in order for you to feel at peace about the relationship. If you need to, plan a counterrejection, telling off your lost loved one in an imagined conversation. Some end by forgiving their lost partners. By rehearsing and later actually communicating with them, many abandonment survivors become more confident of their ability to act in their own best interest.

You might find it helpful to create a closure event. Some of my clients send a carefully written letter. Others arrange to meet their old partner with or without the assistance of a third party like a therapist or attorney.

"My anger toward Lonny had been coming out in little digs and lots of tears just about every time I tried to sit down with him to discuss how we would divide things up," said Marie. "But one day, I decided that it was time to calmly tell him what I thought and how I felt. Whether he heard me, or even cared, is not important. The important thing is that I described what it was like to grieve his loss in such a painful way. I told him exactly what I thought of him for putting me through it. It was the beginning of letting go."

As Marie discovered, you grow by expressing your anger and other complicated feelings to your lost partner. In doing so, you assert your emerging self.

THE ABILITY TO BE SEPARATE

The ability to be separate allows us to be who we are when we are in a relationship. It means being able to openly disagree with the other person. We can express anger without fearing that the other person will break the connection. It means feeling entitled. We can ask for what we want because we haven't lost ourselves in the needs and expectations of the other person.

The *ability to be separate* buoys us through the most stressful times, such as when we physically separate from a loved one after a breakup.

Being separate poses a special challenge for those who have been through childhood abandonment traumas. Their underlying *fear of abandonment* makes it difficult for them to disagree or show anger in their relationships. They're people-pleasers. They're co-dependent. They have a need to be compliant, co-operative, and agreeable, not just in the presence of their significant others, but with nearly everyone else in their lives.

Abandonment survivors of childhood are often compelled to merge with the needs and expectations of others. Emotionally they're unable to tolerate any break in their connections, even with casual acquaintances. Instead, they accede to whatever the other person expects from them. Their own identity is submerged in the need to be loved. When someone else breaks a connection, even a casual connection, the rebuff can be devastating.

Do you have a problem separating yourself from others' needs and expectations? Remember that if children had early separation traumas, their amygdalas are primed to look for signs of an impending breakup, which lowers their thresholds for rejection. The first step to conquering your fears is to acknowledge you have them.

During the rage stage you have an opportunity to change the way you respond when a relationship comes to an end. Communicating with your lost loved one—standing your ground and sharing your own thoughts and feelings—is one way to practice becoming separate.

This development is a slow process, but you'll reap the rewards each time you resist the temptation to let your needs be overshadowed by someone else's.

"I felt uncomfortable about how the evening at the concert went with Roberta," said John. "I had to overcome my initial impulse to bury the whole thing and act like it didn't bother me. After all, I understood where her anger was coming from; I had been there myself. But I was bruised by some of the things she said and the way she acted that evening.

"I know from past experience that I am capable of holding on to feelings, especially anger and hurt, for a long time. This

time, I thought, maybe I should try something different. Maybe I should just tell Roberta how I felt.

"So I told her, 'Roberta, last week, when you reacted to me like I was some sort of nuisance in your life, I felt angry and defensive. I'm telling you this because I would like to be open with you about my feelings. It's not easy for me. I'm vulnerable, too.'

"She responded with a simple, brief, 'You're right. I apologize.' It wasn't her reaction, it was being able to say what I felt that made me feel better. I was able to let go of those nagging feelings."

The *ability to be separate* allows us to sustain our own identity within a relationship. The rage process enables us to break the bonds that have robbed us of our self-expression. Once free of those bonds, you can begin to dismantle old people-pleasing patterns and assert your own preferences and needs.

REALISTIC SELF-APPRAISAL: BEYOND SELF-RECRIMINATION

As an active member of Alcoholics Anonymous, Keaton used its twelve step program to help him focus on behavior he was willing to change.

"I learned in AA that the only person I was supposed to control was me. But with Gabby, in spite of what I rationally knew, I had still been too controlling. When I became involved in abandonment recovery, I was able to address the insecurity and rage left over from my childhood that I'd been acting out all of my adult life. I realized how those feelings affected the way I acted toward other people.

"So I began making amends, beginning with Gabby for all of the times I held her hostage because of my own insecurity and took my anger out on her. I knew she had some responsibility for what went wrong, too. But it was up to her to take

ownership for that. I just made amends for my own part. It helped me feel more complete about things."

Like Keaton, many abandonment survivors rewrite the closure of their relationships by acknowledging things about their own personalities they would like to work on. Making amends and taking responsibility for your part in a troubled relationship can help resolve some of its unfinished business.

POSTTRAUMATIC EXPRESSIONS OF ANGER

One of the posttraumatic features of childhood abandonment trauma is difficulty controlling the way we express anger. Many have trouble asserting anger in a productive way. We flip-flop between overreacting or underreacting. Our attempts to fight back often miss the mark.

"It feels like I've gone through my life as a declawed cat," explains Holly. "I know all the right things to say, but when the moment comes to stand up for myself, I freeze. I let people get away with too much, but fear keeps me from putting them in their place. When I feel rejected, it goes right to the bone. I don't have claws to protect myself."

Like Holly, many abandonment survivors of childhood are sensitive to rejection and hostility. They avoid confrontation, steering clear of its emotionally charged consequences. Why? Because of amygdala-driven fear: fear of reprisal, fear of rejection, fear of *abandonment*.

What happens when abandonment arouses your body's fight-or-flight response, but you have no way to release mounting tension? Abandonment is an internal stress, not the type of threat that forces you to take a physical action as you would fending off the attack of a hungry predator. Nevertheless, your stress hormones surge, your heart races, your pupils dilate, your attention fixates, and your sprinting muscles are energized. Yet there is no physical release.

Some report that they do in fact get into physical fights with their partners. But for the most part, the buildup of aggressive energy is contained, then later unleashed on unsuspecting victims.

One of the reasons aggressive feelings are so often displaced is related to the special nature of abandonment grief—it's often endured in silence and secrecy. There are few socially sanctioned outlets for expressing it.

Is this bottled-up anger at the source of the condition so often diagnosed as agitated depression?

DEPRESSION

The anger framework wouldn't be complete without a discussion about *agitated depression:* that is, depression marked by irritability and a low threshold for frustration. As we learn more about the psychobiology of depression, we understand that depression is multifaceted. The effects are observed on many levels—psychological, physiological, neurochemical, and even molecular—all of which interact to create a complex condition that we experience as *being depressed.*

Anger Turned Inward Psychotherapists have long referred to depression as anger turned inward or *retrogressed rage.* From this description, many have concluded that the best way to reverse the depression is to *get the anger out*—to express it. Whether that works or not is a matter of debate, but careful analysis does show that people who have difficulty releasing their anger are more prone to depression. They also show diminished immune resistance. We have already talked about how submitting rather than fighting lowered the immune resistance of laboratory rats.

Depression and Stress Hormones

Researchers have found that people diagnosed with depression have elevated levels of glucocorticoids. These are the same stress hormones Sapolsky found in excess in the blood of subordinate baboons—the ones that took all of the flak from the higher-ranking members of the group. Likewise, our bodies increase production of glucocorticoids as we struggle with emotional crises of a breakup. The situation temporarily subordinates our desires to someone else's. Higher glucocorticoid levels may contribute to the temporary state of agitated depression.

Antidotes to Depression

There are antidepressants and other medications that may well prove beneficial for you by restoring biochemical balance, but keep in mind that we naturally produce biochemicals associated with well-being. In other words, our bodies have their own mechanisms for rebalancing. As Candice Pert, author of *Molecules of Emotion*, puts it, "Each of us has his or her own 'natural pharmacopoeia'—the very finest drugstore available at the cheapest cost—to produce all the drugs we ever need to run our bodymind in precisely the way it was designed to run. . . ." The flow of our own endogenous drugs is affected by what we do, the love and physical contact we receive, and the overall quality of our relationships.

OTHER HORMONAL CHANGES

In addition to the glucocorticoids, adrenaline, norepinephrine, CRF, and ACTH you release during an emotional crisis, your body undergoes other hormonal changes to prepare you for sustained self-defense. Your pancreas releases glucagon, which raises your blood sugar levels and insulin production is inhibited to conserve energy. Prolactin, which suppresses reproduction, is released. Progesterone and testosterone production is inhibited so that the enormous energy required to sustain your reproductive capacity can be deployed for self-defense. Growth hormone is inhibited so that nutrients and energy normally consumed by various systems can be diverted toward a *fight-or-flight* campaign. Vasopressin, an antidiuretic hormone, is released, and we void dead waste so that we are better able to sprint across the savannah or engage in battle. Endorphins and other natural opiates are produced to help blunt pain, and cortisol, a stress hormone, is produced to aid in the repair of damaged tissues in the event of physical injury. These are among the hormonal changes triggered by your body's response to the emotional crisis of abandonment.

Positive change precipitates biochemical and hormonal changes, too. Your sympathetic nervous system is aroused not only when you're threatened, but also when you're challenged by things that call for a burst of energy and heightened mental alertness, such as playing basketball or proving a geometric theorem. Rather than threatening or stressful, these activities are generally good for your mental and physical well-being. You can direct the action-ready state of this fourth phase and accomplish a great deal.

Sapolsky's studies are inspirational. Remember that baboons' stress hormone levels increased only when they fought to keep from losing their rank, but not when they were fighting to improve their status within the group. When they fought *to gain something,* their stress hormone levels did not increase. The baboon study suggests that we can manage stress (and the depression that rises from it) by transforming rage energy into activity directed toward a goal.

LEARNING TO CHANNEL ANGER

Many abandonment survivors have trouble recognizing anger and knowing what to do about it once they do.

The poet Maya Angelou described how hard it was for her to take action when she felt people taking little nips out of her. By her own account in *I Know Why the Caged Bird*

Sings, she suffered many types of childhood abandonment: grief and loss; relocation; discrimination; sexual, physical, and emotional abuse; betrayal. A true abandonment survivor of childhood, she was reluctant to fight back when she felt hurt. Her strategy was to let the incidents go, to dismiss them as harmless. She made excuses for others' behavior. Eventually she came to a place of strength and self-conviction and began to speak up for herself. She learned to let people know when the way they behaved made her feel uncomfortable, and she told them how she preferred to be treated. This simple communication helped her overcome wide-scale rejection and fear of abandonment.

Each moment of life, every human interaction is an opportunity to assert your newly developing self.

You can see that rage is a many-faceted concept. It can disguise underlying feelings of hurt or fear, or it can generate depression, anxiety, and fatigue. It can masquerade as inhibition, hypersensitivity, or passivity, to name a few of its faces. Or it can be expressed overtly in acts of physical violence or barbed words.

Rage is likened to the roar of the lion protecting its territory on the savannah. This mighty roar is triggered by a sense of endangerment. It signals the moment he senses his adversaries. Baring his teeth, the lion masks this fear as *strength*. His roar is an assertion of power, signifying his expectation of triumph. But underneath the lion's most ferocious roar is his sensitivity to a potential threat. It is fear turned into aggression, fear expressed as rage. It is a rage that expresses the lion's attachment to life.

RATIONAL THINKING TAKES CONTROL

I've spent many pages in this book explaining automatic reactions to stressful situations in which your ability to think and plan a response can be overwhelmed by your emotional brain's knee-jerk reaction. It is important to understand that the amygdala doesn't dictate your every response. You have a higher brain—the neocortex—that is equipped to make a reasonable appraisal of the situation and plan a strategy for dealing with your anger.

Incoming sensory information reaches the thalamus, where it branches off to two different areas of the brain. The larger branch runs not to the amygdala but to the neocortex. (The smaller of the two branches runs to the amygdala; information travels faster along this route but is far less precise.) The neocortex is where you analyze incoming information, retrieve memories, and compare and sort out what is relevant. In short, it thinks, plans, and reasons.

My point is that we have the capacity to learn from experience, and abandonment has provided us with a rich learning laboratory from which to draw new wisdom. Your neocortex works together with your emotional brain to reasses your former assumptions and plan a new course of life. You can overthrow your idealization of your abandoner, lift yourself from your former position of self-subordination, and assert your own worth.

FOURTH AKERU EXERCISE: IDENTIFYING THE OUTER CHILD

The fourth Akeru exercise is an awareness tool designed to help you better understand your responses to anger and change your behavior.

We have already discussed the inner child—that part of us that holds onto feelings of frustration, resentment, and rage. The outer child acts out the inner child's anger. By becoming aware of your outer child, you are finally able to gain access to your primitive, unconscious defenses that interfere with your relationships and your life plans.

In the hierarchy of self, the outer child is sandwiched between the inner child and the adult:

Adult
Outer child
Inner child

Left unrecognized, your outer child can subvert your best intentions. Recognizing behaviors that stem from your outer child is the first step toward positive change.

Your outer child has been the hidden saboteur in your life. It rationalizes its maneuvering by claiming it wants to protect you. It poses as your ally but acts out rather than asserting your true needs.

Identifying your outer child builds upon the previous Akeru exercises by lending them a new level of personal awareness. In exercise one, you learned to *use the moment* as a source of personal power; in exercise two you began a *daily dialogue* with your innermost needs and feelings; in exercise three, you learned to strengthen the relationship between your needs and actions through a *visualization* exercise that shaped your vision of the future. This fourth exercise helps you to recognize the self-defeating patterns that limit your life progress.

The key to disarming outer child defenses is to acknowledge them. Once you learn to identify the special features of your outer child, you'll expose its covert operations and look for emotional triggers that set them in motion. You'll emerge with a new level of insight that puts you in the driver's seat.

Your task is to isolate and take command of your outer child behaviors, using the same separation technique you used to create Little and Big.

Form a mental picture of your outer child—an image distinct from Little or Big. While Little represents valid emotions, the outer child acts out undesirable behaviors, especially deeply entrenched patterns that stymie your growth. By separating these behaviors from your true feelings, you gain psychological distance from which to observe the interaction between the two.

It may take time to establish a clear representation of your outer child. But once you learn to separate *behavior* from *feelings,* you can dismantle automatic and troublesome responses to the many stresses you encounter.

OUTER CHILD INVENTORY

What follows is a list of 100 easily recognizable traits common to the outer child in each of us. They are presented randomly, reflecting the illogical thinking of the outer child. Your daily exercise is to use this inventory to become aware of your outer child—to spot its behavior and find its hiding places. Remember that your outer child is a misguided expression of your inner child's feelings. Touch base with what your outer child is doing by keeping an active inventory of its behaviors, using the list as a guide.

Each of us has a unique outer child, depending upon our individual experiences, needs, and feelings. The list of 100 traits is by no means exhaustive. And not all of the items will describe you. The more you are able to recognize your own and other's outer children, the more self-awareness you bring to your relationships.

You can circle the items on the following list that relate to you, or just read through them, allowing your awareness to build. The random nature of the list is designed to catch your outer child off guard. Hopefully, this will help you to recognize aspects of your behavior you otherwise wouldn't see.

For best results, read through the entire inventory more than once. You may not recognize your outer child at first glance. Remember that your outer child lives in your unconscious mind, and because some of its characteristics are less than flattering, it may be hard to own them. Stick with it until your outer child begins to emerge. You can add to this list as you discover traits unique to your outer child.

Reviewing and updating this inventory daily is the key to breaking down outer child defenses. By keeping your outer child in focus, you'll move beyond where 90 percent of people are able to go and truly understand the dynamics of your behavior.

Each time you spot an insight or trait related to your outer child, you're keeping your unconsciously driven defenses in better focus. As a result, you'll be able to choose more constructive responses to stress.

Outer Child Inventory

1. Outer child is the selfish, controlling, self-centered part of all of us.

2. Outer child encompasses all of the outward signs of the inner child's vulnerability—all of the scars, the warts, the defenses that show on the outside.

3. Outer child is developmentally around seven or eight. Self-centeredness is age appropriate for the outer child.

4. Outer child wears many disguises, especially in public. Since other people's outer children are usually well hidden, you may think you are the only one with an outer child.

5. Outer child is the hidden Chuckie of the personality. Even the nicest people we know can act like a seven-year-old with a full blown behavior disorder when they feel threatened enough.

6. Outer child is developmentally old enough to have its own little executive ego (much to our chagrin). It's old enough to forcefully exercise its will but not old enough to understand the rights and feelings of others. (Inner child isn't old enough to have its own ego, so it has to appropriate ours.)

7. Outer child steps right in and takes over, even if we had every intention of handling a particular situation in a mature, adult manner. Outer child handles things its own way, leaving us holding the bag.

8. Outer child can dominate your personality if you've had a history of repeated abandonments. Many abandonment survivors of childhood are mostly outer child.

9. Outer child throws temper tantrums and goes off on tirades if it feels criticized, rejected, or abandoned. If Outer seems emotionally disturbed, it's because of what you've been through. Don't blame your outer child—it doesn't react well to blame.

10. Outer child takes revenge against the self. It sees itself apart from self and creates a schism between Big and Little whenever an opening presents itself.

11. Outer child likes to blame its faults on your mate. It tries to get you to imagine that your unacceptable traits belong to your mate.

12. Outer child doesn't like to do things that are good for you.

13. Outer child would rather do something that will make you fat or broke than thin or fiscally responsible.

14. Outer child is a hedonist.

15. Outer child talks about your friends behind their backs.

16. Outer child thrives on chaos, crisis, and drama.

17. Outer child enjoys playing the victim.

18. Outer child distracts you when you're trying to concentrate.

19. Outer child loves to play martyr.

20. Outer child is a world-class procrastinator.

21. Outer child makes huge messes that take forever to clean up.

22. Outer child makes you late for appointments.

23. Outer child loses things and blames it on others.

24. Outer child can find an excuse for anything.

25. Outer child tries to look cool and makes you look foolish.

26. Outer child is the *yes but* of the personality.

27. Outer child is reactive rather than active or reflective.

28. Outer child explodes when it encounters difficulties with its own abilities.

29. Outer child can never be wrong.

30. Outer child hates asking for help. It's stubborn, ornery, blind and pigheaded.

31. Outer child acts like a tyrant but is secretly a coward, afraid to assert its needs.

32. Outer child acts gracious when a friend steps on one of your toes and then holds onto the anger for the next twenty years.

33. Outer child specializes in blame; if it has an uncomfortable feeling, somebody must be at fault.

34. Outer child uses crying as a manipulation.

35. Outer child criticizes others to keep the heat off itself.

36. Outer child has a phony laugh to cover up stray feelings.

37. Outer child acts on its own, rather than consulting us, the adult.

38. Outer child needs total control to avoid having to *feel* inner child's feelings, especially hurt, loneliness, disappointment, or loss.

39. Outer child can't stand waiting, especially for a significant other to return your call.

40. Outer child doesn't form relationships—it takes emotional hostages.

41. Outer child doesn't like to show its vulnerability; it keeps its injuries hidden.

42. Outer child will demand, defy, deceive, ignore, balk, manipulate, seduce, pout, whine, and retaliate to get its needs for acceptance and approval met. It doesn't see this as a contradiction.

43. Outer child has a favorite feeling: anger. In fact, outer child's *only* feeling is anger.

44. Outer child has a hole in its pocket when in comes to either anger or money. Both must be spent right away and damn the consequences!

45. Outer child wants what it wants immediately. Yesterday.

46. Outer child wants to get right in the middle of things when you try to start a new relationship. It becomes more reactive, more demanding, more needy than ever before.

47. Outer child may be found in our mates. Sometimes we marry a person who can act out our own outer child wishes. Hopefully, our mate's outer child doesn't act out *against us*.

48. Outer child may be found in our children's behavior. When we get into power struggles with one of our real

children, we find ourselves battling our own outer child. Sometimes we secretly encourage our real children to fulfill our outer child needs. They act out the anger we don't want to own.

49. Outer child goes off on a rampage if it detects even the subtlest signs of abandonment. This leaves Little in jeopardy, unprotected.

50. Outer child strives for its own self-interest while pretending to protect Little. But your outer child wants one thing only: control.

51. Outer child is a people-pleaser with ulterior motives. It will give others the shirt off your back. And what have you got to show for it? Nothing. You're left cold and naked.

52. Outer child is not old enough to care about others. Only you, the adult, can do that.

53. Outer child tests the people it looks to for security—to the limits.

54. Outer child tests new significant others with emotional games. Its favorite is playing hard to get.

55. Outer child can be very cunning, putting its best foot forward when pursuing a new partner. It can act the picture of altruism, decency, kindness, and tolerance.

56. Outer child can also be seductive, funny, charming, and full of life. When it succeeds in catching its prey, it suddenly becomes cold, critical, unloving, and sexually withholding. Outer child makes us pity the person willing to love us.

57. Outer child is the addict, the alcoholic, the one who runs up your credit cards and breaks your diet.

58. Outer child enjoys breaking rules. Your best friends may have very dominant outer children living within.

Their rebelliousness might be what you enjoy most about them.

59. Outer child actively ignores you, the adult, especially when you try to tell it what to do. Outer child just goes right on doing what it wants to do.

60. Outer child strives for independence. Maybe someday your outer child will become independent enough to leave home, but don't count on it!

61. Outer child gains strength during dormant periods. Then, when you feel vulnerabile, your outer child acts out, jeopardizing the new relationship.

62. Outer child tries to defeat the task of intimacy, which is to get your inner child to become friends with your mate's inner child. Intimacy is when you nurture each other's inner child and don't take each other's outer child too personally.

63. Outer child loves to hook up with your mate's outer child. They instantly get into power struggles. It is futile to try to control each other's outer children. Your best bet is to find something for your outer children to do other than interfere in the relationship. If you can't ignore them, send them out to play.

64. Outer child has enough vanity and pride to try to conquer an emotionally dangerous love, one who is potentially rejecting, distancing, and abandoning.

65. Outer child thinks emotionally unavailable people are sexy.

66. Outer child is attracted to *form rather than substance*.

67. Outer child wants what it wants—emotional candy. This goes against what's good for Little, who needs someone capable of giving love, nurturance, and commitment.

68. Outer child seeks all the wrong people. It can't resist a lover who won't commit.

69. Outer child refuses to learn from mistakes. It insists upon doing the same things over and over.

70. Outer child developed during the rage phase of old abandonments when there was no one available to mitigate your pain.

71. Outer child becomes most powerful when Big and Little are out of alignment.

72. Outer child believes laws and ethics are for everyone else.

73. Outer child obeys rules only to avoid getting caught.

74. Outer child can dish it out but can't take it.

75. Outer child can be holier than thou.

76. Outer child loves chocolate and convinces you that it's good for your heart.

77. Outer child beats up on other people's inner children—especially the inner child of a significant other.

78. Outer child bullies its own inner child.

79. Outer child tries to get self-esteem by proxy by chasing after someone who has higher social status.

80. Outer child can deliver a subtle but powerful blow if it perceives a *social slight,* no matter how small.

81. Outer child covers up in public. Some people are better able to hide their outer child than others. Of course, some outer children are easier to hide than others.

82. Outer child can't hide from your closest family members: they *know.* That is what intimacy is all about: the exposure of your outer children.

83. Outer child can express anger by becoming passive. A favorite disguise is compliance. Outer child uses compliance to confuse others into thinking that it doesn't want *control*. But don't be fooled; outer child is a control freak.

84. Outer child finds someone to take for granted and treats them badly without having to fear rejection.

85. Outer child expects new significant others to compensate it for all of the hurts and betrayals inflicted by old relationships dating all the way back to childhood.

86. Outer child protests against anything that reminds it of being on the rock.

87. Outer child refuses to stay on the rock. Unlike Little, Outer climbs down, picks up a hatchet, and goes on the warpath.

88. Outer child has a chip on its shoulder, which it disguises as assertiveness.

89. Outer child is like the annoying older brother who constantly interferes in the guise of protecting you.

90. Outer child doesn't obey the golden rule.

91. Outer child obeys its own outer child rule: Get others to treat you as you want to be treated, and treat others as you feel like treating them.

92. Outer child needs to be disciplined, but don't expect limit-setting to go smoothly.

93. Outer child provokes anger in subtle ways, then accuses others of being abusive. Outer loves to play the indignant injured party.

94. Outer child submits so it can seethe at being dominated.

95. Outer child knows how to wear the white hat.

96. Outer child is master at making the other person look like the bad guy.

97. Outer child behavior ranges from mild self-sabotage all the way to criminal destructiveness.

98. Outer child can gain control so early, the individual doesn't develop any true empathy or compassion for himself or others. The extreme outer child is a sociopath.

99. Outer child needs to be understood, owned, and overruled by an airtight coalition between the inner child and adult.

100. Outer child holds the key to change. Inner child beholds our emotional truth, but can't change. When you catch your outer child red-handed, wrest the key from its hands and unlock your future.

SEPARATING FEELINGS FROM BEHAVIOR

Outer child has its own covert agenda. The only way to expose and derail that agenda is to maintain your daily inventory. Don't let your outer child remain in an unseparated state, entwined with your feelings, where it can control your responses from within.

Separating feelings from behavior is a crucial step in the healing process. So often people use feelings as an excuse for unacceptable behavior.

"My daughter Cindy had a habit of yelling and screaming at me if she didn't get her way," said Barbara. "I'd let her get away with it, blaming her outbursts on myself. I'd think about how much I'd ignored her lately, or some other emotional thing going on around here—sibling rivalry, pressure in school—any handy excuse either she or I could come up with. The truth was, Cindy's outer child was acting out.

"Then I realized that my own outer child was reacting to hers, and that's why I was never able to parent her behavior.

"Typically, the situation would go something like this. When Cindy talked back to me about one thing or another, I'd feel angry and helpless. My responses fluctuated between ignoring her or screaming right back. She'd usually end up walking away, more out of control than before—slamming her door, blaring her radio, or screaming at me even louder. I'd wind up angrier, more frustrated, and more powerless than before."

Screaming back at her daughter was Barbara's automatic response to her feelings. Her outer child was enmeshed with her inner child's helplessness and anger.

"Once I was able to spot Outer's interference," Barbara continues, *"I could sit down and separate my feelings from the way I was reacting. I could see how Outer wanted to handle the situation—screaming. I could see what Little was feeling—helpless. But now I, the adult, was in control and could see that ignoring the situation or screaming at Cindy was not going to accomplish anything.*

"I sat down to pin down my own feelings. I wrote a Big/ Little dialogue to sort them out. Little let me know that when Cindy started yelling at me, Little felt as upset and helpless as she did when my mother used to yell at me. Little helped me get a real handle on what was going on emotionally when Cindy treated me the same way.

"I decided I wasn't going to react to my daughter the way I did to my mother, or the way my mother used to react to me. It was time to break the cycle. The old way was playing out a childish role with my own daughter! I am the parent. I am the adult. So I started doing things differently.

"After giving it some thought—this was my adult self in control—I came up with a reasonable plan.

"I waited until Cindy was completely out of her temper tantrum, then I invited her to talk. I told her that I was upset about the way we yelled at each other and was looking for ways to improve the situation. Rather than criticizing her, I calmly explained that when she yelled at me, I felt disrespected. I said I wanted to help her find a way to stop doing that—both for her sake and for mine. Cindy agreed that she needed help to break the habit. We made a plan together."

Barbara's struggle with Cindy illustrates how important it is to separate your feelings from your behavior—inner child from outer child. Recognizing outer child patterns helps you function better as an adult.

Like Barbara, your task is to keep tabs on what your outer child is doing. As long as you can keep your outer child in focus, you can gain mastery over your life when stressful situations crop up or afterward, as Barbara did.

ADDING YOUR OUTER CHILD TO THE DAILY DIALOGUE

As you read in Barbara's story, one of the best ways to gain mastery over outer child defenses is to strengthen your bond with your inner child with ongoing daily dialogue. Speaking to Little every day, on good days and bad, helps to satisfy Little's need for love and nurturance. Since the outer child thrives on need-deprivation and unacknowledged feelings, staying connected to those feelings can steal your outer child's thunder.

Many find it helpful to include their outer child in their daily dialogues. Some find it works best to keep the dialogue exclusively between Big and Little, talking about Outer behind its back. Here is a piece of Keaton's dialogue following a date.

Keaton's Dialogue

LITTLE: *I liked Janice. But I was so scared the whole time. I felt so needy, and I couldn't relax.*

BIG: *That was Outer trying to hide your feelings.*

LITTLE: *Well, it's your job, Big, to keep Outer out of the way. He was stiff as a board.*

BIG: *I'm sorry Outer made the date so uncomfortable, Little.*

LITTLE: *Outer was trying to control me. Janice will never want to be with me again. And I liked her. I wish you stopped Outer from ruining the date. You weren't doing your job.*

BIG: *How can I help you with being afraid, Little?*

LITTLE: *Just don't leave me.*

BIG: *I'll stay with you, Little. But tell me, how can I help you feel less afraid, more relaxed?*

LITTLE: *You're ashamed of me when I feel afraid. I can tell. You don't want me to be afraid because it embarrasses you. You don't want me to have those feelings.*

BIG: *I accept you as you are, no matter how afraid you might be feeling. But I would like to help you feel more relaxed.*

LITTLE: *I think you only want me to feel relaxed because you are sick and tired of me feeling this way. You don't like me. You don't really accept me.*

BIG: *If that were true, Little, that would be very upsetting and make you really mad.*

LITTLE: *It does. You're the one who lets Outer get involved! You want Outer to hide my feelings and make them go away. You don't accept me—you just want to change me. I'm too much of a nuisance. I can't help my feelings.*

BIG: *If I am able to accept your feelings and love you for them, then maybe Outer won't need to come in anymore and try to take control.*

LITTLE: *Outer is your job, not mine. But I do want you to be proud of me, no matter how I'm feeling. I don't want you to be ashamed of me and try to hide me, even if I'm feeling insecure.*

BIG: *Next time I have a date, things will be different. If you're afraid, I won't try to cover you up or put you in a straitjacket. I'll let you have your feelings.*

Keaton was not able to bring closure to all of his uncomfortable feelings, but through the exercise, he gained awareness of its emotional triggers and was able to better understand the deeper issues. It brought him in touch with deeply rooted shame.

"It was the first time I realized that hiding my vulnerabilities—being ashamed of my feelings—was actually creating the problem. I decided to be more up front about my insecurity. Not to hide it. If the next person I date gets turned off when I show my vulnerable side, then maybe she's not right for me."

Identifying outer child behavior is a process, not a quick fix. In fact, the outer child thrives on a false sense of closure and easily hides behind the illusion of control. Many abandonment survivors, overwhelmed with a tumult of feelings, may crave immediate gratification—feel-good relief. Mastering the outer child is a slower process but a powerful vehicle for real change.

Another way to include Outer in the daily dialogue is to let Little talk to Outer in the presence of Big. Here's a sample of Marie's diary:

BIG: *Outer, Little has something to say to you, but there are ground rules you need to follow. The rules are, you can't argue or criticize Little. Just listen quietly.*

OUTER: *But . . .*

BIG: *No buts, Outer. You need to hear about the consequences of something that you did.*

OUTER: *(Silence)*

LITTLE: *You ruined everything, Outer. I was feeling sad and upset because Phillip left early. And then you had to go and freak out like a maniac. You just couldn't stop yelling and screaming. And now look what's happened. Phillip is mad at me and I am even more sad and alone.*

OUTER: *But . . .*

BIG: *Remember the rules, Outer.*

OUTER: *(Silence)*

BIG: *Do you remember what you did, Outer, that got Little's feelings so upset over Phillip?*

OUTER: *I was only trying to help.*

BIG: *I know you meant to protect Little, but sometimes by fighting for Little, you make things worse.*

OUTER: *Well, what did you expect me to do? Phillip left early, and I felt very rejected and mad.*

BIG: *Do you remember what you did?*

OUTER: *I yelled and accused him of being selfish and inconsiderate, and I cried.*

BIG: *And what happened next, Outer?*

OUTER: *He got really mad and now he's not calling anymore.*

BIG: *Are you aware how Little feels?*

OUTER: *Yeah.*

BIG: *How?*

OUTER: *She is sad and alone because Phillip is mad at her because I yelled.*

BIG: *That was very good, Outer. Can you understand your part in it?*

OUTER: *Yes. But I was very mad at Phillip for acting like he didn't like me.*

BIG: *Never mind, Outer. You leave handling the feelings to me. Your job is to find enjoyable things to do, not to take over when something goes wrong or when Little gets upset. That's my job.*

Again, these dialogues involving Outer won't instantly resolve a conflict, but they will help you clearly distinguish feelings from behavior. Your task is to keep them separate so that your adult self can better make decisions and control your actions, rather than letting your outer child gain control.

Identifying outer child behaviors benefits your inner child as well. It lets you blame your unacceptable, counterproductive behavior on Outer and attribute only the *pure, valid feelings* to Little. Little can look directly to your adult self for reassurance and love, without taking the rap for Outer's behavior.

Establishing a strong alliance between Big and Little *frees* Outer from its need to defend your feelings. Your adult self now controls how you express your feelings, releasing Outer to use its assertive energy in other, more productive ways.

ADDING OUTER TO THE VISUALIZATION EXERCISE

Another way to put the outer child concept to work is to add it to your visualization exercise.

"When I learned to identify my outer child," said John, "I put him right into my dream house. I visualized Little feeling safe and secure and Outer doing all sorts of new exciting things. I even moved my dream house to the Pacific Northwest where I could imagine Outer free and happy. By adding Outer to my visualization, I began making new goals—a lot were things I'd always wanted to try but never got around to."

Many do not find it necessary to include Outer in their daily dialogues or visualization exercises. They keep Outer in check with the daily inventory alone. That quick, daily reminder is all they need to control their frustrations and reactions and change old patterns.

Daily outer child sightings serve as a powerful vehicle for personal growth and development. As your ability to spot your outer child improves, you act more and more out of free choice, no longer tied to outdated behaviors. You finally determine your own life direction.

SUMMARY OF RAGE

Rage is a time of power surges and blown emotional circuits that plague us at many points throughout the abandonment process.

Rage maintains an internal dialogue that feeds on itself and fans its own flames. It seethes beneath the surface.

Until we recognize our outer child, we act without thinking. We use our anger to justify our behavior. But there is a way to use our rage energy constructively. Constructive rage does not destroy, inflict injury, or perpetuate pain. It does not retaliate. It converts to healthy aggression. It is the energy we need to rebuild ourselves and our relationships.

Recognizing outer child traits allows us to choose our actions rather than be guided by habit and reenact deeply entrenched patterns.

The deconstruction of the outer child holds the key to true recovery.

Chapter Six

Stage Five: Lifting

WHAT IS LIFTING?

Lifting is a time of hope. It is spontaneous remission.

It starts slowly and gathers momentum. You've climbed to the top of the hill. You can see where you've been and where you're going.

You've lifted above the turbulence of rage, disarmed the outer child defenses, and found the way out of self-defeating patterns.

So far, your recovery has been focused on your needs, fears, and defenses. During lifting you begin to nurture relationships with others.

Abandonment has awakened the child within. You've now comforted that child and cared for its long-neglected needs and feelings. No longer covered under layers of defenses, these needs and feelings are the bridge to greater love.

STAGE FIVE: LIFTING

HOLLY'S LIFTING

Holly went on a blind date with a man someone at work had arranged. She fretted about how things would go. It was her first date in over a year.

She wanted him to be impressed by her mature, cheerful attitude. She wanted him to see her as independent. She couldn't let him pick up any signs of desperation. She'd keep her loneliness out of sight.

They went to a movie, then to the diner. Holly chatted about her life, about her volunteer work on the hot line. She tried to talk like someone who was happy and fulfilled. He seemed interested, but she could never tell for sure. She wondered what he might be feeling about her but cast those thoughts aside. What if he picked up what she was thinking?

That was Tuesday. Today was Sunday. He still hadn't called.

She got up and pulled on a sweatshirt to go for a run. She had to get away from the thought that she was being rejected again.

Four miles later, she arrived at a bookstore, her favorite destination. She decided to buy a book and spend the rest of her Sunday afternoon reading. She'd be in good form when it was time to show up at the restaurant for work at five.

KEATON'S LIFTING

Keaton awoke to birds chirping outside his window. Sunday morning, *he thought,* should I bother getting up? *This same time last year, he would have spent a morning like this with Gabby shopping at the nursery for something to add to their garden. He was no longer interested in gardening, not without Gabby. But he did want the Sunday paper.*

Why not walk down to the store to breathe the fresh spring air? *he thought.* Then maybe later he'd get some of that laundry done.

He was surprised to see how many flowers were in bloom. The beauty of brilliantly colored tulips made him think of Gabby, and he briefly felt the tug of loss. But soon he found himself enjoying the gentle breeze.

In town he noticed Holly. He knew her from the abandonment recovery workshops he attended. Something she'd said a few weeks ago stuck with him. He wanted to talk to her about it, but she always dashed out when the workshop ended or became engrossed in a conversation with someone else on her way out the door.

Tucking the paper under his arm, he headed across the street to find her.

During his next session with me he described his attempt to reach out to her.

"Holly," he'd said coming up behind her, "how are you doing?"

She seemed surprised.

"I was just grabbing the paper. Saw you and thought I'd say hello. How's it going?"

Her hair was pulled back in a ponytail. "Great," she said. "How's it going for you, Keaton?"

"Pretty good. Beautiful out, isn't it?"

"It is," agreed Holly.

"What are you doing with yourself?"

"Well, right now, I'm here to get a book."

Keaton paused. "Did you go on that blind date this week?"

"Yes."

"How did it go?"

"It went fine," she said, pulling a book off the shelf.

"Good," said Keaton. "You planning to see him again?"

No answer.

None of my business, Keaton thought. "Do you have some time? We could walk down to the water and talk."

"I don't think so," said Holly. "I have so many things to do today."

"But I'd really like to talk, even for just a few minutes. It's

something you and I have never had a chance to do, and I'd really like to."

"Well, okay," said Holly.

They slowly made their way two more blocks to the bagel shop and sat down at a table outside.

Lifting is best described with "L" words. We *lift* out of the grief and back into life. We experience moments of *levity,* a *lightness* of mood and spirit, even as the memory of our lost relationship echoes through our thoughts. *Life,* in all of its fullness, begins to distract us from our sense of loss and personal injury. The grief has *lessened,* and we've *left* many emotional burdens behind.

For Keaton, the vibrant colors of spring reminded him of his loss. We can see that he was starting to *let go* of his obsessive thinking about Gabby and *let* life carry him forward.

Lifting is what I call this final stage, but we have felt brief moments of lifting throughout the healing process. These momentary respites from grief lengthen to hours and then days as we enter the final stage.

For Holly, lifting involved a deliberate, self-directed effort. She chose to spend her day in positive, constructive ways— jogging, reading, and working—rather than focus on her disappointment over her date.

Whether our elevated mood is spontaneous or, like Holly, we make a deliberate attempt to lift, it is during this stage that we move back into life. At times we feel like our old selves again; at others, we feel a whole *new* self emerging.

Lifting is about new life; it is when we explore new territory, conquer new ground. We have been listening to important messages from within about our needs and feelings and learning from our painful experience. We are taking in new ideas about life and about ourselves and weaving them into new patterns of living. We discern who we are becoming.

We *let go* of our rage toward the one who has left us, and we *let go* of old patterns as well. We know that the past still permeates our lives, but we discover that abandonment has brought us to a new place, that we are better off for what we have experienced.

One of the profound realizations of this stage is that we are getting ready to *love* again. It often begins with feelings of warmth and gratitude toward friends and family who were there for us in our time of despair. It is at this point that we find ways to let them know how important they are to us. We feel love and appreciation for ourselves as well, taking pride in the gains we've made. We're more self-reliant, self-aware, and open to our feelings. We feel our own capacity for love stirring within us as we reach out to make new connections.

Lifting out of abandonment into greater life and love is the goal of this final stage, but it is important that when you lift, you take your feelings with you. One of the common pitfalls of the lifting stage is rising above your feelings, leaving your emotional center behind. You want to avoid this mistake, which can keep you at arm's length from intimacy in new relationships.

As I guide you through the final stage of abandonment, I will show you how you can use the energy of lifting to increase your capacity for life and love. This chapter carries messages of both triumph and caution. I will point out some stumbling blocks to forming relationships that are common to abandonment survivors and describe some of the ways they've learned to overcome them. I will review childhood scenarios that lead to the personality profile of the *lifter* and provide an inventory to help you identify some of the unfinished business left over from previous losses. Finally, I will introduce you to the fifth Akeru exercise designed to help you stay in touch with your feelings as you establish new quality relationships.

THE EMOTIONAL AGENDA FOR LIFTING

What follows are the "L" words that describe the emotional agenda of the lifting stage: *Lessening* the stress and tension, *learning* the emotional *lessons* of abandonment, identifying the personality characteristics of the *lifter,* rediscovering lost hopes and dreams, *loosening* the emotional bonds and *letting go* of past attachments, *looking* for love, *letting go* of shame, and finally, *lifting* the obstacles to new relationships.

Lessening Stress and Tension
Learning Emotional Lessons
Hidden Dangers of Lifting
The 'Lifter' Personality Profile
The 'Lifting' Family System
Lost Hopes and Dreams
Lifting the Barriers to Finding Love
Letting Go of Shame
Letting Go of Emotional Bonds of the Past

Emotional agenda for lifting

LESSENING THE STRESS AND TENSION

Lifting is about returning to equilibrium, both emotially and biochemically.

During the previous stages, we talked about the role your sympathetic nervous system played in emotional crises. It alerted you to danger and prepared you to exert the energy required to fight, freeze, or flee. This was your body's automatic response to a perceived threat—which in your case was abandonment. During lifting, you feel the effects of another branch of the nervous system, the parasympathetic nervous system.

The parasympathetic system works in tandem with the sympathetic nervous system to bring various systems like heart and respiration rate back to normal following a state of arousal. This rebalancing of physiological systems allows your body to resume its normal flow of life. It's one of your body's built-in devices for self-correction.

Holly's story illustrates some of the choices people can make to help this rebalancing along. She may not have been aware of the biochemical processes involved, but her choice to go running most likely produced an increase in endorphins, the body's natural opiate I discussed in Chapter 3. When joggers hit the wall, breaking through to that runner's euphoria, they are experiencing an increase in endorphins, which kick in at about the thirty-minute mark. They feel the analgesic, pleasure-inducing effects of this natural opiate coursing through their bodies.

People often describe having an addiction to physical exercise. Between workouts, their bodies go through withdrawal symptoms akin to withdrawal symptoms from narcotics such as morphine or heroin. The runner's endorphin withdrawal induces a craving for another run, thus prompting a regular exercise routine.

There is an interesting parallel here. We have already talked about how primary relationships involve a number of different types of natural opiates. According to Jaak Panksepp's research on the neurochemistry of attachment, the most potent of the brain's opiates are found at their highest levels in the womb. Following birth, there is a gradual shift to the weaker opiates, presumably to motivate the infant to seek gratification by bonding with its mother. Ideally, this attachment picks up where the infant's opiate withdrawal leaves off. This new bond alleviates the withdrawal symptoms, and the infant produces different levels of opiates as the bond takes hold. Panksepp also suggested that the formation of adult relationships leads to an increase in opiate production, and conversely, a breakup leads to a decrease. It is possible that the opiate withdrawal we feel as we grieve over a lost love motivates us to find a replacement.

We're not slavishly driven by biochemical messages, of course. We're not compelled to seek out another partner immediately. On the other hand, given the opiate withdrawal involved in the grief process, it's no surprise that many abandonment survivors seek out high-energy activities to help them feel better. As in Holly's case, many of these activities do indeed increase endorphin flow.

In the last chapter, I explained how our sympathetic nervous system prepares us for any action, not just for the purposes of self-defense but for any activity that requires mental or physical exertion from mountain climbing, to sex, to tackling a computer problem. When Holly got ready for her run, her sympathetic nervous system rose to the occasion, heightening her mental and physiological alertness and giving her increased energy, all of which she put to work on her brisk run. Given Holly's history (she was a foundling who suffered repeated childhood traumatic losses and abandonments), her emotional memories are likely reactivated regularly as she perceives loss or rejection in her adult life. When she engages in physical exercise and other high-energy activities, she brings greater balance to her life, often in ways that escape her conscious awareness.

Like Holly, many abandonment survivors have found their way to highly focused physical or intellectual activities as a way of offsetting the affects of stress hormones, endorphin withdrawal symptoms, and other biological processes involved in emotional crises. According to Frederic Flach, a psychiatrist writing on the subject of depression, "physical exercise helps to stimulate calcium retention in the bone and prevent it from being deposited in the soft tissues (where it does not belong)." Calcium metabolism is affected by stress and is associated with the biochemical changes of anxiety and depression. Increasing calcium in the bone enhances our mental well-being.

Flach also states, "Vitamins such as the vitamin B complex, and especially vitamin B 6, and minerals such as calcium, magnesium, and zinc make a positive contribution toward the body's ability to cope with stress. Sunlight, by activating vitamin D, also produces calcium retention-in-the-bone, an interesting fact considering that certain individuals become depressed when they are not exposed to adequate sunlight." This suggests that by taking vitamin supplements and exposing ourselves to outdoor activities, we are aiding our bio-physiological recovery from the emotional crisis we've been in.

The goal for lifting is to find a new equilibrium, to arrive at a new set point through the choices we make in new interests and activities.

LEARNING THE EMOTIONAL LESSONS OF ABANDONMENT

Lifting is the realization that you have triumphed. You've been through a powerful life experience that initiated profound personal change. You have gained something remarkable from this crisis. It has brought you in touch with your emotional core. You've reached that core because this crisis hasn't just been about your partner leaving. An old wound opened up again—the cumulative wound that contains all of the losses and disappointments from your past and the primal fears shared by all human beings. The new injury reunited you with the old and universal ones.

You do not want to lose touch with the emotional wisdom you have gained. With it, you can avoid disappointment in new relationships. If you can stay in touch with your feelings, you will be more accessible to others, more compelling, more open.

Lifting is a time to take emotional stock, to review some of the feelings you've encountered as you worked your way through the four previous stages. There were the fears and broken trust you encountered during *shattering;* the empty, longing feelings you endured during the *withdrawal* stage; the self-deprecation and injured self-esteem of the *internalizing* process; and the anger and outer child defenses you identified during the *rage* process. At each stage, the feelings harkened back to earlier losses and abandonments and reawakened old memories. You saw inside the emotional baggage you have been carrying all along.

For all of its pain and turmoil, this emotional journey has helped you to see what you've got buried inside. You now know where your emotional triggers come from and what your most basic needs are. How you choose to handle these feelings is crucial to healing. These deeply guarded emotions may well have sabotaged you in the past; you don't want to become disconnected from them again.

During lifting, your primary task is to honor your feelings.

THE HIDDEN DANGERS OF LIFTING

People emerging from the grief of a lost relationship are anxious to leave painful memories behind. Many would rather run from unresolved emotional issues than stay with those feelings. They may not realize how focusing on those emotions can help. Instead, they lift out of the acute pain of grief and *above* their newly discovered feelings.

Lifting above your feelings means that you're leaving more than your lost relationship behind. It means losing contact with your oldest, deepest, and most basic needs. Lifting above, or *overlifting*, means that you're using one or more of a variety of defenses: You're ignoring feelings, self-medicating them, denying their existence, avoiding situations that trigger them, or staying so busy that you don't have time to feel them.

The simple truth is that you can never really leave your emotional baggage behind. When you lift, whatever changes have taken place within you, whether you remain conscious of them or not, become a part of the way you respond emotionally. Ignoring those feelings means adding a new row of bricks to the barrier between your internal self and external self—between Little and Big. You become emotionally unconscious once again.

If abandonment is a knife wound to the heart, then lifting is the last stage of healing, when new tissue forms over the wound. In *shattering*, you felt searing pain as the knife severed the dense tissues of attachment. In *withdrawal*, you were tormented by the nagging pain of the fresh, open wound. During *internalizing*, the wound became highly susceptible to infection, threatening to damage your self-esteem. With *rage*, you felt the tautness and tenderness of flesh knitting back together. Finally, you've arrived at *lifting*, when layers of new tissue form over the wound, protecting it. The danger is that scar tissue can form, sealing you off from the outside world. With these emotional calluses comes a loss of *feeling*.

When you attempt to *lift above* rather than *with* your feel-

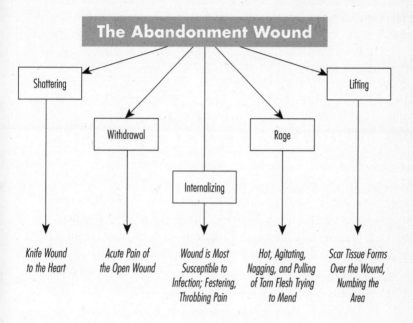

The abandonment wound

ings, you risk becoming insensitive to both yourself and to others. Your task is to stop emotional calluses from forming. Otherwise, they create an invisible shield that make it hard for others to get close. People who might want to become an important part of your life are denied access to your most basic feelings, feelings that form the basis of true emotional connection.

We all know people who come out of painful heartbreak deeply affected yet strangely out of touch with themselves and their feelings. They've become emotionally detached and harder to reach than before. We can only imagine the unresolved feelings that fester within, sapping their energy. They have *lifted above* their feelings and begun to live at emotional half-life. They have quietly altered their beliefs about themselves and their worth, yet they go on as if nothing happened. On the outside, everything seems okay, but they are closed off from the world of emotion. They may have lifted out of the acute grief of abandonment, but they have left behind a great deal of themselves.

How we handle our lingering, still-tender feelings determines why some of us will be positively transformed after a loved one leaves and why others will become remote, detached, and less likely to reconnect.

The Overlifting Personality Profile

As a child, Pamela had a long and difficult recuperation from heart surgery. She languished in bed, watching other children play outside her window and concluded that she must not be as special or deserving. After divorcing her husband, she spent years lifted above her feelings.

"I fell off the horse once and never got back on again. My husband had an affair over twenty years ago. I was devastated, and we got divorced. That was that. I've been single ever since.

"I made a couple of lame attempts to date, but nobody was interested in me, or me in them. I didn't want to risk getting hurt again. Who needed it? As long as I had a way to support myself financially, I was fine by myself. It only became a problem when I was forced to use my vacation time. I had no interest in going anyplace because I didn't feel like going by myself."

The truth is that all of us have done our share of both types of lifting: *lifting with* our feelings intact as well as *lifting above them.* Sometimes lifting above is a healthy way to cope with a difficult crisis. Family and friends may have thought of us as *resilient.* We've all learned to lift above feelings too painful to endure or those we didn't want others to see. At one time or other, we learned to bite the bullet when in pain, pretended to feel brave when we were really afraid. We learned to laugh when we felt like crying. We used these defenses to get through emotional ups and downs.

Emotional resiliency in childhood is a good thing. It is the process by which the life force took you in its hold and helped you move forward. But if, like Holly, Keaton, and Pamela, your childhood involved a great deal of emotional turmoil, you may have done more than your share of lifting. Perhaps you lifted *above* your hurts and fears so often that you lost conscious connection with your emotional core. Lifting above your feelings may have become an automatic response to stress by the time you reached adulthood. In some cases, overlifters are emotionally guarded and detached, obsessed with success or material gain, and closed off from intimate relationships. In extreme cases, overlifters can become the callous sociopaths who lack empathy for anyone's feelings, including their own.

But most of the time, overlifters are people we see every day who have learned to go on with their lives in spite of painful experiences. Their degree of emotional detachment may or may not be apparent to themselves and the people trying to get close to them.

What are some of the identifying characteristics of people who routinely disconnect from their feelings?

You may recognize yourself as someone who tends to *lift above* feelings if you answer yes to the majority of the following questions. Or you may recognize someone important to you (perhaps even the one who left you). Recognizing the characteristics of a lifter can help you regain access to your feelings.

Lifter's Questionnaire As a child:

Did you play the clown in your school days?

Did you try to hide uncomfortable feelings around your friends?

Did you find ways to become invisible?

Did you use diversionary tactics to cover feeling embarrassed or humiliated?

Did you isolate yourself from family or friends when struggling with a problem?

Did you become emotionally stoic and refuse to cry when you believed you were being overpunished?

Did you feel anxious at times, mad at others, but whatever the feeling, disguise it or disown it?

Did you hide your insecurity on dates?

As an adult:

Do you tend to wear a jovial mask in public, even when you feel disappointed in yourself or uncertain about your life?

Do you sometimes think other people are capable of feeling things that you are not?

Do your acquaintances and friends tend to share their feelings with others and not with you?

Do you feel you are missing the emotional essence of an experience?

Are you sometimes more a human doing than a human being?

Are you always on the go? A task master?

Do you live in your head? Are you overfocused, closing out real experience and other people?

Or are you underfocused? Do you go into an emotional haze and become numb to what is going on around you?

Do you have a childhood history of hyperactivity? Were you vibrating above your feelings? Or conversely, were you inactive and underachieving so that you could avoid focusing on uncomfortable feelings?

Do you sometimes feel detached or disconnected from others?

Do you avoid expressing important feelings directly, even positive feelings, afraid that your voice will shake or that you'll cry?

Do you have difficulty showing affection? Tenderness? Sexuality?

Do you feel echoes of old feelings—insecurity, loneliness, anxiety, loss—that blend together into an emotional soup? Do you have trouble naming feelings and identifying their source?

Do you wake up sometimes with an emotional hangover? An emotional hangover is similar to an alcoholic hangover, except you feel drained, spiritually dead, unable to single out one feeling from the mix of blended emotions.

Is there a lack of intimacy and emotional connectedness in your primary relationships?

Is your partner detached, hard to connect with emotionally? If so, might your partner's behaviors mirror back your own tendency toward lifting?

Are your best friends or significant others hard to reach emotionally? If so, are you letting the people around you do your lifting for you?

LIFTING FAMILY SYSTEM

Where do overlifters come from? Why do some people hold onto their painful feelings while others bury them?

The truth is that just about any kind of family background or early experience can lead to the development of overlifting defenses. In the previous stages, I described some of the childhood scenarios in which children pick up emotional baggage: There were the *shattering* losses like the death of a parent or sexual abuse; the *withdrawal* scenarios where children experienced prolonged need deprivation because family members were emotionally unavailable; the *internalizing* scenarios in which children were routinely criticized, scapegoated, and rejected; and the *rage-provoking* scenarios in which children were overcontrolled, exploited, or otherwise emotionally or physically abused.

What follows are some sample childhood scenarios that can lead to lifting as an automatic defense. Some of them will remind you of your own families; others may bring to mind the families of people close to you.

Overlifters may come from families where:

• Adults were emotionally detached and you mirrored their behavior. Feelings didn't count, so they weren't addressed.

• Parents held onto feelings and held grudges against other relatives. The message was that feelings are not something to be worked through.

• Parents or other family role models were overemotional, histrionic, overreactive. You distanced from them in order to protect your own emotional space.

• Parents didn't tolerate anger. They mistook anger for disrespect. So you had to squelch your strongest feelings.

• Parents were emotionally controlling and overinvolved in your feelings. They wanted to fix things, in other words, make your feelings go away. They dismissed your disappointments and fears, telling you what you *should* and *shouldn't* feel. You got the message that it wasn't good to have uncomfortable feelings.

• The structure was authoritarian. Obedience and performance counted more than feelings.

• Adults were perfectionistic and demanding. You neglected your feelings in order to meet unreasonably high expectations.

• Parents or other adults presented a false self to the world, hiding feelings and acting as if everything was okay.

• Adults lacked empathy or sensitivity. You and your siblings acted out by getting into fights with each other to release the built-up tension.

• Things were chaotic. Constant upheaval and disappointment created intense feelings. Adults unpredictably lashed out or emotionally withdrew from the children.

• Adults frequently broke promises to children, possibly due to alcoholism or other illnesses. You learned not to expect too much, setting low expectations for relationships to avoid chronic disappointment.

• Parents humiliated you when you expressed feelings; they admonished you for crying, ridiculed fear. You learned to hide and cover feelings.

• Parents' relationship lacked intimacy, or conversely, parents were intimate only with each other. You were left on the outside looking in.

It is important to bear in mind that parents generally do the best job they can to meet their children's needs. The irony is that most of us manage to pass our own emotional wounds along to our children in spite of how hard we try to avoid it. These hand-me downs are transformed into various behaviors, attitudes, and character traits and may pass from generation to generation. It is pointless to try to pin blame for our struggles on our parents. You'd have to go back many generations—to the historical events that shaped the lives of your ancestors—to get to the bottom of things.

As we try to understand what kind of influence our childhood experiences have on our adult behaviors, the aim is never to be judgmental or to place blame. Our aim is to accept responsibility for our own lives and to examine our emotional baggage. Like our parents, we all make mistakes. None of us can claim that we've never created an emotional barrier in a relationship.

Note to Parents

The thing that we want to avoid as parents is making our children feel badly about themselves. Children can easily be made to feel helpless and insignificant. It doesn't take much to help children to feel integral to our lives. We need to empower our children rather than *over*power them with our own needs. Listen to their needs and nurture their interests, hopes, and dreams. Help them build skills and confidence so that their status within the family and among their peers is securely established.

FINDING A LOST PART OF YOURSELF

Almost everyone has aspirations that were never pursued and dreams still waiting to come true.

As a child, John loved to listen to symphonies on the radio at his grandmother's house when he stayed there on weekends. He taught himself to play her piano and made up tunes, then lyrics to go with them. He begged his parents to give him piano lessons, but they said they couldn't afford it. They encouraged him to play sports instead. An athlete John was not, though he tried his best at Little League.

When his grandmother died, John, then a teenager, tried to get his parents to move her old piano to their apartment. But they said there just wasn't enough room. Finally, he gave up and fed his musical appetite listening to the radio and buying an album here and there with extra money he earned from his paper route.

As an adult, John's interest in music waned. He found the symphonies he'd once loved now put him in a melancholy mood. Instead, he turned his attention to other things.

After an emotional crisis, he began searching for interests to help him get into the moment. It was then that John rediscovered the pleasure of listening to music. He drove to the seacoast, tuned in his car radio to a classical station, and watched the waves roll in. As he sat with his eyes closed, he was swept away by a Beethoven symphony.

There may be parts of you that were simply lost or forgotten. Cumulatively, these neglected interests created an empty space, a hungry hole you've been trying to fill ever since. Perhaps like John, tuning into the moment has helped you rediscover some of them. Perhaps you got in touch with forgotten dreams during your dialogues with your inner self. Now that you are a fully cognizant adult, you are in a position to revisit these lost pieces of yourself and give new life to them.

Hopefully, you have gained some awareness of needs asserting themselves within you, and you have more insight into how your past has contributed to the way you deal with your emotions. The more conscious you are of the feelings you carry forward, the better you'll manage your future.

The primary task of lifting is to let go of old attachments and lift from its grief, *with your feelings intact.*

LETTING GO OF THE PAST

Loosening the emotional bonds that connect you to your lost partner is the primary task of the final stage of grieving. It is a time when, as Herbert Weiner put it, "you reinvest your emotional currency elsewhere." It is a time for restructuring and reorganizing your life.

Lifting involves certain emotional tasks that differ slightly from those confronting the widow or widower. The difference has to do with the type of emotional baggage you're carrying, namely baggage packed with unresolved feelings of doubt and shame.

Shame is not unique to abandonment, however. At some level, all grief involves shame. Anyone who deals with intense and prolonged emotional pain feels a certain shame when they can't control the pain, however strong or persistent. Society tells us we should be able to moderate emotional pain, make it go away. Because we have been raised with these beliefs, we feel that if we can't snap out of it as fast as we think we should, we are lacking in fortitude. We come to feel ashamed of our emotional weakness.

"The pain was so overwhelming after my husband's heart attack," said Lydia, "that it got to a point that I kept my grief to myself. Who would understand why two years later I still

*wanted to die? Even I believed I'd gone off the deep end—that
I was some sort of emotional extremist."*

The widow and the abandonment survivor are both ashamed
of their dependence upon another human being for survival. But
the abandonment survivor is left to deal with yet another layer
of shame—the terrible shame of being thrown away.

*"Losing Lonny nearly killed me," said Marie. "I missed him
so terribly. But having him withdraw his love from me like that
was a whole other type of torture. I felt emotionally mur-
dered—violated and humiliated by my best friend."*

The sense that we carry some kind of stigma is not unique
to abandonment. Both the widow and those who've watched a
loved one walk out the door feel marked by loss.

*"I felt singled out by the fact that a random heart ailment
took my husband's life. Why did tragedy have to strike my
family? Why not someone else's? What did I do to deserve it?"*

As the widow tries to move on with her life, she may feel
shell-shocked, filled with trepidation that fate has singled her
out for profound losses. As we try to move forward, we feel a
similar dread.

*"What if someone else decides to toss me away?" questioned
Michael. "Am I so unworthy that no one will ever accept me
and keep me? How am I ever going to trust anyone or any
relationship again?"*

The widow may have residual feelings of self-doubt, deep
regret, and even anger over being left behind after her husband's
death, but unless her loss was the result of a suicide (a profound
form of abandonment), she is unlikely to feel the loss as a personal affront. She knows at some level that death is beyond

anyone's control. She is focused on mortality rather than questioning her sense of *self*.

The healing agenda for the widow is consumed with filling an emotional void. She searches for a new purpose to go on living. We have an emotional void, too, but ours feels like a punishment for some wrongdoing. Our agenda is to find a salve for our narcissistic injuries, and undo the self-doubt that has infected our sense of worth.

The widow who had a history of previous abandonments may also have some self-doubts as she emerges from her bereavement, especially if the loss of her loved one reawakened fears and insecurities left over from previous breakups and rejections. To close these wounds, she, too, may need to prove her sense of worth as she makes her way back out into the world. But the widow who does not have such a history has a more straightforward task—to adjust to living alone. She may not need to reach out for a love replacement right away; she doesn't need to fix her damaged pride, because she doesn't carry a fear that nobody wants her.

But as we begin to lift out of grief, we're focused on vindicating the harsh dismissal of our worth. We want our wounded egos stroked.

These needs affect the choices we make as we lift out of abandonment and reach out for new relationships.

LOOKING FOR LOVE

No matter what your success in making connections has been in the past, you may have some fears about finding love again. Will you be as happy as before? Will you wind up alone? To address them, you need to explore new lifestyles and relationships.

Some abandonment survivors crawl into a cave and lick their wounds for years.

"I'm still not ready," explains Michael. *"I just need to be by myself for a while until I'm strong enough to risk—to trust someone else."*

There are others who choose to stay on their own because they enjoy their newfound emotional independence. They've discovered some of the advantages of being single and don't want to give them up.

Carole said, "I was happy to have that constant turmoil behind me—the roller coaster of trying to make a relationship work. I appreciate the peace and calm of being by myself, and I want to keep it that way—indefinitely. I'm finally free."

Marie, on the other hand, felt the need to reconnect within the first year. This meant learning to accept her emotional needs.

"I didn't want to admit it at first," she said, *"but after being on my own for a while, I discovered that I am one of those people who do better when I'm in a relationship.*

"I fought the idea at first. I thought I should be able to make it on my own. And besides, I didn't want to risk getting hurt again. But something terribly important was missing in my life, and I knew it. I finally listened to what my feelings were trying to tell me.

"That's when I met Phillip. We were just friends at first. I found him extremely nurturing, not just to me, but to his children and to just about everyone around him. He was able to come right out and talk about whatever he was feeling— whether he was happy, angry, worried, or insecure. And he was very in tune with my insecurities and feelings. He had been through a similar loss much earlier in his life, and he was able to understand where I was at. His affection for me made me feel good for a change; it took away some of the pain.

"But as far as getting emotionally involved with him—I held

back. My friends warned me not to get involved too fast with anyone. 'You're not ready,' they said. 'It's too soon. You shouldn't need someone else to make you happy,' *they kept telling me.*

"It was listening to what Little needed. That helped me decide more than anything else," said Marie. "Once I learned to listen, I couldn't turn my back on what she was crying for. I realized there was no shame in admitting that I needed to be with someone."

Many of my clients have come to recognize that, given their history and the extent of their recent emotional injury, they would do best to get back into a relationship as soon as they feel capable. Equally important is to find someone who can truly care about them, someone who is emotionally responsible and unlikely to abandon a working relationship.

LETTING GO OF SHAME

Many recognize the need for a relationship, but finding one poses a great challenge. Even the most caring, attractive, and loyal people have difficulty forming primary relationships.

Most of them know they have unresolved fears, but it isn't always easy to see how these fears create barriers to starting new relationships. They try to make connections but are ultimately frustrated and confused when those connections lead nowhere.

"Why can't I find someone?"

"What's wrong with me?"

"What's keeping me from connecting with someone?"

Fruitless connections bring us back to the issue of shame. By its very nature, shame is one of the feelings people are most likely to want to distance themselves from. Along with the *shame,* they attempt to bury evidence of insecurities and personal inadequacies they believe give them away.

Given Holly's history of repeated and prolonged childhood

separations, she is an extreme example of what can happen when we *overlift* from shame. She shows us both how hidden shame can create a barrier to forming relationships and how unmasking it can lead to change.

"The problem for me," admits Holly, "is that no matter how much I needed to be with someone, no one wanted to be with me. After a lifetime of trying, I still wasn't able to get into a relationship."

It is easy to see that Holly wasn't the cause of the abandonments that plagued her childhood. Her birth parents chose to leave her behind, and later, her adoptive parents rejected her in other ways. Yet she carried a profound sense of personal failure. She felt guilty and ashamed, as if she were responsible.

"I came to believe that the reason nobody wanted to keep me was that I just wasn't lovable enough. I didn't rate having real parents. If I was special like other people, they wouldn't have pushed me away. I really believed I was missing something that would make people love me—that there was something very wrong with me."

Holly found ways to lift above the intense doubts and fears, but underneath, the feelings of rejection accumulated with each severed bond. She systematically and silently built a case against herself, condemning herself as undeserving. She came to feel ashamed of her feelings. She didn't want people to see how she felt for fear that it would only draw attention to her supposed defects. She took even a hint of rejection as evidence that her unlovableness was showing.

By the time she reached adolescence, Holly had become a chameleon able to disguise the outward signs of this undeserving self. Inwardly she carried an invisible wound; outwardly she presented an I'm-okay mask to the world. But hiding her feelings did not mean that she could stop them from interfering. On the contrary, burying them distanced her from them and from a rich emotional life. She often came across as if she were *staging* her reactions. People sometimes sensed an empty quality to her cheerful gestures.

We saw evidence of Holly's trouble when Keaton asked her about her date, and she chose simply not to answer. Likewise, she used a facade on her blind date to keep any signs of her loneliness out of sight.

The need to separate internal and external selves is common to those who suffered traumatic childhood separations, especially if it led to a pattern of rejection in adult relationships. Anyone who's been through the agony of not being able to find someone knows the shame over feeling "not good enough." Experience has taught these folks that exposing their neediness almost automatically turns off the other person, so they learn to hide the feelings that most desperately need attention.

The irony is that disowning these feelings is often the very thing that keeps them from connecting with others. Both people must be emotionally open for a genuine relationship to form. If you cover up deeply held desires, you're far from emotionally present. Pretense creates an invisible shield to intimacy.

Shame puts many in the double-bind of wanting to get close but not wanting the other person to know what their real needs are.

Holly told me about how she decided to take a leap and share her real feelings with Keaton at the coffee shop that Sunday afternoon.

"It's an impossible bind—being lonely," she'd admitted to him. "I could never tell someone I'm dating how insecure I feel—that I feel like a failure or a reject. They would see me as too needy and pathetic and run right out the door!"

By covering up her vulnerability, Holly had been leaving less emotional surface area for the other person to bond with. Unable or unwilling to bring her real needs along on her dates, she'd left the essence of *who she was* behind. Having condemned her feelings as unattractive, she *abandoned* a significant part of herself—her emotional core.

For Holly, it became a vicious cycle: Shame created the secret, the secret created the isolation, isolation created the loneliness, loneliness created the shame. Hiding her feelings was the process by which her invisible wound became an invisible barrier to relationships.

Remember, it is not your feelings themselves, but the secrecy surrounding them that causes the problem. Secrecy feeds the shame. Keeping the secret creates the deceit which forms a gap between you and someone you might want to get close to.

Holly said that she was initially disappointed in Keaton's response to sharing her feelings.

> *"Why not be open with the guy you went out with last week?"* he'd suggested. *"Tell him what you've been through and what you're really feeling."*
>
> *"Yeah right,"* she said. *"You must be crazy!"*
>
> *"Truthfully. Put it out in the open. What have you got to lose? See what happens."*
>
> *"I might as well be wearing a neon sign that says 'disposable merchandize'"* she told Keaton. *"This guy would immediately notice the scar on my face and how out of proportion I am, and all of that other stuff."*
>
> *"I've never noticed any of that,"* he said.

People who struggle with repeated romantic failures believe that if they let someone in on what is really going on, they'll only draw attention to their inadequacies. Once someone spots these red flags, they will be discarded.

Holly's negative beliefs about herself were so strong, she dismissed Keaton's remark as an attempt to make her feel better.

"How come you can tell me about all of your insecurities and I don't get turned off?" Keaton countered.

"That's because we're not on a date," explained Holly. "If we were, by now you'd be running in the other direction."

"No I wouldn't," said Keaton. "That's not me. In fact, I feel more comfortable with you now that you've explained it all."

"You don't get it," said Holly. "If you and I were trying to check each other out romantically, all my insecurities would come out. These huge emotional suction cups I have would begin to show. One look at my suction cups aimed in your direction and you'd be out the door."

"I'm sitting right here," said Keaton.

"That's only because I'm not showing that side of me to you now," she protested. "And that's because I'm not trying to date you."

"I guess that means I'm not dating material," said Keaton. "What if I told you my own theory about that, about why you wouldn't consider me a potential date?"

"Okay," said Holly.

"This is about me, not about you," he began. "I would like to get to know you on a deeper level, but I feel inadequate. True or false, I feel I'm not at your level, not as well educated as you are, and probably not as smart. I see you as more sophisticated. You've been places I haven't. I don't have the kind of things to offer you that you deserve.

"Those are my feelings." Keaton continued. "They are about me. They may be accurate. They may not. But whatever they are, they are what I believe. Does hearing all of this turn you off?"

"Not really," said Holly.

"Then how DO you feel about what I said?"

"Well, I feel . . . I don't agree with . . . maybe . . . but I liked it," she'd muttered. "I mean your honesty. I feel honored that you trusted me."

"Honored, yes, but do you think any less of me?" asked Keaton.

"I think more of you."

Both Holly and Keaton related this incident to me, each from their own perspectives. Holly expressed surprise over how good it felt to be sharing real feelings with someone, and how close she felt to Keaton when he shared his vulnerability to her. Keaton described what a relief it was to be emotionally honest with someone, how connected he felt to Holly. Breaking their secrets of shame was helping them dismantle their invisible barriers, at least with each other—an important step in healing the source of their relationship problems.

LIFTING THE OBSTACLES TO RELATIONSHIPS

The frustration for many of my clients is not meeting people but staying in quality relationships that can grow with them. When your attempt at a new relationship falls apart, you feel right back where you started—alone.

Shame and heightened *fear of abandonment* can lead to choices that are counterproductive to forming long-lasting relationships.

Below are some pitfalls that those who've suffered repeated losses tend to fall into.

LOOKING TO GET SELF-ESTEEM BY PROXY

In search of reassurance for their injured sense of self, many seek out a great catch to compensate for their damaged self-esteem. There is nothing wrong with dating someone whose accomplishments you feel proud of. The danger is that in the focused search for someone with the right image, you might overlook a potentially caring and emotionally available partner. Remember, you're seeking intimacy, not a narcissistic extension to fix your wounded ego.

A Trophy for Your Ego

"I had such a need to prove myself," admits Keaton, *"that I couldn't come down to earth and accept someone at my own emotional level. I went after the type who could be a trophy for my ego. All I wanted was to prove that I was somebody. The women I felt comfortable with—the ones who made me feel safe and secure—were the ones with the same kind of insecurities I had, so they couldn't prove anything at all, except how pathetic I was. I didn't give them the time of day. I was only interested in someone who could flaunt a big ego. If I could get someone like that to like me—someone who was high on herself, then she could make me feel that I rated also."*

Choosing Flattery

"After Howard left," said Barbara, *"my sexual self-esteem was very low. I mean, I felt absolutely devastated as a woman. I needed to find out if anyone out there would even be interested in me. I wasn't ready to risk a relationship yet. I just needed to be flattered by some attention."*

Choosing Worth by Association

"When I finally got around to graduating from college," says Holly, *"my younger brother was already a surgeon. So, as if I didn't have enough problems, I decided I only wanted to date doctors. It was my way of trying to get worth by association. Only highly successful doctors would do. Anyone less would make me feel like I wasn't meeting my family's standards.*

"At the time, I wouldn't have known what human warmth and companionship looked like if it came up and hit me in the face. All I could do back then was try to get these extremely successful doctors to like me. That's how I got into a pattern where I was the one doing all of the chasing and pursuing and never the one being sought after."

CHOOSING A HIERARCHY INSTEAD OF AN EQUAL PARTNERSHIP

Many abandonment survivors become attracted to people who are emotionally inaccessible. You might meet someone who is a good match for you socially, but a bad match emotionally. Their emotional needs may be different from yours, they may have less fear of abandonment, more self-esteem, or be less vulnerable to rejection. These emotional incompatibilities can create a hierarchy in which you subordinate yourself to the other person. It creates a dynamic that heightens your abandonment fears and arouses your self-doubts.

Choosing a Dominant Personality

"I think what attracted me to Howard in the first place," admits Barbara, *"was his dominant personality. He didn't have any of the insecurities I did. In fact, he was fearless. He'd never been left by anyone, whereas I went through many heartbreaks as a teenager and in college. Howard knew I was afraid of losing him. The fact that I had more fear of loss than he did allowed him to feel completely sure of me—and emotionally dominate me. He acted like he would have no trouble replacing me in a flash. Because he was so fearless, I was always the one who gave in, the one doing everything to hold the relationship together. I don't think Howard realized he was doing it, but he used my fear of abandonment to control me—and I let him do it!"*

Choosing the Less-Than Position

"I came to recognize a pattern," says Michael. *"I've always been attracted to people who have stronger egos than I have. More confidence, less sensitive to criticism. But it always left me in the less-than position—emotionally, that is. All my success with my career and investments counted for nothing. I was*

always the one groveling to be loved. I realize I have to break out of this pattern and be more open to someone who can match me emotionally. I need the emotional playing field to be equal next time. I'm not going to be emotionally one down again. I'll look for someone who has similar fears and needs. Why should I waste my time on the ones who can't relate?"

Changing the Trophy

"Now that I look back," says Roberta, "it was insecurity about myself that landed me with a person like Travis—the maestro himself. He may have been good for my self-image, but he wasn't the right person for Little. I must have kept a muzzle on her, because I didn't have a clue about what my most basic needs were as a person—or who Travis was emotionally.

"The whole time I was with him, I was too busy struggling to find my balance with him. But it always felt like he had the upper hand emotionally. I'm sure Little was whispering in my ear the whole time, but I wasn't listening. I was too busy trying to get Travis to change, trying to change my trophy into a real person, trying to get Travis to become the warm, caring person I needed him to be in order to make my insecurities go away. The fact that we were emotionally incompatible never even occurred to me. My expectations at the time were unrealistic. Travis was Travis. I know that now. But I put all of my energy into trying to get him to change instead of taking responsibility for my own feelings."

Choosing Someone Who Has What I Don't Have

"Every time I was interested in someone, it was because they had what I wanted," says Banford. "They were always more educated than I was, or came from a richer background, or had more charisma and more friends, or more something . . . more anything that I wanted but didn't have. I was trying to get it through them vicariously. The flip side of this was that when I *was with someone like this, I would feel even more inadequate, always worrying whether I was good enough for them. So, I was choosing people who made me feel bad about myself. What a waste of energy!"*

Choosing Someone Who Is Not Like Me

"I was only attracted to people who had a proven track record of successful conquests in relationships," says Holly. "This was the opposite of what I had, which was no track record at all. If they were the ones who usually did the leaving, then I was more attracted to them than ever. What made them attractive is that they were desired by others, and they knew it. On the contrary, if they showed any outward signs of having the self-loathing or loser status I had, I was completely turned off. They'd remind me too much of myself. I wouldn't even consider getting to know someone who had any obvious flaws, especially anything that showed on the outside. If they were too overweight, or pigeon-toed, or had a quirky personality, I didn't want anything to do with them. I wouldn't be able to stomach seeing my own insecurities and imperfections reflected back in theirs. If they had the same low self-worth I did, I wouldn't be caught dead with them. But then I wondered, wasn't I just dismissing others who had the same problems I did? Wasn't it just another way of negating who I was?"

MAKING AN EMOTIONAL CHOICE BASED ON HISTORY

The people you are attracted to may not be right for you emotionally, but you're drawn to them anyway. Something about them—often something less than flattering—reminds you on some level of your father or mother. The person could be rejecting or critical, controlling or domineering, emotionally distant or unavailable. When you encounter someone like this as an adult, it arouses the feelings of longing and insecurity you experienced in your relationship with one of your parents—

feelings of emotional hunger that you've come to associate with love.

"I fell madly in love with Travis," admits Roberta, *"because he was so confident and commanding. But it turned out he was just like my father . . . commanding, all right—downright demanding, self-centered, withholding, and rejecting. But I always wanted my father to love me, and I transferred my efforts to Travis."*

As Roberta helps to illustrate, when you come into contact with someone who reminds you of a powerful figure from your past, your amygdala-driven emotional memories are triggered, arousing your deep-seated desires: your desire to be loved, nurtured, and accepted.

People who can set off this sense of deep longing are pushing your love buttons, the emotional triggers established by childhood attachments. You don't need to be conscious of these physiological connections to feel emotionally drawn to this person, just as you once looked to your mother or father. This complex process is what you have come to feel as an attraction. So off you go, pursuing those who arouse some of your most negatively charged emotional memories, feelings you have come to associate with the *right chemistry* for love.

The antidote is to recognize this pattern and avoid recreating your emotional past. Your goal is to seek emotionally substantial relationships.

The Familiar Emotional Setup

"My wife was always pushing me away—from the day I met her," says Richard. *"She almost never said anything nice or encouraging to me. It was no different from the way my mother treated me, so I never knew there was a better way. It never occurred to me that I wasn't getting the emotional support I deserved out of my marriage.*

"I think what got me involved with my wife in the first place was her rejecting attitude. I was so busy trying to please her, I didn't have time to question whether I deserved better. It was an emotional setup I was used to. The problem was, I set myself up for emotional disaster—because one day, she told me to get out, out of my own house. She wanted her space. Talk about rejection! Now that I'm over the shock, I'm beginning to question why I had let myself be treated like that for so long."

Choosing Someone Who Puts Me Down

"I didn't realize I had an attraction, a weakness for the put-down types," admits Thomas. *"I had to find that out the hard way—from dating women who treated me like I was beneath them. It reinforced exactly how I felt about myself, having been browbeaten by my father all my life. The worse they treated me, the more I'd look up to them for acceptance. Eventually, they'd dump me. That's what it took for me to finally see the pattern—getting dumped one too many times. Now I realize there are many sensitive, caring, supportive women in the world. I have to retrain myself to believe that I have a right to be appreciated and respected."*

CHOOSING RELATIONSHIPS BASED ON ATTRACTION

Being attracted to someone is a very compelling feeling. Sometimes we're attracted to people for all the wrong reasons: They arouse our insecurities and emotional hunger and keep us in a state of longing. We find others attractive for the right reasons: they support and nurture our needs and feelings. These feelings of attraction help form a bond that can lead to a lasting relationship. Eventually the intense feelings of attraction or infatuation wear off, and in its place is a strong emotional tie. This works out well for many people, if they made the right choice. But as we have seen, it doesn't lead to quality relationships for everyone.

Some of us are only attracted to people who are emotionally unavailable. Fear is almost always at the heart of this pattern. By chasing after emotionally unavailable targets, we avoid the risk of intimacy altogether.

Whether you fear getting into a real relationship or not, this attraction paradox is a common stumbling block. Unless you recognize that your fickle sense of attraction is leading you down dead ends, you'll stay locked in a vicious cycle.

This cycle brings us back to the subject of emotional conditioning. Traumatic experiences from your past have created automatic responses to signs of emotional danger. Your past may have conditioned you to associate insecurity with attraction. The adrenaline rush created by the *fear of abandonment* has become confused with the yearning of romantic love. You can no longer differentiate love and emotional hunger.

Misreading Emotional Cues

"By not going out with anyone for over five years," says John, *"I managed to let all sorts of unresolved feelings incubate without realizing it. Then I met a woman who caught my attention. Talking to her the first time, I felt the hackles stand up on the back of my neck. I took this to mean she was someone worth pursuing. I said to myself,* Oh, I finally feel something. Here is someone special. Someone for me. *I didn't realize that the reason my hackles went up was because I was sensing emotional risk. I misread the cues.*

"The woman was completely sure of herself. I worked to match her level of self-confidence, though she didn't seem to care what I thought of her. Somehow that made me think she was really special. It should have made me realize that she was really not interested. Wow, I said to myself, she's really getting a reaction out of me. I'm really feeling something. *Then she never returned my phone calls. I felt dismissed, like a nobody, a failure.*

"Now that I'm finally beginning to understand what my real

needs are, I doubt I would find someone like her very interesting. She wasn't open and vulnerable enough for me. She wouldn't be able to understand where I was at inside. I'm not faulting her for that; it's just that we were on different emotional levels. Next time my hackles go up, I'll know they signal emotional danger, not here comes the right person.

Attracted to Emotional Danger

"I didn't know I was in love unless it felt like I was on the verge of being abandoned," says Jacqueline. "If I wasn't feeling completely love starved or in grave danger of being dumped, then I wasn't turned on. If I felt comfortable with a guy, it meant we were just friends. I wouldn't give a guy who liked me the romantic time of day. If he was easy to get, then my fears weren't set off, and if my fears weren't set off, then I didn't feel anything, and if I didn't feel anything, then I'd assume he was someone to just be friends with. A guy had to make me feel intensely insecure, or I wasn't turned on."

The Chemistry Has to Be Right

"I met this woman," says Jay. "The chemistry felt right, but she turned out to be the exact opposite of what I needed. She was completely unreliable. She started dating someone else while we were seeing each other and didn't even tell me. She was intimate with both of us. When I found out, I was devastated. But I still didn't let go. I pursued her all the more.

"I think it was the emotional challenge she presented that got me going in the first place. I was so insecure all the time that I became her emotional slave. The only good news about this bad situation was that it helped me forget about Carlotta for a while.

"But why did I need an untrustworthy woman to get me going? I realized that it all goes back to what happened with my mother. I was eleven when she ran off with some guy and

never came back. As a teenager, I thought about her a lot and imagined what it would be like living with her. I wasn't able to track her down until after I got married. Now that I'm divorced and out there hunting again, I find myself turned on by women who have that abandoning quality like my mother obviously did. It's taken a lot of hard lessons, but I'm finally onto this weakness, this attraction I have for the wrong woman."

Attracted to the Bad Ones

"It's only now," explains Allana, "that I realize my love life has a short circuit in it. If the guy turns out to be a bastard, a cheater, or a leaver, chances are, I'll be drawn like a moth to a flame. But if he's for real, I feel nothing. I've been running away from the good ones and running toward the ones who can't commit for years. But I've finally learned: If I'm attracted, it means that the guy's probably no good. Instead of doing what the romance novels tell you to do—to follow your heart—I've learned to go in the opposite direction—to run, not walk, in the other direction.

"Next I'll try to stop running away from the good ones—the ones who can give me what I want. I know its because I'm afraid of getting hurt. But it doesn't feel like fear. It just feels like not being attracted. I'm going to have to open myself more, because I've really figured out that whether I'm conscious of it or not, it's just fear of abandonment *that drives my feelings into hiding.*"

Staying Away from Emotional Candy

"I've learned to stay away from the emotional candy. Now I'm looking for substance," says Holly. "How else can you break out of a bind where you're only turned on by people who are unavailable! The only thing to do is get to know people who are on my emotional level—the ones who can understand *what I've been through and accept me for it—and still want to be with me."*

"I'm listening to my needs instead of my need to prove myself," says Keaton. "I think I'm ready to come down to earth and get to know someone I can be really honest with. At least I'm open to it. The kind of relationship I'm looking for isn't an attraction—it's about trust and caring. And there would be acceptance and tolerance of each other's problems. We would respect each other's feelings."

ADDICTED TO INFATUATION

By the time you recognize that you're in a destructive relationship, you are already addicted to infatuation, making it that much harder to break the vicious cycle.

Infatuation is a psychobiological state of arousal. You are so heavily intoxicated on opiates and other neurochemicals of infatuation, you don't feel your usual inhibitions.

Infatuation can lead you to make choices that can jeopardize your emotional well-being in the long run. Under the influence, you are more likely to take emotional and physical risks (such as engaging in unsafe sex). You remain oblivious of the other person's faults, too inebriated on love chemicals to consider the emotional consequences of your decisions.

The biochemistry of romantic love increases sex drive, which of course, is highly adaptive in terms of promoting the procreation of the species. Romantic intoxication makes it easy for two relative strangers to get physically close, but it can obscure the emotional hazards of the relationship.

Searching for That Emotional High

"For years I was addicted to the high," admits Gwen. "As soon as the romantic intensity died down and the emotional high was gone, I'd move on. I knew the romantic feeling was

a temporary state of insanity, but it was something I had a real craving for. The problem was that as soon as I felt sure of the other person, my sexual desire for him dissolved—I'd suddenly lose interest.

"I wasn't ready to handle the emotional responsibility of a relationship," she continues. "The minute someone felt genuinely attached to me, I would be out the door looking for someone else to turn me on—someone harder to get who could create that romantic high.

"There were two different me's. When I was infatuated, I would do anything for the guy. If he needed me to, I would cut off my arms or legs or climb Mount Everest for him. But as soon as the romantic high wore off, I became angry, edgy, and mean—like a junkie who needs a fix. I'd blame it all on him, like it was something he did to cause me to feel turned off.

"When I finally realized what I was doing, I put the brakes on. But changing my behavior was like breaking an addiction. It was time to look for a relationship that could have a longer-acting effect, rather than the constant quick romantic highs I was hooked on."

CHOOSING EMOTIONAL SAFETY

Many abandonment survivors seeking emotional substance find partners who are good for their inner child but who aren't good for their adult selves. They find mates who seem good for Little, but not for Big.

Looking for a Safe Bet

"I went from one extreme to the other," says Jay. "After being with the type of woman who cheated on me and treated me rotten, I started seeing a woman from the opposite end of the spectrum. She was overly devoted to me. She was unsure of herself and had even more emotional needs than I did. I had it

all *ahead of her—education, finances, social abilities, you name it.*

"*The part that felt good was that she was a safe bet. She posed no threat to me emotionally. In fact, she acted like I was God's gift. It was just what I needed—well at least Little Jay was happy for a while. Eventually, though, the differences between us began to wear on both sides. We really couldn't give each other what the other needed—which was to be in a relationship with an equal. So we worked it out and eventually parted ways. Now we're just friends.*"

Some are fortunate enough to strike an emotional compromise between the needs of both the adult self and the child self. It involves give and take and questioning long-held values. Reworking your beliefs about the kind of person who's right for you means putting hard-won emotional wisdom to work.

Learning to Tolerate Feeling Secure

"*Bill and I had gone together for a long time,*" says Virginia. "*But then I broke it off, because I didn't think he had enough to offer me. That was years ago. When I ran into him a few months ago, I felt immediately comfortable with him. But back then, that's what the problem was—I felt too secure with him. I didn't feel enough emotional intensity. I wasn't mature enough to recognize that a good relationship doesn't mean being emotionally challenged all the time.*

"*I remember how much I trusted Bill, how safe I always felt with him. I obviously didn't appreciate it back then, but it's exactly what I need now—to be with an emotionally solid person. I had taken Bill for granted all of those years we were together because I wasn't ready to recognize my own emotional needs. I was still impressed with people's status and other outward things about them. I didn't feel Bill had the panache and the other things I needed. I hadn't realized how valuable Bill's honesty and loyalty were. Since then, I've graduated from the school of hard knocks: the school of abandonment. I've been through so many broken relationships, gotten involved with too many people who didn't have it together emotionally. Bill and I have begun to see each other again, and I'm able to appreciate him this time."*

Settling

Some would describe Virginia's decision to see Bill again as settling, but she doesn't see it that way.

"I'm not settling just because I've recognized my need for security and to be loved. I used to think something was wrong with me for needing to feel secure. But now I'm with someone I can trust and count on for a change. If I choose to be with someone who has emotional substance rather than panache, that's not settling, that's an opportunity to create a real relationship."

Abandonment recovery does not advocate settling or clamping on to someone who will become an emotional drain later on. The lesson here is that there are many beautiful people who are capable of love and commitment who may not match old expectations or the societal notions of a good match. You may not become high on them, feel the right chemistry, or gain status by associating with them. There is no perfect mate. There is only the love, caring, and respect you create between yourself and an emotionally capable person.

AKERU EXERCISE FOR LIFTING

Lifting is a time for reconnecting, whether you're reviving old interests and aspirations, forging closer relationships with the people in your life, or reaching for a new partner. Connective energy is the procreative life force; it is what binds people one to another and to the world around them.

As I lifted out of my own abandonment, I realized I was more aware of my needs and desires than ever before. I'd met someone and was comfortable being with him. I understood what it meant when he shared his feelings openly with me. It was a gift of trust. Through this emotionally honest exchange with another person, I discovered the meaning of my crisis. I found the seed that I'd been looking for. At the heart of any successful relationship is sustained emotional openness. My own experience taught me the benefits of staying *with* my feelings—even uncomfortable ones.

I began to think about the day my mother told me about how she and my father had left me at the hospital. She bravely disclosed something she may have felt guilty about in order to share a valuable truth. I wondered what other gestures of my mother's emotional courage and generosity had gone unacknowledged. She passed away soon after my partner left me, and I began to think there was probably so much more about my mother—hidden aspects of her—that I hadn't fully understood. I began to think about the other people in my life. What was really going on inside their heads and hearts? What emotional pieces were accessible? What was hidden? How could I connect with them in ways that I had not before?

With these questions and reflections, I realized I'd reaped a valuable harvest from the most intense of life experiences. What I learned was that connectedness is the key to life. Only love counts.

I had always known the central importance of love, but now I recognized it on a new level, and it transformed my life. Surviving abandonment served a purpose. Difficult though it was, it helped me understand that *the ultimate gift of abandonment is the opportunity to increase our capacity for love.*

We all have capacity for love, a capacity that can expand on a daily basis if we continue to grow. Some believe we use only a small percentage of the human brain's potential. I believe that we live our lives using only a fraction of our capacity to express and experience love.

As a society, we tend to define a narrow path for love. The abandonment experience increases our capacity for love because it brings us in touch with our feelings. It forces us to recognize the power of human attachment. It teaches us that vulnerability is a human condition.

Unless we let calluses form, abandonment has made us more aware of the needs of others, more responsive, more capable of overcoming the obstacles to making genuine contact. Indeed, many humanitarians report that their own abandonment experiences inspired their life's work. Oprah Winfrey, for example, taps into her emotional legacy as she reaches out to support others. It is obvious that she is not closed off from her feelings. In fact, they are immediately accessible to her. She draws on them to make a personal connection with the people she reaches out to on every show. At the heart of a socially conscious person is a greater wisdom about love.

So many of the people who visit me tell me they suffer from an emotional emptiness—a feeling that love is missing from their lives. The love they are usually referring to is the kind they expect to fall into by meeting the right person. For some, it actually happens this way. But there are many other ways to reach love. This powerful human bond is far more than a feeling that suddenly overwhelms you. Love is something you can create.

Most of us can remember special moments when love was a feeling that washed over us. But the more elemental truth is that you can generate love within yourself, even when you are feeling most isolated. Love is an action, an attitude, a creative process. It grows with wisdom and often relies on initiative and self-discipline. Commit yourself to take the necessary steps toward reaching it.

Your task is to practice your life in such a way that your capacity for love begins to overtake your old emotional agenda. Many of my clients have agendas mired in the need to remedy insecurities. As their love capacity expands, it obliterates the need for narcissistic gratifications. The key is to remain open to your feelings—to be on honest emotional terms with the world around you.

This brings us to the fifth Akeru exercise. Its mechanism for growth is built into the previous four exercises—the ones for staying in the moment, talking with your inner self, visualizing your dream house, and keeping an outer child inventory. Here we add the element of *love* to each of the previous four exercises.

When you make love the goal of the exercises, you unify them into a life plan. Love is the substrate that integrates all that you have learned so far.

ADDING *LOVE* TO THE EXERCISE FOR STAYING IN THE MOMENT

You already understand the importance of *getting into the moment*. The moment is where all of your power is—the power to experience life through your five senses. Getting into the moment allows you to make immediate contact with the sights and sounds of the world within and around you. Now, when you get into the moment, bring your capacity for love with you. At least once a day, make a conscious effort to practice being mindful and open when you are with another person, be it a stranger, relative, friend, child, or lover.

"The first 'victim' I practiced this on was a waitress at the diner," Carlyle explains. "When she came by to bring me coffee, I prepared myself to become fully present with her, to bring all that I had to bear into the moment of this ordinary encounter. Not that I meant for her to notice anything unusual was going on. I made eye contact with her and asked her sincerely how her day was, but that was it.

"As she served my coffee, I had no way of knowing anything about what her life might be like, whether she was happy or disappointed with her day. But each time she filled my cup, I remained completely open to her presence and began sending

her positive thoughts, wishing her well. I brought all of my most caring intentions with me into the moment with her. This woman may not have known it, but she received all of the love that I was capable of in that moment."

You can also practice getting into the moment with someone you know.

"I met my best friend for lunch," said Roberta. "Right in the middle of the salad course, it occurred to me that this was an opportunity to practice the moment with her. So I just made myself completely aware of everything about her and how it felt to be with her right then and there. Whether she realized it or not, she had my full, undivided attention probably more than any time before."

You will probably find that you will not be able to maintain this intensity for very long. It is easy to be distracted by peripheral thoughts or become overly involved in the content of the conversation, rather than stay focused on the process of the moment. It may last only for a few minutes, but it is a chance to practice being open to your own and your friend's feelings.

Like Roberta, you'll discover your capacity to generate love—love as defined by *being there*.

You can also practice being in the moment with a significant other. Rather than allowing yourself to be caught up in your own emotional needs or distracted by things going on around you, you bring your full capacity for love to bear upon your partner. Imagine what would happen if you practiced this exercise together, each of you tuning into everything about the other person and the moment you're sharing together.

ADDING *LOVE* TO THE DAILY DIALOGUE WITH LITTLE

All it takes to add the element of love to your daily dialogue is to ask Little, "What do you need from the other people in your life?" "Is there enough love?" "What can I do to bring more love into your life?" "What would you like to feel with someone special?" "What type of loving people would make you feel secure?"

The issue of love becomes grist for powerful dialogues between Big and Little, giving rise to new insights and motivating you to take positive action.

"I opened up the issue of love to Little," said Roberta, *"and she started asking me to get closer to a man I had recently met at work. Somehow, I knew he was wrong for me. So I explained:*

BIG: *But he's the emotionally unavailable type, Little.*

LITTLE: *I want him anyway. I like him.*

BIG: *But he's not right for us. He'll just leave you feeling sad and needy. I thought you wanted to be loved and accepted, Little.*

LITTLE: *I do.*

BIG: *Then we need to set our sights on someone else.*

LITTLE: *I just want to feel loved. It must have been Outer who was trying for that guy.*

BIG: *You're right. I'm glad one of us figured that out, Little. Because that guy would just be a waste of time. He would bring up that same old emotional starvation stuff. Remember how that felt?*

LITTLE: *Go out and find someone who can make me feel good, Big. And keep Outer out of it!*

Indeed, Outer is a handy vehicle on which to blame the old self-defeating patterns you're trying to break. The antidote is to listen more carefully to what Little is really asking.

Remember, Little's primary needs are to be appreciated, accepted, nurtured, and loved—and *not* to be abandoned. Make a pact with Little that you will do everything within your power to bring the love that she or he needs into your life. You will need to check in on a daily basis with Little. This tight coalition with Little leaves your outer child's craving for the unsafe person out of the loop and strengthens your ability to make emotionally responsible choices.

BUILDING *LOVE* INTO YOUR DREAM HOUSE

You can include love in your visualization exercise by imagining that your dream house already contains all of the love that you need. Imagine it's about two years in the future, and all of the relationships you desire are in place and you are happy and secure. You and Little are completely at peace because you now have all of the love you need. Feelings of hurt and anger toward your lost partner have been released, forgiven, and forgotten. This is a big task, an important one, but in your visualization it is already behind you. All you need is in your reach: commitment, security, intimacy, affection, tenderness, openness, respect, trust, admiration, and companionship.

Within your dream house, imagine that you are exhilarated by the knowledge that the quality of your life is only getting better. Your ability to generate love has created a beacon of warmth so powerful that its message reaches all the people in your life and touches them in a special way.

One of the benefits of performing the visualization in this way is that it reveals clues about how to overcome the actual obstacles in your life. Having assumed that the visualization is two years in the future and that you have already achieved this love, you can use hindsight to answer questions such as, "What internal barriers did I have to remove to get to this place of love?" "What did I do to overcome them?" From this future perspective, most people find their answers surprisingly helpful.

Now imagine that you have magical powers. What gifts of love and caring would you bestow upon the other people in your life? If your power were unlimited and your capacity for love boundless, what resources and benefits would your magical powers bring to the people in your community? What special gifts would you give to those in the larger world and the people of future generations?

Now consider what places within your dream house are best suited to pondering these questions. Do you need to make any architectural changes in order to create an environment more conducive to love? Make whatever changes in its size and location that will help you to include this love factor in your life. Place significant people you need within the house as visitors or life companions.

"I moved my dream house to a neighborhood full of children, with lots of community activity," said Barbara. *"I guess I was thinking about my children's needs and also my readiness to be neighborly—to reach out."*

Having made whatever renovations, additions, and deletions that are necessary, your visualization now contains the essential element of *love,* which you can reinforce on a daily basis just by conjuring up its image. Your ability to increase your capacity for love is incorporated in the setting and structure of your dream house. This exercise summons the resources of your imagination to focus your energy on your goals. As you continually renovate your dream house to suit your ever-changing needs, you expand your sense of entitlement and confidence.

OVERCOMING LOVE OBSTACLES IN YOUR OUTER CHILD

Your outer child is usually at odds with your ability to increase your love capacity. In fact, the outer child is the saboteur of intimate relationships. Your task is to identify outer child behaviors and attitudes that interfere with your attempts to bring love into your life.

Your outer child can become particularly troublesome when

you are trying to start a new relationship, when you feel especially vulnerable. As you test the waters of a new relationship, Outer might be testing the other person—sometimes to the limits—by overreacting, clamming up, or clamping on when you know the person may not be right for you.

Many who come to me for help describe how difficult it is to withstand the usual emotional ambivalence that is normal to any new relationship.

"I know that wavering back and forth is to be expected with a new person," said Marie, "but I had a hard time tolerating the uncertainties. Even though I wasn't sure whether the relationship could work, I felt abandoned—abandoned by my own feelings. The whole time I was getting to know Phillip, I felt out of control."

"When I tried to date," said Roberta, "the insecurity I felt reminded me of what I went through with Travis. It kicked up the old emotional dust and turned me into a basket case every time I tried to see someone. Outer was trying to act out the whole time. I had to lay low for a while before I could get control and become ready to make myself vulnerable again."

Indeed, new relationships can activate old emotional memories and create uncomfortable anxieties. Your outer child can act swiftly and spontaneously to defend against your heightened vulnerability. Anything that reminds Outer of the child on the rock can set its defenses into motion. Your attempts to parent this part of yourself aren't always quick enough to prevent Outer from taking control.

The best hedge against this interference is to maintain your outer child inventory on a daily basis. Keep Outer in focus. Try to anticipate its next move. This increased self-awareness gives you greater control. Let the adult in you decide how to handle a situation. When your outer child acts against your need to be in a secure, loving relationship, your task is to take responsibility for its behavior. Make amends to anyone you may have lashed out at, even yourself. (This is what the twelve step program that originated with Alcoholics Anonymous calls for in its *tenth step:* Promptly admitting when you are wrong and making immediate amends.) Thus you, not your outer child, make decisions about your relationships and your life.

INCREASE YOUR CAPACITY FOR LOVE

By adding love to each of the four previous exercises, you are creating an integrated plan: a life plan for increasing your capacity for love. You are enhancing this capacity on many different levels: through your ability to experience the moment, relate to Little's needs and feelings, visualize your ultimate goals, and gain control over Outer's self-defeating patterns.

Keeping a diary of your progress increases your motivation to practice the exercises on a daily basis. Taking time each day to chart your progress sharpens your focus and allows you to plan positive actions into your day.

All it takes is a little quiet time to jot down your thoughts. Keep a running account of the times you are able to be in the moment with another person. Give yourself credit for being able to respond to Little's need for love; outline the steps you plan to take that day on Little's behalf. Document your progress as your real life begins to resemble the vision contained within your dream house. Maintain a record of outer child sightings, especially the ones that sabotage your relationships; create a plan for changing your behaviors and being in control that day.

The progress note may look something like this:

Daily Progress

1. Was I able to be in the moment with another person? _____
_____

   Today's plan for the moment: _____
_____

2. Did I respond to what Little was really asking for? _____
_____

   Today's plan on Little's behalf: _____
_____

3. Am I able to visualize the fulfillment of love in my dream house?
_____
_____

   Today's renovations: _____
_____

4. Did I identify my outer child? Did I take control? _____
_____

   Today's action plan _____
_____

5. Did I make love a goal of my daily activities? _____

As you integrate the exercises into daily practice over time, they begin to take on a less formal structure and become part of your everyday experience, incorporated into your actions and thoughts. You are able to live in the moment, address your most important needs and feelings, reach for new goals, and respond to others as an adult. As you grow, your capacity for love grows with you.

SUMMARY OF LIFTING

Lifting is a relief from insecurity, longing, and grief. It is a time to reflect upon the emotional truths revealed to us through our abandonment and take stock of the emotional baggage we have been carrying all along. This knowledge is gold, rich in personal wisdom.

Lifting is the time to honor our feelings. If we can keep our emotional center open, its energy becomes self-generating, the impetus for continual healing and lifelong personal growth.

Chapter Seven

Making a New Connection

A Five-Point Action Plan

W E have been on a journey together through the five stages
of abandonment. Along the way, our experiences often
reminded us of earlier times. Becoming reacquainted with our
oldest and most basic feelings has made us more self-aware.
Abandonment opened us up to emotional truths and brought
us in touch with universal life forces. It has been intense and
powerful because we have been here before. Abandonment mir-
rors developmental stages we went through as children, as we
made our way from infancy to the world beyond the home.

Stage One: In the *shattering* stage of abandonment, you were
forced to survive the severing of a primary relationship and to
reenter the world in a state of stark separateness. Infants likewise must withstand the birth trauma, the jolt of being separated from the womb. In this first stage, then, both
abandonment survivors and infants are forced to survive as separate individuals.

Stage Two: In the second stage of human development, infants form a bond with their caregivers to receive the nurturance

they need for survival. In the second stage of abandonment, you experienced the same drive toward attachment, but the object of your attachment was no longer available. Your needs were thwarted, causing intense *withdrawal* symptoms. At stage two, both infants and abandonment survivors experience the powerful opiate-driven need for attachment.

Stage Three: In the third stage of human development, children *internalize* the sense of security they've gained through relationships with their parents. They transfer feelings of safety, trust, and confidence onto their own newly forming *sense of self*. During the third stage of abandonment, you likewise *internalized* emotions, but the feelings you incorporated contained the message that you were unworthy. Like a young child, you transferred feelings derived from a primary relationship onto the *self*.

Stage Four: The fourth stage of human development is when children and adolescents, secure in the love and support of their family, feel confident enough to assert their place in the world. In the fourth stage of abandonment, called *rage,* you likewise returned to the external world, but you asserted the needs of your injured sense of self. In the fourth stage, both children and recovering adults move forward into the external world to meet their emotional needs. The difference is that you sought compensation for your injuries.

Stage Five: In the last stage of human development, emerging adults seek to form primary bonds. In the final stage of abandonment, *lifting,* you may experience the same desire to reconnect. But there is a need to protect yourself from further injury. In the fifth stage then, young adults and those recovering from the loss of a love are propelled to form new attachments. As an abandonment survivor, you gained valuable insight into the emotional baggage you carry forward into your relationships.

Abandonment recapitulates the process of starting out in life; you retread all of its developmental stages. You've grown from infancy to adulthood all over again, this time as a fully cognizant adult. You've created a new sense of self and perhaps set a new course for your life. You've converted the pain of abandonment into a touchstone for personal change.

Indeed, you have gained much from your experience.

From **shattering**, you gained strength and self-reliance. You survived the experience of being alone. You faced the anxieties that had you stuck in old patterns. You discovered your capac-

STAGES OF HUMAN DEVELOPMENT		STAGES OF ABANDONMENT
Survive the Birth Trauma	**1**	Birth Trauma is Reexperienced
Attach to Primary Care Giver	**2**	Wrenching Tear in a Primary Attachment
Transfer Attachment to Self	**3**	Transfer of Negative Feelings Onto Self
Assert Self to the World Outside	**4**	Assert Self in Conflict to Outside World
Find Another to Bond With	**5**	Wounded Self Seeks Another to Bond With

Abandonment follows the same path as the stages of human development

ity to deal with the feelings rising from cumulative wounds—injuries from abandonments past and present. You learned to use the power of your senses to *stay in the moment*.

From **withdrawal**, you gained the wisdom of your inner feelings. You identified unfinished business left over from old emotional traumas—the need-deprivations that led to your emotional hunger and, perhaps, unhealthy ways of dealing with it. You learned to put your emotional wisdom to work by creating a daily dialogue with your inner feelings. Ultimately, you addressed your most basic emotional needs directly, rather than medicating them with substances, people, obsessive thoughts, or compulsive behavior.

From *internalizing,* you gained integrity as you learned to voice deeply held aspirations, values, and goals. You identified feelings left over from past episodes when your sense of self had been injured. You discovered how to use your imagination as an internal resource for healing. You have built self-esteem, expanded your vision, and targeted your goals.

From *rage,* you learned to redirect your anger into healthy aggression. You identified emotional baggage left over from old frustrations. You exposed outer child behaviors that until now interfered with your life and relationships. You've become more alert to these behaviors and learned to assert your needs with greater control over attitudes and behavior.

BENEFITS OF ABANDONMENT RECOVERY

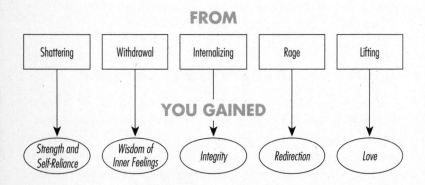

FROM

| Shattering | Withdrawal | Internalizing | Rage | Lifting |

YOU GAINED

| Strength and Self-Reliance | Wisdom of Inner Feelings | Integrity | Redirection | Love |

Benefits of abandonment recovery

From *lifting*, you learned to remain open to your own vulnerability and to reach out for a higher level of love. You revived lost hopes and dreams and reestablished emotional contact with yourself and others. You created a life plan for increasing your capacity for love on a daily basis.

In short, you *swirled* through the stages of abandonment—*s*hattering, *w*ithdrawal, *i*nternalizing, *r*age, and *l*ifting—and emerged from its funnel-shaped cloud with greater *s*trength, *w*isdom, *i*ntegrity, *r*edirection, and *l*ove than before.

FIVE-POINT ACTION PLAN FOR MAKING A NEW CONNECTION

What follows provides a rough framework in which these changes can take direction.

Action 1: Step outside your usual circle of friends and activities to explore new interests and try out new roles.

Action 2: Initiate new contacts with at least ten people and explore different aspects of your personality that may not have found expression before.

Action 3: Come clean about your feelings and your culpabilities about past relationship failures with at least three of these contacts.

Action 4: Become your higher self.

Action 5: Share your higher self with significant others.

ACTION 1: STEP OUTSIDE YOUR USUAL EXPERIENCE

Explore the territory beyond your usual circle of friends and activities to discover facets of your personality that have been denied. You will discover new interests, strengths, and capabilities you may not have realized before. This expansion gives you maximum opportunity for positive change. Here are some opportunities people I work with have taken advantage of:

• Having discovered his old interest in the piano, John decided to buy one. This meant moving into a new apartment big enough to accommodate it. His renewed commitment to music was how he happened to buy the concert tickets—the ones that led to his evening at the concert with Roberta.

• Roberta signed up for flying lessons and joined a poetry reading group.

• Holly joined a bicycling group and prepared to go on a six-week tour through Italy and France.

• Keaton took evening courses at the New School for Social Research, his first class being Modern Cinema. He planned to join Holly on her bicycle trip during his two-week vacation from work in August.

• Richard joined a dating service.

• Jay took up jogging, joined a volunteer outreach organization, and bought a vacation home on the west coast of Florida.

• Barbara went to a chef's school to learn macrobiotic cooking. She started a small catering business on the side.

• Marie finished sailing lessons. She continued her relationship with Phillip. They bought a sailboat and plan to sail up the East Coast to Maine.

• Michael changed jobs and took up racquetball.

• Caryle bought a colonial-period house and undertook its restoration. He needed lots of help and found that his new community was behind him; he became a leader in the town's civic association.

The key to change is opening your life to new experiences. Even small changes in your daily routine can lead to new discoveries about who you are becoming.

"I felt that I had been stuck in my job situation long enough," said Banford. *"The people at work didn't seem to respond to me the way I wanted them to. Even when I did things entirely differently, changes I made went unrecognized. So I changed jobs. It took a colossal effort. I spent all my free time visualizing my new job, then redesigning my résumé and going on job interviews. But I finally landed a job. I was on a whole new playing field.*

"I started out on new footing and created a whole new image. It was to my advantage that nobody knew me, because I was able to set things up the way I wanted right from scratch. The people I worked with just bought into it. I was able to change the way I usually related to people much easier because they weren't reacting to me with the same old biased expectations."

Making changes in your life creates room for expansion and growth. It allows for *internal* changes to take root in fresh soil. Your task is to get out there and try new things, join new groups, and change your routines. Give each new experience time to show you its hidden benefits.

ACTION 2: INITIATE NEW CONTACTS

Initiating new contacts helps you explore aspects of your personality that are not always apparent to yourself or others. I don't mean you should mislead others about yourself, pretending to be something you're not, simply that new situations reveal interests you haven't had the opportunity to express. Perhaps you haven't yet recognized certain talents or had a chance to develop them. Perhaps you haven't met people who could relate to certain interests. Many refer to these aspects themselves as *alter egos*.

Opportunities will come about as a result of the new activities you are becoming involved in, through friends, dating services, or chance encounters. You will discover facets of your developing self and be able to choose new directions for your life.

"I didn't know I could have a truly sharing relationship," said Janet. *"I'd spent so many years bickering and fighting with my husband. It was a revelation to discover how pleasant and agreeable I could be, just by being with someone who would meet me halfway."*

In reaching out beyond your usual social boundaries, do not dismiss someone because you're not instantly attracted to him or her. Your goal is not to fall in love at first sight. It is to discover your emerging strengths by socializing with a variety of people.

"I had no idea that I had a femme fatale in me," said Barbara. *"But I went out on a few dates and discovered that, at least with one or two of them, I was able to knock 'em dead. None of these men were really right for me, and I don't think I was ready yet. But it was a pleasant surprise and gave me a whole new sense of what I had to offer."*

Reach out to others who might share some of your special interests, as well as those whose interests extend beyond your own. So what if romance isn't in the cards. You might make a friend, a professional contact, or simply a memory of an interesting encounter.

"One of my new friends has a great sense of humor and finds everything I say funny," said Keaton. *"She laughs at almost everything that comes out of my mouth. And it makes me even*

funnier. I found one of my alter egos is a stand-up comedian—
except that I'm better when I'm sitting down."

A word of caution. When you reach out, you may find that
your inner child becomes impatient and needy. It may prompt
you to clamp onto the first person who comes along. Avoid
clamping on to anyone at this point. Just make contacts with
as many people as possible to maximize opportunities to discover your emerging self.

ACTION 3: COME CLEAN

Coming clean means finding someone you can be open with,
someone you can tell about your feelings, your breakup, and
more importantly, how you may have contributed to your failed
relationships.

Your goal in coming clean is twofold: to take responsibility
for your role in the difficulties you may be having and to un-
cover the kind of acceptance a human relationship can offer.

"What if I can't find anyone I can trust?" my clients often ask.

In fact, there are many people worthy of your trust, who, if
you ask them, will listen to you nonjudgmentally and won't try
to fix it or give you advice. Indeed, there are people who will
reciprocate by sharing their own foibles. Why not try an old
friend, a new friend, or the person you're now dating?

If there is no one in your life at the moment that you can
trust, your task is to go out and find them. They do exist.

When you come clean with another person, you break
through the shame barrier, exposing your deepest fears and insecurities.

One week Holly did it in an abandonment recovery group
session:

"I didn't know what I was doing wrong, but I have had
trouble getting into a relationship. Until now, I'm been too
ashamed to admit I've been having a problem. Now I realize

that anyone who'd been through the kind of crises I've been through would have the same problems. I used to think there was something about me that made people want to run away. But I know now that it isn't about whether I'm worthy or not. It isn't about me, it's about what happened to me. *I am worthy, alone or not. I have a lot of love to give and that makes me valuable."*

Coming clean for Holly helped her give up a facade she'd maintained for years. Being honest about her real fears allowed her to become her real self. She'd given up her false cheerfulness and traded it in for genuine depth of feeling and vulnerability.

"The first time I told someone how I felt," said Keaton, "I felt extremely vulnerable, but as I felt the other person accepting me, I felt free. It was almost like I'd been leading a double life. Finally, I felt accepted for what I really am, warts and all."

If you've been using the outer child inventory, you have some specific ideas about the behaviors that have interfered with your relationships. For many, this eases the work.

"When I tell people about some of my outer child traits," said Banford, "they get a kick out of it. They catch on to the idea, and get in on the fun of volunteering their own outer child traits. It opens up a really great exchange."

As you let others know about your outer child, you can more easily express your *inner child's* needs. Unencumbered by outer's defenses, you can be more emotionally present and honest. As you continue to come clean in your relationships, the abandoned child is released from the bondage of secrecy. Abandonment recovery workshops are a safe place to practice coming clean. But to feel the real benefits, try sharing openly with at least three people outside your support group.

Sharing with more than one person ensures that you reveal

different aspects of your emotional honesty and get a range of responses. If you come clean to a single person, you might come to think of the cleansing experience as an exception to the rule, rather than a newly developing capacity to be on emotionally honest terms with others.

Being rigorously honest with yourself and with select others cleanses your abandonment wound. Once you are able to break through the secret of shame, healing begins on a deeper level.

ACTION 4: INCORPORATE YOUR ALTER EGO INTO YOUR EGO: BECOME YOUR HIGHER SELF

"I found out that my higher self was really a loving and caring person," said Jay. "I was getting to know this woman who was in my business group. She had just been diagnosed with a degenerative bone disease. She had three young children, and it was becoming really hard for her to function. Such an unlucky break for such a nice person.

"I went out of my way to help her. I went to battle with her health insurance company and got her financial benefits secured. I even helped her husband get a better job. Half of the things I did for her, she never knew about. As I helped her, I discovered a whole new Jay."

As you continue reaching out for new activities and sharing yourself honestly and openly, you'll begin to realize your capacity for growth on many levels. With an expanded recognition of your capabilities and needs as a person, you are able to set new standards for yourself and new expectations for relationships to come. You are becoming your higher self.

"What really convinced me that I was changing," Jay continued, "was when my oldest kid broke up with his girlfriend. He was down in the dumps, but he wasn't in the habit of coming to his dad with his feelings. The old Jay wouldn't have known how to respond. The new Jay was determined to drag

*the story out of him. I really felt for the kid, and I wanted him
to know it and to support him. Voilà! Suddenly I was acting
like a nurturing father! I wish someone had been there for me
like that when I went through all the stuff I did as a kid or
when I was going through my breakup with Carlotta. But at
least I could be there for my own kid. Now I want to practice
this new Jay with a woman. I am ready for a real relationship."*

ACTION 5: SHARE YOUR HIGHER SELF WITH OTHERS

For those of you who have made finding a significant other
a primary goal, it's important to avoid those who might tempt
you to revert to old patterns.

*"I met this guy," said Roberta, "who was spectacular. He
owned a marina and lived on a house barge that he designed
himself. He had exquisite taste and lots of money to express it
with. By the fifth or sixth date, I discovered that I was deferring
to him, trying to please him. It was a prescription for failure.
What I needed was to feel comfortable, not perpetually impressed—comfortable enough so that I could feel impressed
with myself for a change. I thought, If only I could find someone
who I could feel as comfortable with as I do with John. Then,
that gave me a new thought—about John."*

Like Roberta, your goal is a relationship based on substantial
emotional benefits such as trust and comfort, rather than an
emotional high that raises your self-esteem by extension. You
are looking for someone who can complement the substance
and sensitivity you have gained through your experience.

*"I told Roberta that I had very strong feelings for her," said
John. "I admitted that it felt as if I was reaching again, reaching
for love that was out of my grasp, that this was just my old
pattern again. But I cared for her and wanted to express it to
her, just the same. I also knew how to take care of myself. 'Just*

let me have my feelings for you,' *I told her.* 'No strings attached. If you respond, you respond. If you don't, I can take care of myself. But just give it some time.' "

Giving love a chance is the lesson for Action 5. To do that, you need to surrender the losses of the past. Accept yourself as you are. You have a unique constellation of feelings and endowments. No one else can judge you or direct the course of your life. Your task is to honor it all. Bring all that you are into the moment with you. There is nothing to be gained by defending yourself against your feelings of vulnerability, wishing them away, or holding yourself to blame for having them. The vulnerability, self-doubt, and shame rising out of your past are as much a part of your personal truth as your talents and accomplishments are. They are worth sharing and may be the very reason someone new feels comfortable with you.

In the kind of relationship you're looking for, you can wear your vulnerability openly, without shame. Remain open to your partner's most basic fears, needs, and vulnerabilities as well.

"I've decided this time, I'm hanging in," said Roberta. "It helps that John is willing to accept full responsibility for his feelings. He even admits that it may be unhealthy for him to be pursuing someone who isn't returning his feelings. But I like John as a person. I respect his honesty. He knows just about all of my vulnerabilities, and I know his. We're very comfortable with each other. My values are changing. I'm looking for different things in life now. I know what love is. My big question is, has it already found me and I just can't see it yet? I've decided to stick around and find out."

We are all looking love in the face at almost every moment. Many of us may even think we've already found it. Yet whether we have found a relationship or not, there is always much more love to embrace in the relationships we already have and the ones we are creating.

The key to reconnecting is to cherish the gift that abandonment has given you, to remain open to your vulnerabilities and to the vulnerabilities of others. Maintaining emotional contact creates a bridge to true relationships.

Coda: Theater of the Absurd

W HAT *would be the opposite of the secrecy and silence of abandonment? Why not give it a parade!*

THE ANNUAL ABANDONMENT DAY PARADE

All of the people in this imaginary parade would be abandonment survivors; they'd all get to wear the badge of the wounded.

At first, you'd see what appeared to be a ragtag group of people marching down Main Street. But among the thousands would be exquisitely dressed, perfectly postured, and undeniably strong individuals. You would sense dignity and triumph, especially from the most wounded, who carry the banners. These are the parade's heroes. The incredible openness, depth, and humanness of the marchers moves the crowd to tears.

Right behind the Grand Marshal Most Wounded carrying the baton are the people in the wheelchairs. They are the ones whose emotional histories have left them so profoundly impaired, they have difficulty forming primary relationships. Many of them live their lifetimes alone. Their wounds are hidden, but they have been awarded the purple heart of abandonment.

Just behind them are the ones who have been recently abandoned. They need to be carried on floats as they are in too much pain to walk. The floats carry these many thousands of broken-hearted through the admiring, respectful crowds.

Behind the recently abandoned come throngs of people on foot, many of them on crutches or holding each other up. These are the abandonment survivors of childhood whose adult lives have been stricken with *fear of abandonment*. Many of them are tied to the wrong people, too afraid to let go of what little security they have. Others have known the emotional turmoil of constantly being in and out of relationships.

Many of the people on the sidelines are not sure why they are clapping and cheering for the marchers, but the spirit of the marchers moves them to tears. Some of them are almost ready to join the parade to celebrate their own woundedness. Others are more reluctant to get in touch, not willing to bring their pain out of silence. They have yet to discover that the site of the deepest wound is the site of the greatest healing.

A number of the people on the sidelines are torn. They are aware of their own pain, but they want to retain their option to abandon others. They are not yet ready to take a stand against abandonment, to denounce it as an unacceptable practice. Some of them might be able to change. Perhaps they will join the parade next year.

Standing back out of sight are the wounders themselves. Many of them have paused momentarily to observe the parade from a distance, wondering if maybe they are missing something—something the marchers seem to possess. Others may even have fleeting thoughts that there could be something seriously wrong within that allows them to inflict so much pain on others.

The *hard-core* abandoners avoid the parade altogether and

go on about their business, oblivious to the pain they have inflicted on those who have loved them. Paradoxically, many of them were abandoned themselves, but the experience left them calloused, numb, and desensitized, rather than more compassionate.

At the finish line, the grand marshals and standard bearers intermingle long into the night. This is the opportunity for the most wounded to meet each other. Many permanent unions are born here. People discover each other's lovability and refuse to be put off by stigmas. They vow to heal each other through loving relationships. They possess the capacity for profound loyalty and devotion, determined never to abandon each other. It is the greatest gift of love to offer the other: freedom from fear.

The antidote to abandonment has been found: commitment to love.

Notes

IN *identifying information about neuro-biology I am indebted to the writings of Robert Sapolsky, Joseph LeDeux, Myron Hofer, Jaak Panskepp, and Daniel Goleman. I've incorporated their lucid explanations and insights into my text without stopping to credit them each time. Rather, I use this space to fully acknowledge their contributions as well as those of many others who have investigated the underlying structure of human experience.*

(Attention reader: Complete information regarding references cited in the notes is provided in the bibliography.)

CHAPTER ONE:
THE FIVE STAGES OF ABANDONMENT

11 "the invisible drain," A phrase coined by Peter Yelton, CSW, colleague, friend, and abandonment guru.

CHAPTER TWO:
SHATTERING

22 the difference between grieving and depression: See Freud, Sigmund, *Mourning and Melancholia*.

22 Alby anecdote: Courtesy of Peter Yelton.

26 For excellent descriptions of the sympathetic nervous system response: See Larry J. Seiver, and William Frucht, *The New View of Self*, p. 35. Also consult Robert M. Sapolsky, chaps. 2 and 3 in *Why Zebras Don't Get Ulcers*: Daniel Goleman, chap. 5 and app. C in *Emotional Intelligence*.

26 reactivation of early separation distress: Myron Hofer points out that separation distress is made possible in the infant by the development of neural networks of the limbic system. In the evolutionary ladder, separation distress is the first innate anxiety state. It is adaptive to ward off threat of separation from mother . . . In animal studies, it has been shown that rats react to their very first experience of separation. See Myron Hofer, "An Evolutionary Perspective on Anxiety," in Anxiety as Symptom and Signal, pages 25–27.

Our original emotional experiences (i.e. separation distress) are imprinted in the brain and can return in the form of what Daniel Goleman has described as, "wordless blueprints . . . potent emotional memories dating from first five years of life between the infant and its caretaker." He writes that since these memories were laid down before the neo-cortex and hippocampus were fully developed, there would be no "matching set of articulated thoughts" for the vague sensation of reawakened anxieties from childhood. See Daniel Goleman, *Emotional Intelligence*.

27 prenatal memories: Anthony DeCasper's research has shown that babies prefer sounds they heard before birth—namely their mother's heart beat and voice. See Decasper and Fif, "Of Human Bonding" *Science* 208(1980). William Smotherman's research shows that conditioning occurs prenatally and therefore has implications for the care of premature infants. Rat fetuses can be conditioned to avoid unpleasant smells to which they are exposed before birth. See William P. Smotherman and Scott R. Robinson,

"The Development of Behavior Before Birth," in *Developmental Psychology* 32 (1996) pp. 425–434.

27 the infant calms: Jaak Panksepp researches the way in which social connectedness is mediated by the brain's endogenous opiate system. Opiates help to reduce isolation distress. See Panksepp, Siviy and Normansell, "Brain Opioids and Social Emotions," *The Psychobiology of Attachment and Separation.* According to Myron Hofer, another researcher in this field, physical contact (i.e. a mother rat licking her distressed infant) comforts by stimulating opiate release. See Hofer, "Hidden Regulators."

28 split thinking: Abandonment is an emotional crisis often severe enough to create symptoms similar to borderline personality disorder. One of the indications of this temporary regression is the tendency toward either/or thinking—seeing the self and/or others as alternatively all good or all bad. Freud explored the issue of ambivalence about self and others. Kohut, Kernberg, Masterson and others described the 'splitting' phenomenon. For a treatment perspective, see Jerome Kroll, *PTSD / Borderlines in Therapy.*

29 symbiotic feelings: Hofer provides new substance to the term symbiosis when he suggests that the "mutual regulation" that has been found to take place between mother and infant involves multiple physiological and psychological processes. Mother and infant serve as external regulators for the other. See Hofer, "Hidden Regulators," p. 29.

29 symbiotic regression: Another indicator of temporary borderline functioning (see note 37).

30 need to be with others: Baumeister's studies emphasize that the stress of separation is mitigated by a sense of belonging. See Roy F. Baumeister and Mark R. Leary, "The Need to Belong" *Psychological Bulletin,* (1995) p. 509. Hofer's research offers credence to this on a neuro-chemical level—social companions offer some comfort by stimulating opiate release. See Hofer, "Hidden Regulators."

30 the arousal of old emotional memories: See Joseph LeDoux, "Emotion, Memory, and the Brain," *Scientific American,* (June, 1994) pp. 50–57.

31 children are attached to their abusers: Judith Harris, *The Nurture Assumption: Why Children Turn Out The Way They Do*, p. 151.

34 the body's alarm system is triggered: See Goleman, *Emotional Intelligence*. Also, see Edward Wilson, *Consilience, The Unity of Knowledge*, pp. 113–114.

35 immune-system response: According to Steven Maier and other researchers, stress is immunosuppressive. Different stressors such as 'social defeat' or 'maternal separation' produce different mixes of autonomic nervous system activity and hormones. See Steven F. Maier, Linda R. Watkins, Monika Fleshner, "Psychoneuroimmunology: The Interface Between Behavior, Brain and Immunity," *American Psychologist*, Vol. 49., (December 1994) pp. 1004-1017. Herbert Weiner, makes the point that the immune system is under the control of the sympathetic branch—encompassing bone marrow, thymus, spleen, gut and lymph nodes. See Herbert Weiner, *Perturbing the Organism: The Biology of Stressful Experience*, p. 204. See also *J. K. Kiecolt-Glaser and others, "Marital Quality, Marital Disruption, and Immune Function," *Psychosomatic Medicine*, 49, no. 1 (1987), pp. 13-34.

36 intense emotional battle: See Sapolsky, *Why Zebras*.

36 alcohol depresses anxiety: Roy Wise explains why some people faced with an abandonment crisis tend to self-medicate with alcohol and other substances. He states, "Drugs of abuse activate positive reinforcement mechanisms directly and centrally on the brain . . . They may do so with much greater intensity than can ever be summoned by environmental stimuli like food, water, or the reinforcing beauty of nature, art, or music." See Roy A. Wise, "The Neurobiology of Craving: Implications for the Understanding and Treatment of Addiction," *Journal of Abnormal Psychology* 97, no. 2 (1988), p. 127. Those who greatly over-consume may unwittingly increase the depression and despair associated with the abandonment experience. William McKinney found that alcohol ameliorated the despair response in rhesus monkeys; however, in higher doses, it exacerbated this condition. See William T. McKinney, "Separation and Depression: Biological Markers," in *The Psychobiology of Attachment and Separation*, p. 215.

36 becoming addicted to alcohol: Ronald Ruden examines the psychobiology of the 'gotta have it' impulses leading to addictions—high dopamine production in nucleus accumbens, low serotonin levels. See Ruden and Myalick, *The Craving Brain: The Biobalance Approach to Controlling Addiction*, pp. 5–6.

36 Shame: For a discussion regarding theoretic psychological origins of shame, read Melanie Klein, *Love, Guilt, and Reparation and Other Works 1921–1945* and Helen Block Lewis, *Shame and Guilt in Neurosis*. For a psychobiological perspective see Alan Schore, *Affect Regulation and the Origin of the Self: The Neurobiology of Emotional Development*, pp. 348–354, 415–430.

37 Richard's shame: For a perspective which highlights men, read Terrence Real, *I don't Want to Talk About It*. He discusses the tendency for men who have been socialized in Western society to feel ashamed of their vulnerability, grief, and emotional needs. Healing begins when men drop the macho defense of suppressing their grief, begin to explore their emotional truths, and share feelings.

38 Shame about feeling pain and grief: Jerome Kagan suggests that attributing *suffering* to *weakness* has a long history. He quotes Pierre Janet as saying, "Sadness is always a sign of weakness and sometimes of the habit of living weakly." See Jerome Kagan, *The Nature of a Child*. See also Michael Lewis, *Shame: The Exposed Self*, and Helen Block Lewis, *Shame and Guilt in Neurosis*. For a self-help book addressing shame, consult John Bradshaw, *Healing the Shame that Binds You*.

38 shock—numbing to surroundings: See D. D. Kelly, "Stress-induced Analgesia." *Annals of the New York Academy of Sciences* (1986).

39 posttrauma: Comprehensive research on posttrauma is found in Bessel A. van der Kolk, Alexander C. McFarlane, and Lars Weisaeth, *Traumatic Stress: The Effects of Overwhelming Experience on Mind, Body, and Society*. Also consult Judith Lewis Herman, *Trauma and Recovery*.

41 trauma related to abandonment: Hofer found that older children as well as older rats who had experienced earlier separations, responded to signals of impending separation without requiring the actual loss to elicit the response. This 'conditioning' was found to have long reaching effects—an indication of 'posttraumatic' reaction. See Hofer, "Hidden Regulators" p. 211. Daniel Goleman in *Emotional Intelligence,* referred to PTSD as a "limbic disorder," "a condition of learned fearfulness," and "a lowering of neural setpoint." He writes that if a child had early trauma, the amygdala is primed to find danger later on; the threshold to activation of SNS is lowered. Alan Schore refers to "abandonment-depression," demonstrating its impact on the development of brain structures (orbito-frontal systems affecting ventral tegmental limbic circuits) in *Affect Regulation,* pp. 416–422. (See note 126.)

41 list of posttrauma characteristics: I was guided to extrapolate many of the characteristics on this list from those delineated in Van der Kolk, McFarlane, and Weisaeth, *Traumatic Stress,* pp. 203, 259.

43 acting impulsively: Van der Kolk suggests that for many posttrauma victims feelings can often lead directly to actions without going through a linear process of rational planning to avoid negative consequences. Ibid., 188.

43 Angry outbursts as a sign of separation-trauma are well documented: Virginia Colin writes that one of the traumatic reactions to separation is a display of aggression. As an example, she cites a study in which sixty white middle class subjects who were going through divorce showed high incidence of aggressive impulses. In some cases, "all pretense of rational thinking was abandoned—subjects attacked former spouses through burglaries, poisoning pets, kidnapping and brandishing weapons." Virginia A. Colin, *Human Attachment,* p. 340.

43 predisposing factors for developing PTSD: Jerome Kagan cites research suggesting that genetic variation plays a role. Inhibited children may have inherited different thresholds of excitability, which is related to higher concentrations of norepinephrine (NE) and/or a higher diversity of NE receptors in the locus ceruleus. Jerome Kagan, *Galen's Prophecy: Temperament in Human Nature,* pp. 51–52. Susan Vaughan writes about the way in which the deep brain nuclei seem to set the tone of the whole cerebral cortex. She suggests that the "absence or presence of important 'others' during early childhood may affect the deep brain nuclei directly . . . which can lead to the development of depressive symptoms" later on. See Susan Vaughan, *The Talking Cure: The Science Behind Psychotherapy,* pp. 141–142. Also consult Myron Hofer, "An Evolutionary Perspective on Anxiety," *Anxiety as Symptom and Signal,* pp. 17–38.

44 current trauma: Abandonment is undoubtedly a traumatic event—a sustained emotional crisis, whether or not it leads to the development of a posttraumatic disorder. Neuroscience points to the role of the neurotransmitter norepinephrine (NE) in the development of protracted anxiety, suggesting that there is a deregulation of norepinephrine in the locus ceruleus, a structure of the emotional brain or limbic system. Goleman in *Emotional Intelligence* writes that NE deregulation involves the following PTSD symptoms: anxiety, fear, hyper-vigilance, being easily upset, being easily aroused, readiness for 'fight or flight' and indelible encoding of intense emotional memories. For more about NE, see Researchers Seiver and Frucht, *New View,* p. 35. They write that fear is a condition in which one's attention turns outward thus more norepinephrine (NE); conversely, when attention turns inward, NE declines. This may explain why the emotional crisis of abandonment causes our attention to rivet upon our lost relationship. We suffer obsessive thinking and prolonged hyper-vigilance.

Traumatic stress also involves an increase in the production of a stress hormone, CRF (corticotropin releasing factor). Increased secretions of CRF leads to the 'sweating, chills, shakes, flashbacks, startle response' that we experience during the initial throes of abandonment. Opiates are also involved, creating a generalized numbing to life going on around us, withdrawal symptoms, a state of anhedonia, and a dissociation of feeling. The short term advantages of these trauma-induced biochemical changes include: vigilance, arousal, readiness, imperviousness to pain, being primed for sustained physical demand, indifference to other events.

45 shock: An interesting point about the numbing affect of shock is made by Van der Kolk, McFarlane, and Wisaeth, *Traumatic Stress*, p. 227: "After two decades of the original trauma, people with PTSD developed opioid mediated analgesia in response to a stimulus resembling the original trauma which we correlated with secretion of endogenous opioids equivalent of 8 mg of morphine." For additional discussion about the endogenous opiate system mediating the 'numbing effect' associated with grief and other forms of trauma, consult Panksepp, Siviy, and Normansell, "Brain Opiods," pp. 5–7; David Benton and Paul F. Brain, "The Role of Opioid Mechanisms in Social Interaction and Attachment," *Behavioral Processes,* (1988) pp. 219, 220; and Myron Hofer, "An Evolutionary Perspective," pp. 222–223. See also Kelly, "Stress–induced Analgesia."

45 depersonalization: Extensive discussion about feelings of disconnectedness and dissociative states is found in Herman, *Trauma and Recovery*. See also Van der Kolk, McFarlane, and Weisaeth, *Traumatic Stress*, pp. 51–73, 303–330.

46 separation anxiety: Eric Fromm asserts that separation anxiety underlies all psychological disturbance and distress. See Eric Fromm, *The Art of Loving*. For a general definition of anxiety that seems to speak for separation distress, here is Hofer's: ". . . a behavioral state that occurs in response to signals of danger and that entails a special set of response tendencies that have resulted in avoidance of similar dangers during events in the organism's past development and in the evolution of the species." See Hofer, "An Evolutionary Perspective," p. 36.

46 reality distortion: Reality distortion so prevalent to the emotional crisis of abandonment, is explained at a neuro-scientific level. For one example, see Candace B. Pert, *Molecules of Emotion,* p. 143.

47 self-destructiveness: tendency toward self-mutilation and other acts of self-abuse. See Van der Kolk, McFarlane, and Weisaeth, *Traumatic Stress,* p. 189.

48 substance abuse and addiction: Many addicts, including heroin addicts, report having traumatic early histories of abandonment.

Researchers have found that in distressed laboratory rats, the inhibition of distress vocalization (crying when infant is separated from its mother) is *particularly* sensitive to opiates. According to Benton and Brain, "Opiod Mechanisms," p. 221: "the general impression gained from several lines of investigation is that opioids have a relatively specific influence on separation induced distress in the young of the species so far examined." See also Wise, "Neurobiology of Craving," and Ruden and Myalick, *The Craving Brain.* (See notes S 47 and 75.)

48 explosive rage as a symptom of PTSD: See Van der Kolk, McFarlane, and Weisaeth, *Traumatic Stress,* p. 217.

49 abandonment survivors as trauma victims: In my view natural selection in evolving our species must have factored in abandonment/separation as a threat to human existence. The very same equipment that enables us to react automatically (autonomically) to other types of danger, seems adapted to the need to sustain the human bond upon which our earliest survival is dependent and by which our species is able to procreate. When that bond is threatened, we are conditioned to react: Our emotional brain *warns* us autonomically of any perceived threat to our primary attachments, *punishes* us with anxiety for allowing our attachments to be broken or abandoned, and *rewards* us (with endogenous opiates) when we are able to maintain stable life-enhancing attachments.

The series of far-reaching reactions whose condition we call *post-traumatic stress disorder* (PTSD) represents early conditioning—the organism's ability to learn-by-experience. Through this process we learn the approach/avoidance mechanisms we perceive as necessary for survival. Where abandonment is concerned, the intrusive anxieties and inhibitions we experience posttraumatically can be seen as the organism's way of protecting the human bond which is the infrastructure of species survival. Of course, abandonment is but one of many potential threats to survival. There are also snakes, enemies, falling from cliffs—all of which are processed by the neuroanatomy of conditioning, and yield sometimes extreme "conditioned responses" (which we readily identify as symptoms of PTSD); but "fear of abandonment" is a naturally occurring condition of post-separation experience, representing a baseline of emotional reactivity, a kind of emotional platform unique to each individual, upon which future occurrences—grizzly bears, car accidents, rapes, separations from parents or later attachments—are further engraved. In other words early separation anxieties set the tone for future experiences.

51 emotional experience molds the brain: an extensively researched area of neuroscience still in theoretical stages. Researchers find that childhood experiences help to mold the structure of a child's maturing brain. Rats once separated from their mothers are more anxious the second time around. Separation effects the development of the rat's brain and biochemistry. During separation trauma, the body produces cortisol, a stress hormone known to cause growth hormone to decline. Speculation has it that this leads to slower growth of an important brain connection involved in regulating experience (cortico-limbic circuits). At a later stage of childhood, the connections to and from the vagus nerve—a part of the brain that primes the body for fight-or-flight response—are affected. This sets the brain at a high level of reactivity, creating anxiety disorders to emerge in adolescence or adulthood. It is known that stress affects the learning processes as well. This should tell parents and other adults how important it is to attempt to mitigate the effects of abandonment in children.

For additional comprehensive analysis, see Allan Schore, *Affect Regulation* and John Madden, ed. *Neurobiology of Learning, Emotional and Affect,* 1991. For an overview, see Hara Estroff Marano, "Depression: Beyond Serotonin," *Psychology Today,* Vol. 32(April, 1999) pp. 30–76.

52 amygdala: The work of Joseph LeDoux on the amygdala and limbic system is helping to reshape our understanding of human experience. See LeDoux, *Emotional Brain,* 1996. See also Kagan's description of the projections of the central nucleus of the amygdala to other targets in *Galen's Prophecy,* pp. 100–107.

53 conditioned response: For the best read on classical conditioned response, consult the original text of I. V. Pavlov, *Conditioned Reflexes,* 1922. For a discussion of how the immune response can be conditioned in Pavlovian manner see Maier, Watkins, and Fletcher, "Psychoneuroimmunology," p. 1007. See also report about the placebo effect which operates according to a Pavlovian conditioning model in Sandra Blakeslee, "Placebo Prove So Powerful Even Experts are Surprised," *New York Times, Science Times* section, 13 October 1998.

53 looking at abandonment fear as a conditioned response: In my view separation distress and fear of abandonment are among the most common sources for early amygdala-driven emotional conditioning (see note 64). The intense emotional feelings associated with abandonment is a feeling 'all of its own.' Panksepp suggests that separation-distress involves distinct neurobiological systems, giving rise to distinct emotional responses (albeit sharing much of the neurochemistries with other emotional states). See Panksepp, *Advances in Biological Psychiatry,* p. 269.

I have observed that the activation of this emotional state does not require extraordinary circumstances; on the contrary 'fear of abandonment' is universal to human experience; it seems to develop in even the most uneventful infant-to-caretaker relationships as a natural consequence of the infant's dependence on a life-sustaining source. The universality of this response suggests that abandonment/separation is one of the primary avoidance conditions for which the emotional brain is equipped. For this reason, the work of Ledoux and Van der Kolk in their respective areas, has much to inform the subject of abandonment, and can help us understand why this universal experience harkens back to our earliest fears and represents a true emotional crisis profound enough to mimic (at least temporarily) some of the most severe forms of psychiatric dysfunction such as psychosis and major depression.

54 fear of abandonment: Baumeister and Leary suggested a link between death anxiety to fear of loneliness or separation anxiety, helping us to understand the intensity of fear of abandonment. See Baumeister and Leary, "Need to Belong," p. 507. (See note 61.)

55 hippocampus: Again, indebtedness to LeDoux, *Emotional Brain.*

56 amygdala is not its own kingdom: LeDoux explains, "Although the amygdala stores primitive information, we should not consider it the only learning center. The establishment of memories is a function of the entire network." See LeDoux, "Emotion, Memory," p. 56. Antonio *Damasio* also cautions against an oversimplistic or mechanistic view of the human mind, entreating us to appreciate the dynamic interaction of multi-levels of experience— neurological and environmental. See Damasio, *Descartes' Error: Emotion, Reason, and the Human Brain.*

56 impact of childhood traumas: Herbert Weiner states, "Separation . . . may be especially poignant for adults if it recapitulates a childhood loss . . . Patients at risk for major depressive disorders (beyond genetic factors) include separation from mother (but not from father) before the age of seventeen. See Weiner, *Perturbing the Organism,* p. 75. For an insightful look at this type of loss see Hope Edelman, *Motherless Daughters.*

57 some people develop PTSD, some don't: Jerome Kagan in his discussion about inhibited versus uninhibited children, suggests that there are predisposing factors that contribute to the development of far reaching anxiety to stimulating events. See Kagan, *Galen's Prophecy,* pp. 217–219. (Also, see note 58.)

57 responsiveness of antidepressants to bereavement: William McKinney points out that separation can have the same symptoms as "endogenous" depression and can respond to the same medications. Specifically, drugs that affect certain neurotransmitter systems interact specifically with separation. See McKinney, "Separation and Depression," p. 213. For a comparison of the effectiveness of antidepressants and psychotherapies, read David Healy, *The Antidepressant Era.* (See note 62.)

61 getting into the moment: a natural pain-analgesic and life-enhancement technique—staying in the moment—was emphasized to me by Zachary Studenroth during a personal dialogue. For additional help with this exercise, there are many excellent books; see Jon Kabat-Zinn, *Full Catastrophe Living.*

66 for intensifying the moment and getting into your senses, read Hannah Merker, *Silences* or Diane Ackerman, *Natural History of the Senses.* For increasing awareness of the world we live in, see

Michael Pollan, *Second Nature*. See also Sogyal Rinpoche, *The Tibetan Book of Living and Dying*, 1994.

68 healers are those who have worked through trauma:" from a dialogue with Peter Yelton.

CHAPTER THREE:
WITHDRAWAL

74 opiate mediated withdrawal symptoms: Jaak Panksepp states that the "main characteristics of narcotic addiction, namely the development of dependence, tolerance, and withdrawal," are strikingly similar to the characteristics of social bonding, "specifically the feelings of attachment, alienation/weaning, and separation-distress arising from the disengagement of social bonds." See Panksepp, Nelson, Bekkedel, "Brain Systems for the Mediation of Separation Distress and Social Reward," *Annals NY Academy of Sciences* 807 (1997): p. 82. With regard to separation distress, he states, "No other behavior is as powerfully and consistently modified by low doses of opiate receptor agonist;" see Panksepp, Siviy, and Normansell, "Brain Opioids," p. 6. Myron Hofer's research addresses the impact of grief on the opiate network of mind-brain. Rats put out a distress cry when they are totally isolated. When the mother hears the cry, she comes to the cage and licks the pup, and the distress vocalization shuts off. But if the rat pup is injected with an opioid blocker (naloxone), the licking does not shut the cry off. It is the opiate secreted by the licking that calms the distress state down, not the licking itself. See Hofer, "Hidden Regulators," p. 23. See also Benton and Brain, "Opioid Mechanisms."

75 the need for someone to belong to: Baumeister suggests that grief often takes the form of an especially severe depression. . . . "not [only] as a reaction to the loss of the person but as a reaction to the loss of a *linkage* with another person;" see Baumeister and Leary, "Need to Belong."

75 people can be just as shattered by loss of a bad relationship: For research which demonstrates this point, see Julia K. Vormbrock, "Attachment Theory as Applied to Wartime and Job-Related Marital Separation," *Psychological Bulletin*, 114 (1993): pp. 122–144.

76 background object: Much of this discussion is based upon the teachings of Richard Robertiello, psychoanalyst and author. See Robertiello, *Hold Them Very Close and Then Let Them Go.*

77 taking background object for granted: Myron Hofer emphasizes the point that a primary relationship helps to regulate many hidden psychological and physiological factors. These "hidden regulators" come to be stored in memory as "mental representations that were built originally on earlier childhood interactions that had been regulatory in terms of the functioning of the whole system." Hofer, "Hidden Regulators," p. 222.

77 gaining weight when settling down to a relationship: For a fascinating discussion about the conundrum of stress causing an increase and/or decrease in appetite, read Sapolsky, *Why Zebras*. See also the "weight loss" section in Chapter Three: WITHDRAWAL in this book.

77 parasympathetic nervous system: For a clear explanation of complementary branches of autonomic nervous system which includes sympathetic nervous system and parasympathetic nervous system, see Robert Ornstein and Richard F. Thompson, *The Amazing Brain;* and Richard M. Restak, *Brainscapes: An Introduction to What Neuroscience has Learned about the Structure, Function and Abilities of the Brain.*

78 children need trust in order to be independent: See Donald W. Winnecott, "The Capacity to be Alone," *The Maturational Processes and the Facilitating Environment.*

79 involuntary separation: The term comes from Colin, *Human Attachment,* p. 294.

79 will run riot: This term was introduced to me by Dexter Griffith Jr., my brother and self-awareness consultant.

79 having no sense of control: Being abandoned may resemble the condition of 'learned helplessness' that has been extensively investigated in research laboratories. Animals who have been exposed to uncontrollable stressors have trouble coping with all sorts of other tasks afterwards, such as competing for food. In this they may share many of the same features as humans whose lives have been stressed by having 'no sense of control.' Sapolsky, *Why Zebras*, pp. 252–255. See Martin Seligman, *Helplessness: On Depression, Development and Death.*

79 aloneness: Jaak Panksepp offers speculation about future psychiatric medications for conditions of aloneness—ranging from 'loss-induced depression, to the despair of everyday loneliness.' He suggests, "The development of an orally effective ligand (a neurochemical agent that attaches to neuronal receptors) for oxytocin receptors (associated with social bonding) in the brain should prove to be a powerful alleviator of loneliness and other forms of separation-distress, just as opiates are effective, but without the clinically problematic addictive features of narcotics. Panksepp, Nelson, and Bekkedal, "Brain Systems," p. 85.

For inspirational books about coping with loneliness, see Rae Andre, *Positive Solitude* and Anthony Storr, *Solitude: A Return to the Self.*

81 sexual hormonal changes related to stress: See Sapolsky, chap. 7 in *Why Zebras.*

81 heightened sexual needs: ACTH (adrenocorticotropic hormone) produced during the stress response has been found to act as an endogenous antagonist for opioids (*antanogist* means it blocks the effect of the opioid). This is interesting considering that the opiates heroin, morphine, methadone, are known to decrease libido, retard ejaculation, and contribute to impotence in males. This could explain why the stress incurred during the abandonment crisis (with increased levels of ACTH) might reduce the endogenous narcotic effect and thereby induce greater sexual expression. See G. Serra, M. Collu, and G. L. Gessa, "Endorphins and Sexual Behavior," in *Endorphins, Opiates and Behavioral Processes.*

82 sexual withdrawal: In addition to the generalized sexual withdrawal many abandonment survivors report, a number have expressed a desire to perform oral sex on their lost lovers. Becoming separated is a powerful enough emotional crisis to reactivate amygdala-related emotional memories, causing you to reexperience some of your earliest instinctual needs, which may even include the sucking reflex. The infant's suckling involves the tongue, lips, and internal rim of the mouth—all highly tactile areas. The sucking reflex is innate and universal in human beings, providing nourishment for the newborn and helping to initiate the bond between the infant and its care-giver. The infant suckles the mother's breast, and she in turn feels the relief of her engorged breast and the pleasurable stimulations associated with the experience. It is that sublime oneness we crave throughout our lives and are most bereft of when we are going through abandonment-withdrawal. The component of sexual oral fantasy is only one aspect of the larger issue of physical withdrawal. The sucking reflex is established prenatally, as suggested in Smotherman and Robinson, "Development of Behavior," pp. 425–434. Also consult P. H. Wolff, "The Serial Organization of Sucking in the Young Infant," *Pediatrics* 42 (1968) pp. 943-956.

83 weight loss: Sapolsky explains the impact of stress hormones on appetite and weight loss in *Why Zebras*. Herbert Weiner describes the "rhythmic secretion of corticosteriods in humans . . . (with) five to seven bursts of cortisol (stress hormone) during a 24 hour period." He explains, "corticosteriods are secreted during specific experiences, often life threatening situations (or perception of—such as in the case of abandonment), as well as experimental situations in which unpredictable or uncontrollable electric shock (which is analogous to abandonment pain) is inescapable. See Weiner *Perturbing the Organism,* p. 207. To wit, the feeling of 'having no control' and 'inescapable devastation' are commonly reported by abandonment survivors (see note 103.)

84 hypervigilance: Excellent discussion of this anxious state is found both in Sapolsky, *Why Zebras* and Goleman, *Emotional Intelligence.*

85 grief: See Elisabeth Kubler-Ross, *On Death and Dying;* John Bowlby, *Loss: Sadness and Depression; Attachment and Loss, III,* London, 1980; M. D. S. Ainsworth, "Attachments and Other Affectional Bonds Across the Life Cycle," in *Attachments Across the Life Cycle*; Virginia A. Colin, *Human Attachment.*

85 searching for the lost object: John Bowlby, ibid.

85 waiting and watching: Jerome Kagan states that hypervigilance is the result of the neurotransmitter norepinephrine (NE), "whose

role is to inhibit background neural activity in the sensory areas of cortex so that if a stimulus [a threat] occurs, the signal-to-noise ratio is increased, and sensory neurons will be more likely to respond to the [threat]." See Kagan, *Galen's Prophecy*, p. 52. (Also see note 57.)

86 mistaken identity: Pert, *Molecules*, p. 143.

86 grief operating beneath conscious awareness: According to Myron Hofer, grief is due to the loss and withdrawal of a number of "physical and temporal interactions" with the lost love-object, including the loss of the "mental image of the person." He makes a point that underscores the intensity of the grief process, stating that there are "several cognitive and physical changes in bereavement [that] are strikingly similar to those seen in acute sensory deprivation." See Hofer, *Hidden Regulators*, p. 222.

86 dreams: Abandonees report having dreams with themes of wishful thinking in which the lost object returns, as well as a cascade of other intense feelings (fear, loss, sorrow, sexual arousal, emotional longing, sense of impending doom, panic) associated with the abandonment—all of which gets played out in the bizarre story-drama of the dream script. Extensive research on the brain during REM sleep provides some neurobiological elucidation. Allan Hobson discusses an EEG pattern called "PGO waves" (ponto-genticulo-occipital waves) which send volleys through various portions of the brain, stimulating visual and motor areas causing the characteristic hallucinations of the dream state. The PGO waves also volley across the amygdala-centered limbic system causing the high emotional intensity (including fear) of dream content. Research seems to support the notion of "dream transparency," tending to substantiate Carl Jung's dream theories in which dreams would reflect memories, thoughts and feelings held in the memory buffers, sorted and retrieved to relate to current experience (i.e. abandonment). See Allan J. Hobson, *The Dreaming Brain*.

87 self-corrective mechanisms: This point was emphasized by Robert Gossette who led me to many primary resources regarding parasympathetic system as well as other psychobiological systems cited throughout the text. For interest, see Robert L. Gossette and Richard M. O'Brien, "The Efficacy of Rational Emotive Therapy in Adults: Clinical Fact or Psychometric Artifact?", *Journal of Behavior Therapy and Experimental Psychiatry,* 23, no. 1, (1992) pp. 9–24.

87 withdrawal is *post* trauma: This statement means that withdrawal occurs *after* (or post) the initial trauma. The symptom sequelae are discussed in Van der Kolk, McFarlane, and Weisaeth, *Traumatic Stress.* For additional discussion, see Goleman, *Emotional Intelligence.* He provides an excellent synthesis of post trauma, describing the prolonged arousal of the sympathetic nervous system (such as that which is experienced during abandonment's withdrawal stage) as a deregulation of the limbic system.

87 sustained emotional crisis: For extensive discussion about the impact of sustained stress, consult Sapolsky, *Why Zebras,* and Goleman, *Emotional Intelligence.*

88 patterns of attunement: Hofer describes "hidden regulatory interactions" that come to be experienced by infants as synchrony, reciprocity, and warmth (or dissonance or frustration). These persistent regulatory processes constitute the "internal working model" of our attachments to others and account for the our vulnerability to the "protest and despair" response to loss. See Hofer, "Hidden Regulators." Nathan Fox found that children are attuned to their parents by smile response and heart-rate. See Nathan A. Fox, "Behavioral Antecedents of Attachment in High-Risk Infants," in *The Psychobiology of Attachment and Separation,* p. 401. Tiffany Field showed that children become attuned similarly after they have become involved with a peer group (nursery school). Their circadian rhythms begin to synchronize when they play together. On weekends the cycles more closely approximate the cycles of their parents. Likewise lovers develop concordant patterns of interaction—their pupils dilate (result of autonomic arousal), and their speech patterns become similar as well. Partners create attunement with each other over time. These behavioral and physiological attunements maintain stimulation and arousal modulations—creating a balance of equilibrium and intimacy. See Tiffany Field, "Attachment as Psychobiological Attunement: Being on the Same Wavelength," in *The Psychobiology of Attachment and Separation,* pp. 445–448.

88 pheromones: See Michele Kodis, David T. Moran, and David Berliner, *Love Scents: How Your Pheromones Influence Your Relationships, Your Moods, and Who You Love;* and L. Monti-Bloch, and B. I. Grosser, "Effect of Putative Pheromones on the Electrical Activity of the Human Vomeronasal Organ and Alfactory Epithilium," Journal of Steriod Biochemistry and Molecular Biology 1001 39, no. 48 (1991) pp. 537-582.

88 attachment as a regulatory system: Many researchers converge on this point. According to Hofer, animal studies show that for each response to separation, there is a loss of a specific component of the infant rat's relationship to its mother. In other words, the mother/infant interaction . . . [is] regulatory of a number of systems. See Hofer, "Hidden Regulators," p. 209. Jaak Panksepp states, "distinct neural systems appear to mediate separation distress." See Panksepp, *Biological Psychiatry,* p. 269. Herbert Weiner points out that each target area—muscles, lungs, heart, skin, gut—is controlled by local physiological mechanisms. See Weiner, *Perturbing the Organism.* Paul *McLean* suggests that the affiliative/attachment system is housed within the limbic system, specifically the cingulate gyrus. See McLean, *The Triune Brain in Evolution,* p. 8.

88 factors contributing or co-existing with depression: Neurotransmitters—chemicals that carry messages between the cells of the nervous system—are also involved in depression. The are three most widely associated with the depression. Norepinephrine (NE) is involved in arousing your body's self-defense system and maintaining your heightened state of vigilance. Subjectively you experience this as being anxious and agitated. NE is depleted by stressful situations and the result is depression mixed with anxiety. Dopamine is a neurotransmitter known to mediate the brain's reward and pleasure system, and is believed to be affected by both fear and grief. The neurotransmitter serotonin's impact on self-esteem and mood have been well publicized due to widely prescribed anti-depressant medications such as Prozac. Serotonin levels are related to emotional distress.

For additional information on depression, see Frederic Flack, M.D., *The Secret Strength of Depression;* Candace B. Pert, *Molecules of Emotion;* Peter D. Kramer, *Listening to Prozac;* Sapolsky,

Why Zebras; Aaron Beck, *Anxiety Disorders and Phobias;* David Healy, *The Antidepressant Era.* (See notes 75, 116, and 252.) See also, Hara Estroff Marano, "Depression: Beyond Serotonin," *Psychology Today,* April 1999, pp. 30–76.

88 depression and norepinephrine (NE): consult Jay M. Weiss, "Stress-Induced Depression: Critical Neurochemical and Electrophysiological Changes," in *Neurobiology of Learning, Emotion and Affect.* In addition, the effects of the norepinephrine (and epinephrine, also called adrenaline) secreted during stress are counter-regulated by the opiate system (which include the enkaphalins and endorphins). See Weiner, *Perturbing the Organism,* p. 201.

90 For the allegory of child on the rock, see Susan Anderson, *Black Swan: The Twelve Lessons of Abandonment Recovery,* Part One: "The Little Girl on the Rock," (New York) Rock Foundations Press, 1999.

90 feelings: Another allegory extremely helpful with feelings, particularly fear and sadness, is Hannah Hurnard, *Hind's Feet in High Places.* Antonio Damasio suggests that primary emotions such as fear, sense of loss, etc. are amygdala-based, whereas secondary emotions, such as remorse, jealousy, etc. involve the agency of prefrontal and somatosensory cortices. See Damasio, *Descartes' Error,* p. 134. For an in depth understanding of the origin of feelings, consult LeDoux, "Emotional Brain," pp. 50-57.

91 childhood scenarios of withdrawal: explanation of early insecure attachment is contained in Virginia Colin's work. She points out that childhood loss makes adult grief worse. In one study, a control group of adults going through a separation process were compared to subjects whose childhoods reflected anxious attachments to caretakers. The control group was found to suffer less distress at a time of loss. According to Colin, childhood separation, loss, or threats of abandonment were associated with increased anxiety and depression many years later when the grown woman's husband died. It has been found that if a rat is handled during first weeks, it will secrete less glucocorticoids (associated with anxiety and depressive states) as an adult. (Incidentally, it has been found that optimists have less glucocorticoids during stress.) See Myron Hofer and Robert Sapolsky already cited.

Researchers caution against viewing early childhood precursors in an overly deterministic way. Colin points out that the relationship with parents (an important configuration of attachment theory) is not regarded as the only factor that influences the child's emerging model of self and other. See Colin, *Human Attachment*, p. 302, 338. Michael *Lewis* makes an assertion that it is not the isolated factor of loss of mother that produces later disturbances, but whether the loss of mother constitutes a loss of a significant social contact. He asserts, "children do not possess a preference for social form . . . When motherless monkeys are raised together, . . . they do just fine." See Lewis, *Altering Fate: Why the Past Does Not Predict the Future*, p. 144–149. For more on attachment theory, see Renee A. Spitz, "Hospitalism: An Inquiry into the Genesis of Psychiatric Conditions in Early Childhood," *Psychoanalytic Studies of the Child*, 1, (1945). Mary D. S. Ainsworth, "Infant-Mother Attachment," *American Psychologist*, 43, (1979); Vormbrock, "Attachment Theory," p. 122–144; C. M. Parkes and J. Stevenson-Hinde, *The Place of Attachment in Human Behavior*. For an overview on this subject, see Margaret Talbot, "Attachment Theory: The Ultimate Experiment," *New York Times Magazine*, 24, May 1998, pp. 24-54. For an alternative perspective regarding this subject, consult Harris, *The Nurture Assumption*; and see an overview of pros and cons of attachment theory in Malcolm Gladwell, "Do Parents Matter?" *New Yorker*, 17 August 1998, pp. 54-64.

92 being predisposed to loss and rejection: Kagan explores factors related to "inhibited" and "uninhibited" children in *Galen's Prophecy*. Allan Schore has produced an interesting theoretical context: the human brain develops (cortico-limbic circuits) as a result of child-to-caretaker experiences. See Shore, *Affect Regulation*. (See note 57.)

93 infant macaques: See Hofer, "An Evolutionary Perspective," p. 32.

93 impact of early loss and separation on the brain: Exposing animal infants to early separations from mothers is discussed in McKinney, "Separation and Depression." (See also notes 55, 57, 58, and 125.)

97 hippocampus: for a good overview of the research related to memory see Stephen S. Hall, "Our Memories, Our Selves," *New*

York Times Magazine, 15 February 1998. Also see LeDoux, "Emotion, Memory." Richard *Restak* helps to clarify central role of hippocampus on memory when he stated that fibers from all four lobes converge in the hippocampal region (the area described as the "relay station for memory"). See Restak, *Brainscapes,* p. 14.

98 stress hormones and memories: For extensive research, consult Eric Kandel, *Essentials of Neural Science and Behavior.* Also see Sapolsky, *Why Zebras*; LeDoux, *Emotional Brain*; and LeDoux, "Emotion, Memory."

98 ACTH (adrenocorticotropin hormone): In studies exploring the impact of "repeated separations" on animal infants, researchers found that "ACTH can retard extinction of a previously reinforced behavior, whereas cortisol tends to facilitate extinction and relearning." See Christopher Coe et al., "Endocrine and Immune Response to Separation and Maternal Loss in Nonhuman Primates," in *The Psychobiology of Attachment and Separation,* p. 178.

102 developing a relationship with yourself: See Aleta Koman, *How to Mend a Broken Heart,* p. 93–125.

102 separation therapy: By all means, read the book from which this exercise was taken: See Grace Elish Kirsten, and Richard C. Robertiello, *Big You, Little You, Separation Therapy.* It will provide step by step help with mastering this therapeutic technique.

108 doing exercises gets the whole brain involved: Susan Vaughan states, "When we learn . . . we form new pathways by arborizing our existing neural trees, sprouting new branches (dendrites), which gives rise to new neuronal connections. . . . Brain training (rewiring aberrant brain structures) takes time and the repetition of the useful exercises." To support her hypothesis she cites research that shows the ability of an external event to change internal brain function. In one study they surgically fused two of the monkey's fingers together, so that the two functioned as one. "When the digits were separate, distinct areas of the cortex represented each finger. After the fusion, the cortical representation areas of the third and fourth digits had lost all demarcation from one another—merged into one . . ." See Vaughan, *The Talking Cure,* p. 69–71. This provides support to the idea that when we practice a regimen of exercises on a daily basis, we may be in fact changing brain function and structure, perhaps sprouting new neuronal connections.

CHAPTER FOUR:
INTERNALIZING

121 universality of grief: Darwin said that adult grief had much in common with grief displayed in other species. Extensive research of the animal kingdom corroborates. Symptoms of bereavement in adults are similar to those that occur following the separation of non-human (or human) infants from attachment figures. These symptoms include social withdrawal, sadness, decreased food intake, and sleep disturbance. Researchers David Benton and Paul Brain say that separation-distress and withdrawal from an attached object is associated with crying, irritability, depression, insomnia, and anorexia. The similarity of the symptoms suggests that they reflect common neural mechanisms (including regulation through endogenous opioids). See Benton and Brain, "Opioid Mechanisms."

123 narcissistic injury: For in depth discussion, consult H. Kohut, *The Restoration of the Self*; and O. Kernberg, *Borderline Conditions and Pathological Narcissism. See also* Helen Block Lewis, *Shame and Guilt.*

124 grief's loss/pain: William McKinney describes two commonly observed responses to loss: protest and despair. Protest represents an active response, i.e. crying, motoric demonstrations of grief; and despair (the stage following protest) represents a quiet, withdrawn response, i.e. becoming inactive, socially withdrawn. See McKinney, "Separation and Depression."

124 grief stages: See Kubler-Ross, *Death and Dying;* Bowlby, *Attachment and Loss;* Ainsworth, *Attachments*; and Colin, *Human Attachment.*

124 factors confronting the bereaved: For additional information consult: Hofer, "Hidden Regulators"; Colin, *Human Attachment*; Vormbrock, "Attachment Theory," p. 122-144; R. S. Weiss, *Lone-*

liness: The Experience of Emotional and Social Isolation; and R. S. Weiss, *Marital Separation: Managing After a Marriage Ends.*

126 numbing and shock: (See notes 50 and 59.)

126 anger: (See notes 56 and 63.)

127 ambiguous loss: Pauline Boss: Read *Ambiguous Loss: Learning to Live with Unresolved Grief.*

128 grief work—accepting the pain of loss: For extensive discussions on grief work, consult Bowlby, *Attachment and Loss;* Volumes 1, 2, 3, Basic Books, 1982; Bowlby, John, *Loss, Sadness and Depression; Attachment and Loss, III,* London, 1980; and Kubler-Ross, *On Death and Dying.*

128 necessary losses: Read Judith Viorst, *Necessary Losses.*

128 accepting the temporary nature of the material world: See Rinpoche, *The Tibetan Book.* Also read Pema Chodron, *When Things Fall Apart.*

130 prozac: See Kramer, *Listening to Prozac;* and Richard M. Restak, *Receptors.* It is interesting to note that placebo effect is found to account for a high percentage of improvement in clinical conditions of depression. Comparative studies showed that 73 percent of the improvement among patients treated with antidepressants was duplicated in patients treated by placebo. See Irving Kirsch, and Guy Sapirstein, "Listening to Prozac but Hearing Placebo: A Meta-analysis of Antidepressant Medication," *Prevention & Treatment* 1 (1998); and Irving Kirsch, "Reducing Noise and Hearing Placebo More Clearly," *Prevention and Treatment* 1 (1998). Also see the rebuttal to this in D. F. Klein, "Listening to Meta-analysis But Hearing Bias," *Prevention and Treatment* (1998). Read more on placebo in Blakeslee, "Placebo Prove."

130 subordinating yourself to the abandoner: baboon study is from Robert Sapolsky, "Social Subordinance as a Marker of Hypercortisolism," *Social Subordinance,* p. 634–635.

131 baboons build up stress when they face loss of rank: Ibid., 632.

134 shame of abandonment: The difficulty mitigating the shame of abandonment is emphasized by abandonment guru, Peter Yelton. Jerome Kagan defines shame as stemming from two factors, one which occurs when an individual "believes she had not had a choice over committing a deviation of expectations" (such as losing her relationship through abandonment) and the second which occurs when "others know of the violation" (such as when friends notice the absence of one's mate and observe your isolation). According to Kagan, guilt is developmentally higher than shame because it is cognitively based. When guilt and shame are mixed, they create the painful condition of self-torment (such as that experienced during the internalizing stage of abandonment). See Kagan, *Nature of a Child*, p. 145–147. Also see Michael Lewis, *Shame;* and Helen Block Lewis, *Shame and Guilt.* For a self-help approach, see Bradshaw, *Healing the Shame.*

135 grappling with loss, becoming self examining: See Kubler-Ross, *On Death.*

138 limited capacity to perform the work of conquest: Quotation taken from Michael Balint, *The Basic Fault: Therapeutic Aspects of Regression.* Balint writes about the "basic fault" which he describes mostly in intra-psychic terms, but may be equally explainable in terms of early amygdala-based emotional conditioning, as well, in Alan Schore's terms of orbito-frontal brain development (see notes 55 and 64).

139 immunological issues: See Maier, Watkins, and Fleshner, "Psychoneuroimmunology," Vol. 49, p. 1008. Also see S. J. Shleifer, et al., "Suppression of Lymphocyte Stimulation Following Bereavement," *Journal of the American Medical Association*, Vol. 250, No. 3 (1983) pp. 374-377.

139 people who do not fight back get cancer: See J. J. Eysenck, "Anxiety, Learned Helplessness and Cancer," *Journal of Anxiety Disorders* 1 (1987): p. 87–104.

141 Childhood scenarios creating low self-esteem: Once again, it is important to consider physiological factors that may predispose one to develop low self-esteem or sensitivity to rejection. Donald Klein postulated the existence of psychobiological factors that can cause an individual to experience heightened pain in response to loss. See Donald Klein, "Anxiety Reconceptualized," in *Anxiety: New Research and Changing Concepts,* p. 159–260. Robert Cloninger suggested that people whose levels of norepinephrine (NE) are severely high tend to be highly dependent on emotional supports and intimacy, and highly responsive to social cues and expectations. See Robert Cloninger, "A Unified Biosocial Theory of Personality and its Role in Personality States," *Psychiatric Development* 3 (1986): p. 220–226.

145 for books that deal with issue of self-esteem: See Linda Tschirhardt Sanford and Mary Ellen Donovan, *Women and Self-Esteem;* Nathaniel Branden, *Honoring the Self;* and Stanley Coopersmith, *The Antecedents of Self-Esteem.*

146 need for immediate gratification: During one of his lectures on self-esteem, Sol Gordon emphasized that the "need for immediate gratification" is a key features of low self-esteem. See Sol Gordon, *When Living Hurts.*

148 co-dependent relationships: This issue is clearly defined and thoroughly explored in Melody Beattie, *Codependent No More;* and Charles Whitfield, *Co-Dependence: Healing the Human Condition.*

150 when it all seems to go in circles—overcoming resistance to change: A landmark book exploring the issue of change is Paul Watzlawick, John Weakland, and Richard Risch, *Change: Principles of Problem Formation and Problem Resolution.*

151 visualization: There are many books to aid in this activity, but an excellent foundation for using visualization to achieve success is found in Wallace B. Wattles, *The Science of Getting Rich.* According to Candace Pert, visualization increases blood flow into a body part and increases availability of oxygen and nutrients to carry away toxins and nourish the cells. See Pert, *Molecules,* p. 146.

155 becoming engineer and architect of your life: For excellent support for developing self-acceptance and emotional independence, see David Richo, *How To Be An Adult.*

CHAPTER FIVE:
RAGE

163 rage converted into assertiveness: concept of constructive aggression is from the work of Heinz Hartmann, author of "In Search of Self."

164 rational mind: An insightful synthesis which helps to clarify the question of the "mind" versus the "brain" is offered by Edward Wilson. He refers to the "parallel processing of vast numbers of coding networks" and the "simultaneous internal mapping of multiple sensory impressions," and then asserts: "Who or what within the brain monitors all this activity? No one. Nothing. The scenarios are not seen by some other part of the brain. They just *are.*" Wilson, *Consilience,* pp. 108–115.

164 anger: This discussion is based on the excellent extrapolation of the psychobiology of anger in Daniel Goleman, *Emotional Intelligence,* p. 59–65.

164 two waves of arousal: See Dolf Zillman, "Mental Control of Angry Aggression," in Handbook of Mental Control, p. 373. See also Diane Tice and Roy Baumeister, "Self Induced Emotion Change" in Handbook of Mental Control, pp. 393-401. Goleman referenced many of his comments to Zillman.

166 amygdala as a 'neural name that tune': See Goleman, *Emotional Intelligence*, p. 24.

166 subcortical route to amygdala: See LeDoux, "Emotion, Memory."

166 neocortex: Taken from Goleman, *Emotional Intelligence*, p. 25. According to Antonio Damasio there is an interdependency of emotion and reason. He states, "Emotions are a direct sensing of our own body states, a link between body's survival oriented regulations and consciousness." See Damasio, *Descartes' Error*. See also discussion about neo-cortex and frontal lobes in Kagan, *Galen's Prophecy.*

168 strangling the steering wheel: Metaphor borrowed from Goleman, *Emotional Intelligence,* p. 59.

175 amor fati: a concept found in Irvin Yalom, *When Nietzsche Wept.* In his novel, a protagonist makes an ultimate life-adjustment by learning to *choose his fate (amor fati).*

178 anger is energizing: This discussion is based on Daniel Goleman, *Emotional Intelligence,* p. 59.

180 forgiveness: The benefits of *forgiveness* are discussed in John Amodeo and Charles Whitfield, *Love and Betrayal.*

181 expressing your anger toward the person: Here is an interesting if unwelcome piece of information: According to Sapolsky, when baboons are able to displace their anger on lower ranking members of the troupe, they accumulate lower glucocorticoid levels. In other words, when they're angry, it's good for their health to kick the dog, so to speak. See Sapolsky, "Why Zebras."

181 the ability to be separate: a concept emphasized in personal dialogues with psychoanalyst and author Richard Robertiello. See "Sado-masochism as a Defense Against Merging," Robertiello and Terril Gagnier. Margaret Mahler has written extensively on this subject. See M. Mahler and R. Pine, "The Psychological Birth of Human Infant" and M. Mahler, "On Human Symbiosis."

183 to avoid people-pleasing and other codependent difficulties: Excellent resources are: Beattie, *Codependent No More;* and Charles Whitfield, *Co-Dependence: Healing the Human Condition.*

185 evolution and modern stress: This discussion was taken from Sapolsky, *Why Zebras.*

185 posttraumatic features of anger: See Van der Kolk, McFarlane, and Weisaeth, *Traumatic Stress,* p. 217. See note 56 regarding Colin's study of separated couples who committed uncharacteristic acts of vengeance toward one another. Or see Colin, *Human Attachment,* p. 340.

185 depression: If indeed depression can be seen as anger turned inward, then according to Sapolsky, the depressed individual is "fighting an enormous aggressive mental battle—similar to an animal sprinting across the savannah." This description represents a highly active state involving psychomotor retardation, impulse to self murder, elevated stress hormone levels, increased metabolic rate; the individual is exhausted from a "draining, internal emotional conflict going on within." All quotes are from Sapolsky, *Why Zebras,* p. 201, 217.

186 stress hormones and depression: Seligman's work explores the connection between helplessness (lack of control) and depression. See Seligman, *Helplessness.* For additional discussion about the relationship between depression, anxiety, and the glucocorticoids, consult Flack, *The Secret Strength,* p. 222; Kramer, *Listening to Prozac,* p. 378; Sapolsky, *Why Zebras,* p. 252; and Pert, *Molecules* p. 271–192. For a general text on depression, consult Beck, *Anxiety Disorders.* Also consult Healy, *The Antidepressant Era.*

186 responsiveness of antidepressants: Separation can have the same symptoms as endogenous depression and can respond to the same medications. Specifically, drugs that affect neurotransmitter systems interact with separation. McKinney, "Separation and Depression."

186 natural pharmacopoeia: Pert, *Molecules,* p. 271.

187 hormonal changes caused by stress: Much of these changes were mentioned in Sapolsky, *Why Zebras,* p. 33, 39, 110, 168. For a discussion about the role of glucocorticoids related to immune response, see Maier, Watkins, Fleshner, "Psychoneuroimmunology."

189 frontal lobes: Much has been written about lesions in the frontal lobes and their affect on personality. They are, as Goleman put it, your brain's "emotional managers." This is the region located just behind your forehead in which you coordinate and respond to a wide range of information. They receive internal information from your amygdala, from your memory banks, as well as from the environment. It is where you are able to make sense of a situation, grasp its meaning, manage your emotional response, and organize your actions toward a goal.

The frontal lobes work hand in hand with your amygdala and other structures within the emotional system—they have neuron circuits leading to the amygdala and back. Many of you have heard about an outdated surgical procedure called a lobotomy in which the prefrontal lobes were removed or disconnected from the rest of the brain. The well-intentioned goal was to alleviate severe emotional distress. Unfortunately the person suffered a total lack of emotional responsiveness to life.

Your right frontal lobe is the domain of negative emotions— anger, fear, sadness—while the left frontal lobe is responsible for dampening the impact of those negative feelings. They work together in concert with the emotional brain to regulate your emotional life. People who have suffered strokes to their *left* frontal lobe are unable to regulate anger and fear and are prone to catastrophic worries. If their *right* frontal lobe is damaged, they show an *absence of negative emotion,* and are according to Goleman, "unduly cheerful, joking around during their neurological exams, seemingly unconcerned about the results" (anecdote taken from Goleman, *Emotional Intelligence,* p. 26).

Also see Damasio, *Descartes' Error,* p. 54-61, 71. His collected evidence shows an interactive link between emotion and working memory. Also see Oliver Sacks, *The Man Who Mistook His Wife for a Hat;* and Oliver Sacks, *An Anthropologist on Mars.* Also, read a lucid synthesis on the subject in Goleman, *Emotional Intelligence,* p. 25.

189 inner child: The seminal work was in Kirsten, G. and R. Robertiello, *Big You.* For additional discussion see John Bradshaw, *Homecoming: Reclaiming and Championing Your Inner Child.*

189 outer child: Abandonment guru Peter Yelton CSW nurtured the development of this concept.

CHAPTER SIX:
LIFTING

213 letting go: Viktor Frankl's personal account testifies to the capacity for human beings to let go of pain from the past and gain wisdom and strength from it. See Viktor Frankl, *Man's Search for Meaning.* Also see Morrie Schwartz, *Letting Go.*

214 parasympathetic nervous system (PNS): For one reference explaining the workings of this complementary branch of the autonomic nervous system, consult Restak, *Receptors.* Also see Damasio, *Descartes' Error.* To explain the role of PNS and acetylcholine's affect on sleeping and dreaming, see Hobson, *Dreaming Brain*.

215 joggers hitting the wall: Flack, Frederic, M. D. *The Secret Strength of Depression*, p. 218.

215 opiate reduction following birth: See Panksepp, Siviy, and Normansell, "Brain Opioids."

218 the dangers of lifting above: Paul Ekman conducted experiments which I interpret to suggest the futility of pretending about one's feelings. He had subjects perform facial expressions, i.e. of happiness, which led to happy feelings. But one of his significant findings was that the make-believe smiles produced different *patterns of brain waves* from real smiles, signifying that the internal experience is different. This suggests to me that one can improve one's mood by acting as if, but one cannot eliminate the reality of one's true emotional response to life. Paul Ekman, "Facial Expressions of Emotion: New Findings, New Questions," *Psychological Science* 3 (1992): pp. 34–38,

221 lifters who lack empathy: See Ken Magid, and Carole A. McKelvey, *High Risk Children without a Conscience*.

225 parents passing their inner child wounds along to their children: See Alice Miller, *The Drama of the Gifted Child*. Transgenerational dynamics is central to the work of family therapist, Murray Bowen. See his book *Family Therapy*.

226 parents and self-esteem: Several recommended books are Louise Hart, *The Winning Family;* Haim G. Ginott, *Between Parent and Child*. H. C. Clemes, and Reynold Bean, *How to Raise Children's Self-Esteem;* Richard Robertiello, *Hold Them Very Close, Then Let Them Go*. For a slightly different view of parenting, see Michael Lewis, *Altering Fate* in which the author suggests that children are not destined by biology or parents. The controversy over how much impact parents have upon children's development rages on. See Harris, *The Nurture Assumption;* and for a report on originators of this point of view, read Gladwell, "Do Parents Matter?" (See note 124.)

226 losing and finding a lost part of yourself: the process of self discovery is covered in Robert Moore and Douglas Gillette, *The*

Lover Within—written mostly from a men's movement point of view, its principles are applicable to all of those who are regaining their ability to experience their deepest human needs and feelings.

227 loosening the bonds: This phrase comes from Weiner, *Perturbing the Organism,* p. 76.

227 shame of feeling so much pain: Kagan, in *The Nature of the Child,* discusses the shame associated with prolonged suffering. (See notes 48 and 49.)

231 the decision to find a replacement: Roy Baumeister advances a "substitution theory." He reports that re-marriage tends to eliminate many negative consequences of divorce. His research suggests that substitute partners help to mitigate the traumatic impact of one's separation experience. "When new relationships fail to form, the emotional distress associated with the [ex-spouse] may actually increase rather than decrease over time . . . implying that substitution is an effective way of recovering from relationship dissolution." Baumeister and Leary, "Need to Belong," p. 516. John Bowlby supports the notion of "replacement" or "substitution" in his observation that children's anxiety over separation from their mothers seemed to be greatly reduced if they were accompanied by a familiar other person at the time.

From a different perspective, Vormbrock, describing the protest, despair, and detachment cycle of "separation grief," refers to a research study suggesting that when a primary object is lost (unlike finding a substitute primary object), friends and supportive family were not sufficient to mitigate the anxiety associated with separation from the primary object. See Vormbrock, "Attachment Theory," p. 123.

231 letting go of shame: See John Bradshaw, *Healing the Shame.*

236 finding a quality relationship: For interesting perspectives read Allan Fromme, *The Ability to Love;* and Michael Sky, *Sexual Peace: Beyond the Dominator Virus.*

241 romantic love: at the biochemical level romantic love—in addition to the endogenous opiates—involves *oxytocin*, a neurochemical that has been implicated as the bonding chemical. It has been called the *interpersonal* hormone. According to researcher

John Capitanio it is involved in milk ejection, uterine contraction, and sperm transport. It has been known to disrupt memory consolidation (so women can forget the intense pain of childbirth); there is evidence that human infants release it during labor. See John Capitanio, Michael Weissberg, and Martin Reite, "Biology of Maternal Behavior," in *Psychobiology of Attachment and Separation*, p. 68. Damasio adds that oxytocin is released during stimulation of the genitals and nipples, or orgasm . . . It influences a whole range of grooming, locomotion, sexual, and maternal behaviors. But most significantly, it facilitates social interaction and induces bonding between mating partners. See Damasio, *Descartes' Error*, p. 122.

242 the familiar emotional set up—getting used to it: According to Sapolsky organisms will habituate to a stressor if it is applied over and over because it is predictable by then, and triggers a smaller stress response. See Sapolsky, *Why Zebras*, pp. 213-215.

246 addicted to infatuation: Virginia Colin suggests that there are similarities between adolescent romantic love (in which our culture is steeped) and infant-to-caregiver attachment. The adolescent's (or adult's) mood depends on his perception of whether his desired object is responsive or rejecting; "just as the baby's feeling of joy and distress depends on his perceptions of [mother's] availability or responsiveness (parentheses mine)." See Virginia Colin, *Human Attachment*, p. 297. See also Field, "Attachment."

248 security: For a look at the formation of security based relationships see Vormbrock. She suggests that there are two basic psychobiological systems involved in human bonds—the caregiving system and the attachment system. For example, it is possible that a person has difficulties depending on others (avoidant attachment style) but is quite comfortable with others depending upon him or her (secure caregiving style). The combination of attachment and caregiving styles might characterize adults who tend not to initiate intimacy unless their partner feels helpless and is in need of emotional reassurance. See Vormbrock, "Attachment Theory," p. 122–144.

249 the validity of falling in love: Two willing partners can create attunement with each other over time through physical proximity, sharing goals and life's mission. Arranged marriages are practiced throughout much of the non-Western world, and many believe these arrangements are more successful than the marriages based on falling in love. For a discussion of how attachment is formed— through physical proximity, sharing life goals, etc., consult Colin, *Human Attachment.*

250 capacity for love: Excellent resources include: Fromm, *The Art of Loving;* and Diane Ackerman, *A Natural History of Love.* For additional perspectives see Marianne Williamson, *A Return to Love;* and Harville Hendrix, *Getting the Love You Want.*

251 making the connection: Read Bob Greene and Oprah Winfrey, *Make the Connection: Ten Steps to a Better Body and Mind.*

CHAPTER SEVEN:
MAKING A NEW CONNECTION

267 initiating new contacts: for some fun reading and practical advice, read Sharyn Wolf, *Guerilla Dating Tactics: Strategies, Tips and Secrets for Finding Romance.*

268 alter ego: The concept of alter ego (which literally means "other eye") is traced back to Cicero, meant to refer to "other" or "second" self. See *Webster's Unabridged Dictionary,* 2nd ed., "alter ego."

Bibliography

S OME of the following references relate to lay readers, some are academic works aimed at professionals, and still others are novels I recommend to clients to help them identify their feelings. In some areas I've included two works on the same subject, representing different positions in an ongoing theoretical debate.

Ackerman, Diane. *A Natural History of Love.* New York: Vintage Books, 1995.

——. *A Natural History of the Senses.* New York: Random House, 1990.

Ainsworth, Mary D. S. "Infant-Mother Attachment." *American Psychologist*: 43 (1979).

——. "Attachments and Other Affectional Bonds Across the Life Cycle." In *Attachments Across the Life Cycle.* New York: Routledge, 1991.

Amodeo, John, and Charles Whitfield, *Love and Betrayal.* New York: Ballantine Books, 1994.

Anderson, Susan. *Black Swan: The Twelve Lessons of Abandonment Recovery.* New York: Rock Foundations Press, 1999.

Andre, Rae. *Positive Solitude*. New York: HarperCollins, 1991.

Balint, Michael. *The Basic Fault: Therapeutic Aspects of Regression*. Evanston: North Western University Press, 1992.

Baumeister, Roy F. and Mark R. Leary, "The Need to Belong: Desire for Interpersonal Attachments as a Fundamental Human Motivation." *Psychological Bulletin* (1995).

Beattie, Melody. *Codependent No More*. Center City: Hazelden, 1987.

Beck, Aaron. *Anxiety Disorders and Phobias*. New York: Basic Books, 1990.

Benton, David, and Paul F. Brain, "The Role of Opioid Mechanisms in Social Interaction and Attachment." In *Behavioral Processes*, edited by R. J. Rodgers and S. J. Cooper. New York: John Wiley and Sons, Inc. 1988.

Blakeslee, Sandra, "Placebo Prove So Powerful Even Experts are Surprised," *New York Times, Science Times* 13 October 1998.

Boss, Pauline. *Ambiguous Loss: Learning to Live with Unresolved Grief*. Cambridge: Harvard University Press, 1999.

Bowen, Murry. *Family Therapy*. New York: J. Aronson, 1978.

Bowlby, John. "The Nature of the Child's Tie to his Mother." *International Journal of Psycho-analysis* 39 (1958).

———. *Loss: Sadness and Depression; Attachment and Loss, III*, Basic Books, 1982.

Branden, Nathaniel. *Honoring the Self*. New York: Bantam Books, 1983.

Bradshaw, John. *Healing the Shame that Binds You*. Deerfield Beach: Health Communications, 1988.

———. *Homecoming: Reclaiming and Championing Your Inner-Child*. Bantam Doubleday Dell, 1992.

Capitanio, John, Michael Weissberg, and Martin Reite. "Biology of Maternal Behavior." In *Psychobiology of Attachment and Separation,* edited by Martin Reite and Tiffany Field. San Diego: Academic Press, 1986.

Chodron, Pema. *When Things Fall Apart*. Boston: Shambhala, 1997.

Clemes, H. C., and Reynold Bean. *How to Raise Children's Self-Esteem*. New York: Price Stern Sloan, 1978.

Cloninger, Robert. "A Unified Biosocial Theory of Personality and its Role in Personality States." *Psychiatric Development* 4, no. 3 (1986) 167–226.

Coe, Christopher, Sandra Wiener, Leon Rosenbert, and Seymour Levine. "Endocrine and Immune Response to Separation and Maternal Loss in Nonhuman Primates." In *The Psychobiology of Attachment and Separation,* edited by Martin Reite and Tiffany Field. San Diego: Academic Press, 1985.

Colin, Virginia A. *Human Attachment.* Philadelphia: Temple University Press, 1996.

Coopersmith, Stanley. *The Antecedents of Self-Esteem.* San Francisco: W. H. Freeman and Company, 1967.

Damasio, Antonio. *Descartes' Error: Emotion, Reason, and the Human Brain.* New York: A Grosset/Putnam Book, 1994.

Decasper, A. J., and W. P. Fif. "Of Human Bonding: Newborns Prefer Their Mother's Voices," *Science* 208, no. 4448 (June 6, 1980).

Edelman, Hope. *Motherless Daughters.* New York: Delta, 1974.

Ekman, Paul. "Facial Expressions of Emotion: New Findings, New Questions," *Psychological Science* 3, no. 1 (1992) 34–38.

Eysenck, J. J., "Anxiety, Learned Helplessness and Cancer," *Journal of Anxiety Disorders* 1 (1987) 87–104.

Field, Tiffany, "Attachment as Psychobiological Attunement: Being on the Same Wavelength." In *The Psychobiology of Attachment and Separation.* San Diego: Academic Press, 1985.

Flack, Frederic, M.D. *The Secret Strength of Depression.* New York: Bantam, 1988.

Fox, Nathan, A. "Behavioral Antecedents of Attachment in High-Risk Infants." In *The Psychobiology of Attachment and Separation*, edited by Martin Reite and Tiffany Field. San Diego: Academic Press, 1985

Frankl, Viktor. *Man's Search for Meaning.* New York: Pocket.

Freud, Sigmund. *Mourning and Melancholia.* 1917.

Friday, Nancy. *My Mother Myself.* New York: Delacort Press, 1977.

Fromm, Eric. *The Art of Loving.* New York: HarperCollins, 1989.

Fromme, Allan. *The Ability to Love.* New York: Pocket Books, 1965.

Gershon, Michael D. *The Second Brain.* New York: HarperCollins, 1998.

Ginott, Haim, G. *Between Parent and Child.* New York: Avon Books, 1969.

Gladwell, Malcolm. "Do Parents Matter?" *New Yorker*, 17 August 1998, pp. 54-64.

Goleman, Daniel. *Emotional Intelligence*. New York: Bantam Books, 1995.

Gordon, Sol. *When Living Hurts*. New York: Dell Publishing, 1983.

Gossette, Robert L., and Richard M. O'Brien. "The Efficacy of Rational Emotive Therapy in Adults: Clinical Fact or Psychometric Artifact?" *Journal of Behavior Therapy and Experimental Psychiatry* 23, no. 1 (1992) 9–24.

———. "Irrational Beliefs and Maladjustment: When are Psychometric Effects Clinically Meaningful?" Paper presented at 1990 Convention of American Psychological Association, Boston, Mass., August 11, 1990.

Greene, Bob and Oprah Winfrey. *Make the Connection: Ten steps to a Better Body and Mind*. New York: Hyperion, 1999.

Hall, Stephen S., "Our Memories, Our Selves," *New York Times Magazine*, 15 February 1998, pp. 26-57.

Harris, Judith. *The Nurture Assumption: Why Children Turn Out The Way They Do*. New York: The Free Press, 1998.

Hart, Louise. *The Winning Family*. New York: Dodd, Mead & Company, 1987.

Hartmann, Heinz. *In the Service to Others: Reflections of a Retired Physician on Medicine, the Bible and the Jews*. Prometheus Books, 1988.

Healy, David. *The Antidepressant Era*. Cambridge: Harvard University Press, 1997.

Hendrix, Harville. *Getting the Love You Want*. New York: Henry Holt & Company, 1988.

Herman, Judith Lewis. *Trauma and Recovery*. Basic Books, 1992.

Hobson, J. Allan. *The Dreaming Brain*. New York: Basic Books, 1988.

Hofer, Myron. "An Evolutionary Perspective on Anxiety." In *Anxiety as Symptom and Signal*, edited by S. Roose and R. Glick. Hillsdale: Analytic Press, 1995.

———. "Hidden Regulators, Implications for a New Understanding of Attachment, Separation, and Loss." In *Attachment Theory: Social, Developmental and Clinical Perspectives, edited by S. Goldberg, R. Muir, and J. Kerr)*. Hillsdale: Analytic Press, 1995.

Hurnard, Hannah. *Hind's Feet in High Places*. Illinois: Living Books, 1975.

Kabat-Zinn, Jon. *Full Catastrophe Living*. New York: Delta, 1990.

Kagan, Jerome. *Galen's Prophecy*. New York: Basic Books, 1994.

―――. *The Nature of a Child*. New York: Basic Books, 1984.

Kandel, Eric. *Essentials of Neural Science and Behavior*. Appleton: Appleton and Lange, 1995.

Kandel, Eric, James Schwartz, and Thomas Jesse, eds. *Principles of Neural Science*. Appleton and Lange, 1992.

Kelly, D. D. "Stress-induced Analgesia," *Annals of the New York Academy of Sciences* 1986.

Kernberg, O. *Borderline Conditions and Pathological Narcissism*. Northvale: Aronson, 1975.

Kiecolt-Glaser, J.K., L.D. Fisher, P. Ogrocki, J.C. Stout, C.E. Speicher, and R. Glaser. "Marital Quality, Marital Disruption, and Immune Function." *Psychosomatic Medicine* 49, no. 1 (1987).

Kirsch, Irving. "Reducing Noise and Hearing Placebo More Clearly." *Prevention and Treatment* 1 (1998).

Kirsch, Irving and Guy Sapirstein. "Listening to Prozac but Hearing Placebo: A Meta-Analysis of Antidepressant Medication." *Prevention & Treatment* 1 (1998).

Kirsten, Grace Elish and Richard C. Robertiello. *Big You Little You, Separation Therapy*. New York: Dial Press, 1977.

Klein, D. F. "Listening to Meta-analysis But Hearing Bias." *Prevention and Treatment* (1998).

Klein, Donald. "Anxiety Reconceptualized." In *Anxiety: New Research and Changing Concepts,* edited by Donald Klein and Judith Rabkin. Philadelphia: Raven Press, 1981.

Klein, Melanie. *Love, Guilt, and Reparation and Other Works 1921–1945*. New York: Free Press, 1984.

―――. "On the Theory of Anxiety and Guilt." In *Envy and Gratitude and Other Works 1946–1963*. New York: Delacorte Press, 1975.

Kodis, Michele, David T. Moran, and David Berliner. *Love Scents: How Your Pheromones Influence Your Relationships, Your Moods, and Who You Love*. New York: E.P. Dutton, 1998.

Koman, Aleta. *How to Mend a Broken Heart*. Raleigh: Contemporary Publishing, 1997.

Kohut, H. *The Restoration of the Self.* Madison: International Universities Press, 1977.

Kramer, Peter. *Listening to Prozac.* New York: Penguin Books, 1992.

Kroll, Jerome. *PTSD—Borderlines in Therapy: Finding the Balance.* New York: W.W. Norton and Company, 1993.

Kubler-Ross, Elisabeth. *On Death and Dying.* New York: Simon and Schuster, 1969.

LeDoux, Joseph. "Emotion, Memory and the Brain." *Scientific American* (June 1994).

———. *Emotional Brain.* New York: Simon and Schuster, 1996.

Lewis, Helen Block. *Shame and Guilt in Neurosis.* Madison: International Universities Press, 1971.

Lewis, Michael. *Shame: The Exposed Self.* New York: The Free Press, 1992.

———. *Altering Fate: Why the Past Does Not Predict the Future.* New York: Guilford Press, 1998.

Madden, John, ed. *Neurobiology of Learning, Emotion and Affect.* New York: Raven Press, 1991.

Magid, Ken, and Carole A. McKelvey, *High Risk Children Without a Conscience.* New York: Bantam Books, 1987.

Mahler, Margaret. *On Human Symbiosis and the Vicissitudes of Individuation.* Vol 1 of *Infantile Psychoses.* Madison: International Universities Press, 1968.

Mahler, M. S. and Pine, R. and Bergman, A. *The Psychological Birth of the Human Infant.* New York: Basic Books, 1975.

Maier, Steven F., Linda R. Watkins, and Monika Fleshner. "Psychoneuroimmunology: The Interface Between Behavior, Brain and Immunity," *American Psychologist,* Vol. 49 (December 1994) pp. 1004-1017.

Marano, Hara Estroff. "Depression: Beyond Serotonin." *Psychology Today,* April 1999, 30–76.

McKinney, William T. "Separation and Depression: Biological Markers." In *The Psychobiology of Attachment and Separation,* edited by Martin Reite and Tiffany Field. San Diego: Academic Press, 1985.

McLean, Paul. *The Triune Brain in Evolution.* New York: Plenum Press, 1990.

Merker, Hannah. *Silences.* New York: HarperCollins, 1994.

Miller, Alice. *The Drama of the Gifted Child.* New York: Basic Books, 1997.

Monti-Bloch, L. and B. I. Grosser. "Effect of putative pheronomes on the electrical activity of the human vomeronasal organ and alfactory epithilium." *Journal of Steroid Biochemistry and Molecular Biology 1001*, 39, no. 48: 537-582.

Moore, Robert, and Douglas Gillette. *The Lover Within*. New York: W. Morrow, 1993.

Ornstein, Robert, and Richard F. Thompson. *The Amazing Brain*. Boston: Houghton Mifflin Company, 1984

Panksepp, Jaak, and Stephen M. Siviy and Lawrence A. Normansell. *"Brain Opioids and Social Emotions."* In *The Psychobiology of Attachment and Separation,* edited by Martin Reite and Tiffany Field. San Diego: Academic Press, 1985.

Panksepp, Jaak. *Advances in Biological Psychiatry*. Vol 1. Greenwich: JAI Press, 1995.

———. "The Emotional Brain and Biological Psychiatry." In *Advances in Biological Psychiatry*, 269–286. Greenwich: J.A.I. Press, 1996.

Panksepp, Jaak, Eric Nelson, and Marni Bekkedal. "Brain Systems for the Mediation of Separation Distress and Social Reward." *Annals NY Academy of Sciences* 807 (1997) 78–100.

Parkes, C. M., and J. Stevenson-Hinde. *The Place of Attachment in Human Behavior*. New York: Basic Books, 1982.

Parkes, C. M., J. Stevenson-Hinde, and P. Marris, *Attachments Across the Life Cycle*. New York: Routledge, 1991.

Pavlov, I. V. *Conditioned Reflexes*. Mineola: Dover Publications, 1922.

Pert, Candace B. *Molecules of Emotion*. New York: Scribner, 1997.

Pollan, Michael. "Second Nature." *Atlantic Monthly Press*, 1991.

———. *A Place of My Own: The Education of an Amateur Builder*. New York: Dell, 1998.

Real, Terrance. *I don't Want to Talk About It*. New York: Scribner, 1997.

Rensberger, Boyce. *Life Itself: Exploring the Realm of the Living Cell*. New York: Oxford University Press, 1996.

Restak, Richard M. *Receptors*. New York: Bantam Books, 1994.

———. *Brainscapes: An Introduction to What Neuroscience has Learned about the Structure, Function and Abilities of the Brain*. New York: Hyperion, 1996.

Richo, David. *How To Be An Adult.* New York: Paulist Press, 1991.

Rinpoche, Sogyal, *The Tibetan Book of Living and Dying.* San Francisco: Harper, 1994.

Robertiello, Richard. *Hold Them Very Close, Then Let Them Go.* New York: Dial, 1975.

Robertiello, Richard, and Terril T. Gagnier, PhD. "Sado-masochism as a Defense Against Merging: Six Case Studies." *Journal of Contemporary Psychotherapy* 23, no. 3 (1993) pp. 183-192.

Robertiello, Richard, and Hollace M. Beer, M.S.W. "Bulimia as a Failure in Separation." *Journal of Contemporary Psychotherapy* 23, no. 1 (1993), pp. 41-45.

Ruden, Ronald A., and Marcia Byalick. *The Craving Brain: The Biobalance Approach to Controlling Addiction.* New York: HarperCollins, 1997.

Sacks, Oliver. *The Man Who Mistook his Wife for a Hat.* Summit 1985.

————. *An Anthropologist on Mars.* New York: Knopf, 1995.

Sanford, Linda Tschirhardt, and Mary Ellen Donovan. *Women and Self-Esteem.* London: Penguin Books, 1985.

Sapolsky, Robert M. *Why Zebras Don't Get Ulcers.* New York: W. H. Freeman and Company, 1994.

————. "Social Subordinance as a Marker of Hypercortisolism," Social Subordinance, Annals New York Academy of Sciences, pp. 626-638.

Schleifer, S. J., S. E. Keller, M. Camerino, J. C. Thornton, and M. Stein. "Suppression of Lymphocyte Stimulation Following Bereavement." *Journal of the American Medical Association,* Vol. 250, No. 3 (1983), pp. 374-377.

Schore, Allan. *Affect Regulation and Origin of Self: The Neurobiology of Emotional Development.* Mahwah: Lawrence Erlbaum Associates, 1994.

Schwartz, Morrie. *Letting Go.* New York: Walker and Company, 1996.

Seiver, Larry J., and William Frucht. *The New View of Self: How Genes and Neurotransmitters Shape Your Mind, Your Personality and Your Mental Health.* New York: MacMillan, 1997.

Seligman, Martin. *Helplessness: On Depression, Development and Death.* San Francisco: W. H. Freeman, 1975.

Serra, G., Collu, M. and G. L. Gessa. "Endorphins and Sexual Behavior." In *Endorphins, Opiates and Behavioral Processes.* New York: John Wiley & Sons, Inc. 1988, pp. 237-247.

Selye, Hans. *Advances in Psychonuroimmunology,* edited by Istvan Berczi and Judith Szelenyi. New York: Plenum Press, 1994.

Sky, Michael. *Sexual Peace: Beyond the Dominator Virus.* Santa Fe: Bear and Company, 1993.

Smotherman, William P., and Scott R. Robinson. "The Development of Behavior Before Birth." *Developmental Psychology* 32 (May 1996): 425–434.

Spitz, Renee A. "Hospitalism: An Inquiry into the Genesis of Psychiatric Conditions in Early Childhood." *Psychoanalytic Studies of the Child* 1 (1945).

Stanford, S. C., and P. Salmon, *Stress: From Synapse to Syndrome.* San Diego: Academic Press, 1993.

Storr, Anthony. *Solitude: A Return to the Self.* New York: Ballantine, 1988.

Suomi, Stephen. "Early Stress and Adult Emotional Reactivity in Rhesus Monkeys." In *The Childhood Environment and Adult Disease.* John Wiley and Sons, Inc. 1991.

Suomi, Stephen, J. "Primate Separation Models of Affective Disorders." In *Neurobiology of Learning, Emotion and Affect,* edited by John Madden IV. Philadelphia: Raven Press, 1991.

Talbot, Margaret. "Attachment Theory: The Ultimate Experiment." *New York Times Magazine* 24 May 1998, pp. 24-54.

Tavris, Carol. *Anger: The Misunderstood Emotion.* New York: Touchstone, 1989.

Tice, Diane and Baumeister, Roy. "Self Induced Emotion Change," *Handbook of Mental Control,* edited by C. M. Wegner and J. W. Pennebaker. Prentice Hall, 1992.

Van der Kolk, Bessel A., Alexander C. McFarlane, and Lars Weisaeth. *Traumatic Stress: The Effects of Overwhelming Experience on Mind, Body, and Society.* New York: Guilford Press, 1996.

Vaughan, Susan. *The Talking Cure: The Science Behind Psychotherapy.* New York: Grosset/Putnam, 1997.

Viorst, Judith. *Necessary Losses.* New York: Simon and Schuster, 1986.

Vormbrock, Julia K. "Attachment Theory as Applied to Wartime and Job-Related Marital Separation." *Psychological Bulletin,* 114 (1993): 122–144.

Wapner, S., Ciottone, R., Hornstein, G., McNeil, O., and Pacheco, A. M. (1983). An examination of Studies of critical transitions through the Life Cycle, In, S. Wapner and B. Kaplan (Eds.), *Toward a Holistic Developmental Psychology.* New Jersey: Erlbaum, pp. 111-132.

Wattles, Wallace B. *The Science of Getting Rich.* 7th ed. Pinellas Park: Top of the Mountain Publications, 1996.

Watzlawick, Paul, John Weakland, and Richard Risch. *Change: Principles of Problem Formation and Problem Resolution.* New York: W. W. Norton & Company, 1974.

Weiner, H., M.A. Hofer, and A. J. Stunkard, *Brain, Behavior and Bodily Disease.* New York: Raven Press, 1981.

Weiner, Herbert. *Perturbing the Organism: The Biology of Stressful Experience.* Chicago: University of Chicago Press, 1992.

Weiss, Jay M., "Stress-Induced Depression: Critical Neurochemical and Electrophysiological Changes." In *Neurobiology of Learning, Emotion and Affect,* edited by John Madden. New York: Raven Press, 1991.

Weiss, R. S. *Loneliness: The Experience of Emotional and Social Isolation.* Cambridge: MIT Press, 1973.

————. *Marital Separation: Managing after a Marriage Ends.* New York: Basic Books, 1975.

Whitfield, Charles. *Co-Dependence: Healing the Human Condition.* Deerfield Beach: Health Communications, 1991.

Williamson, Marianne. *A Return to Love.* New York: HarperCollins, 1996.

Wilson, E. O. *Consilience: The Unity of Knowledge.* New York: Knopf, 1998.

Winnecott, Donald W. "The Capacity to be Alone." In *The Maturational Processes and the Facilitating Environment: Studies in the Theory of Emotional Development.* Madison: International Universities Press, 1965.

Wise, Roy, A. "The Neurobiology of Craving: Implications for the Understanding and Treatment of Addiction." *Journal of Abnormal Psychology* 97 no. 2 (1988), pp. 118-132.

Wolf, Sharyn. *Guerilla Dating Tactics: Strategies, Tips and Secrets for Finding Romance.* New York: Plume, 1994.

Wolff, P. H. "The Serial Organization of Sucking in the Young Infant." *Pediatrics* 42 (1968), pp. 943-956.

Yalom, Irvin. *When Nietzsche Wept.* New York: Basic Books, 1992.

Zillman, Dolf. "Mental Control of Angry Aggression" In *Handbook of Mental Control*, edited by C. M. Wegner and J. W. Pennebaker. New Jersey: Prentice Hall, 1992.

A VERY special group of people provided the wisdom and the substance for this book—my clients. They have taught me how the human spirit can triumph over profound loss and despair. Their voices tell the real story of abandonment and recovery.

I am deeply grateful to my son Adam, my daughter Erika, and Paul for their love, patience and willingness to 'endure abandonment' while I wrote this book; my father Dexter Griffith for imbuing me with creative determination, my mother for her steady beacon of support, my sister Marcia Gerardi, and my brothers, Dexter and Robert Griffith for their love and devotion; their mates Mark Gerardi, Karen Griffith, and Randy Davis, and the cousins, Jessica Gerardi, Kristi, Dylan, and Bryan Griffith; Paul's children, Alex, Jesse Mark, and Laura Cohen; Jill Mackey, Carole Ann Price, and Patricia Malone, for their constant encouragement; and Dilys and Keith Purdy, who helped look after my flock so that I could attend to the writing.

Special gratitude to Peter Yelton, who is my abandonment

guru. Profound and prophetic, Peter is the ultimate abandonment survivor. He let me freely use his wisdom, indifferent to receiving credit. In many places I have used his words. The only thing that matters to him is life experience and human relationship—the priorities of a true sage.

I owe a debt of gratitude to Robert Gosset for his help with the scientific portions of the manuscript. He led me to the relevant primary resources and helped clear up many clouds and confusions.

Special dedication to Carrie who had all the love and affection any child could want. She motivated me to go beyond my own field, searching the recesses of brain science, anthropology, and philosophy to try to understand why she would inadvertantly abandon herself.

I would also like to acknowledge the public figures who have shared the legacies of their own childhood abandonments with us. They reflect the wisdom that can come from the hardest emotional lessons in life.

I am grateful to Teresa Kennedy, who helped get the project launched, Susan Golomb for believing in it and placing the manuscript in good hands, and Lisa Considine whose insight, vision, and excellent help with the manuscript carried the project to completion. I am also grateful to Richard Robertiello, M.D., for his invaluable advice and support during the trials and tribulations; Edward Kannel, who encouraged my writing during my formative years; Hannah Merker, my literary mentor, who helped me keep the faith; and IWWG for being there. I would like to acknowledge my writing group for their feedback, Carolyn Hasler of Huntington Public Library for helping me secure hard-to-find resources; Mayumi Hayashi for helping me to understand the concept of Akeru; and T.K.'s Galley, a perfect little café by the water in Halesite, for providing the hospitality and perfect writing atmosphere.

Index

Photo by Marcia Gerardi

Author's address and Web site
Susan Anderson
P.O. Box 2307
Huntington, New York 11743-2307

Web address: www.abandonmentrecovery.com
email: abandonment@erols.com

From the author of
The Journey from Abandonment to Healing

SUSAN ANDERSON

The Journey from Heartbreak to Connection

A Workshop in Abandonment Recovery

A manual for individual or support group use,
The Journey from Heartbreak to Connection includes exercises
that the author has tested and developed throughout her
years of expertise in abandonment recovery, to help
users develop trust, build new relationships,
and learn to love again.

Praise for
***The Journey from Abandonment to Healing*:**

"If there can be a pill to cure the heartbreak of rejection,
this book may be it."
—Rabbi Harold Kushner, bestselling author of
When Bad Things Happen to Good People

NOW IN PAPERBACK FROM BERKLEY

0-425-19020-X

Available wherever books are sold or at
www.penguin.com